The Trinity

The Trinity

The Central Mystery of Christianity

Hans Schwarz

Fortress Press
Minneapolis

THE TRINITY

The Central Mystery of Christianity

Copyright © 2017 Fortress Press. All rights reserved. Except for brief quotations in critical articles or reviews, no part of this book may be reproduced in any manner without prior written permission from the publisher. Email copyright@fortresspress.com or write to Permissions, Fortress Press, PO Box 1209, Minneapolis, MN 55440-1209.

Cover image: *Roundel with the Holy Trinity*. South Netherlandish. 1510–20. Colorless glass, silver stain, vitreous paint. The Cloisters Collection, 1932; Triangles. © iStock/Thinkstock

Cover design: Ivy Palmer Skrade

Print ISBN: 978-1-5064-3298-4

eBook ISBN: 978-1-5064-3299-1

This book was produced using Pressbooks.com, and PDF rendering was done by PrinceXML.

Contents

	Preface	vii
	Abbreviations	ix
	Introduction	xi
1.	Father, Son, and Holy Spirit in the Old Testament	1
2.	Father, Son, and Holy Spirit in the New Testament	15
3.	The Early Church and the Emerging Trinitarian Reflections	35
4.	The Struggle over the Decision of Nicea	57
5.	Developments in the Middle Ages and in the Reformation Period	79
6.	Post-Reformation Developments	105
7.	Perspectives of the Present Scene	135
8.	A Systematic Discernment	175
	In Conclusion	199
	Recommended Reading List	207

Index of Subjects 209
Index of Names 213

Preface

In the last thirty years books on the Trinity have abounded. There seems to be a fascination with this mysterious topic, especially among systematic theologians. The topic has been mined for many different interests, from liberation theology to feminist interpretations of the Christian heritage and from neo-Reformation theology to interreligious dialogue. With this present book I have no intention of adding to the plethora of treatises on the Trinity. The main question that will concern me is what is really scripturally tenable with regard to the Trinity and what is unwarranted theological construction or even speculation. While we are aware that exegesis without presuppositions is an overly idealistic endeavour, we must nevertheless try to ascertain whether the theological assertions made about the Trinity are in line with the biblical base from which they are derived, or whether they have veered off in a more or less questionable direction.[1]

This critical assessment has nothing to do with little respect for tradition or with renouncing the biblical faith. Quite the opposite! If we want to present our Christian faith in a credible manner, we must try to avoid all speculation, lest we be charged with credulity. And we must show the basis on which we have built our faith. If it is based on our own preferences and ideas, then it borders on ideology. If it is based on God's self-disclosure in Jesus of Nazareth, then we will be able to see God's human face. Only in this latter case can we rest assured that we are following God's ways and not our own. We should take heed here of

---

1. We are therefore very skeptical about the "programme of a scientific analysis" that "distances itself from the *normative claim* of religious texts" and "goes beyond the limits of the *canon*." See the project of Gerd Theissen, *The Religion of the Earliest Churches: Creating a Symbolic World*, trans. John Bowden (Minneapolis: Fortress Press, 1999), 323–26, and the justified response by Udo Schnelle, *Theology of the New Testament*, trans. M. Eugene Boring (Grand Rapids: Baker Academic, 2007), 45–49.

the story of the magi who first thought a king must be born in a castle and therefore pounded on the door of Herod's palace. But, led by God's messenger, they found their way to the Christ child in Bethlehem.

It is my hope that those who trace with me Trinitarian thinking from its biblical base to the present are able to discern some of the unwarranted theological constructions that have been proposed and the human fantasies that have been concocted in contrast to what is biblically warranted. From a biblical perspective, Christianity is a Christ-centered faith that believes that the one God is steering history from creation to its fulfilment in the eschaton, despite the human effort being made to derail the completion of this God-promised destiny.

At this point I want to thank Dr. Terry Dohm, who once more improved my style; Frau Jutta Brandl-Hammer, who secured books from various libraries and was always available when needed; and above all my wife, Hildegard, who supports her husband's sheer endless hours at his desk to finish yet another manuscript.

Hans Schwarz

Abbreviations

ABD   *Anchor Bible Dictionary.* Edited by David Noel Freedman. 6 vols. New York: Doubleday, 1992

ACW   *Ancient Christian Writers.* 66 vols. New York; Paulist Press, 1946–2015

ANF   *The Ante-Nicene Fathers.* Edited by Alexander Roberts and James Donaldson. 1885–87. 10 vols. Repr., Peabody, MA: Hendrickson, 1994

CO   *Ioannis Calvini Opera quae supersunt omnia.* Edited by Edouard Cunitz, Johann-Wilhelm Baum, and Eduard Wilhelm Eugen Reuss. 59 vols. Corpus Reformatorum 29–88. Brunswick: Schwetschke, 1863–1900

FC   *Fathers of the Church.* 127 vols. 1947–2013

LW   *Luther's Works* [American ed.]. 55 vols. St. Louis: Concordia; Philadelphia: Fortress, 1955–86

NIB   *The New Interpreter's Bible.* Edited by Leander E. Keck. 12 vols. Nashville: Abingdon, 1994–2004

NPNF[1]   *Nicene and Post-Nicene Fathers*, Series 1

NPNF[2]   *Nicene and Post-Nicene Fathers*, Series 2

T. Levi   Testament of Levi

T. Mos.   Testament of Moses

TDNT   *Theological Dictionary of the New Testament.* Edited by Gerhard Kittel and Gerhard Friedrich. Translated by Geoffrey W. Bromiley. 10 vols. Grand Rapids: Eerdmans, 1964–76

TRE   *Theologische Realenzyklopädie.* Edited by Gerhard Krause and Gerhard Müller. 36 vols. Berlin: de Gruyter, 1977–2007

WA   *D. Martin Luthers Werke: Kritische Gesamtausgabe [Schriften].* 73 vols. Weimar: Hermann Böhlaus Nachfolger, 1883–2009

Introduction

A few days before his death, Philip Melanchthon, a coworker of Martin Luther, committed to writing his reasons for not fearing death. He writes: "You will be delivered from sins, and be freed from the acrimony and fury of theologians," and "You shall go to the light, see God, look upon his Son, learn those wonderful mysteries which you were not able to understand in this life."[1] Yet exactly these mysteries in the form of the Trinity have exerted extreme fascination for theologians within the last generation. This may in part be due to Karl Barth, who began the doctrine of revelation with the doctrine of the Triune God. Yet he admits: "In putting the doctrine of the Trinity at the head of the whole of dogmatics we are adopting a position which, looked at in view of the history of dogmatics, is very isolated."[2] He surely remembered Friedrich Schleiermacher, who treats the doctrine of the Trinity only in the conclusion of his *The Christian Faith*, where he states, "We have less reason to regard this doctrine as finally settled," and then questions whether this doctrine is so clearly and firmly present in the New Testament.[3] To find our way between Barth and Schleiermacher, perhaps it would be good to consult the creeds of the church, which most Christians hold in common. After all, we should find here references to the Trinity if that doctrine is that central to the Christian faith.

The Apostles' Creed goes back to the old Roman Creed, first attested in the West in the early third century. In the West it has been traditionally used as the baptismal creed and received its present shape

---

1. Philip Melanchthon, no. 6977, Scriptum ca. April 18, 1560, in *CR* 9:1098.
2. Karl Barth, *Church Dogmatics*, vol. 1, *The Doctrine of the Word of God*, trans. G. T. Thomson (Edinburgh: T&T Clark, 1960), 345.
3. Friedrich Schleiermacher, *The Christian Faith*, ed. H. R. Mackintosh and J. S. Stewart (New York: Harper Torchbooks, 1963), 2:747.

in the eighth century. Its form is tripartite. In its first part faith in "God, the Father Almighty" is expressed, and in the second part faith in "Jesus Christ, God's only Son, our Lord." The third part opens with faith in "the Holy Spirit, the holy catholic church," and the communion of saints. While Jesus Christ is connected in the creed to God the Father by calling him God's only Son, such a connection between God and the Holy Spirit is missing. The Spirit is closely associated with the holy catholic church, the communion of saints, the forgiveness of sins, the resurrection of the body, and life everlasting.

Without undue imagination, one could say that these items are so intimately connected with the Holy Spirit that they can be regarded as effects of the Spirit. Certainly the outpouring of the Spirit at Pentecost led to the formation of the church and the gathering of the faithful. Forgiveness, resurrection, and eternal life can hardly be thought of without the life-giving power of the Spirit. But with regard to the Trinity of Father, Son, and Holy Spirit, we can at most detect a triadic connection in the Apostles' Creed, since each of the three divine agents leads to the other in a subsequent affirmation.

The other important ancient creed is the so-called Nicene Creed, also known as the Nicene-Constantinopolitan Creed, which was written either during the Council of Constantinople in 381 or already before. Initially it was the baptismal creed in the East, and later it became the creed for the regular worship setting. In the West today it is frequently used in connection with the Eucharist. Again it is tripartite, each segment devoted to one entity of the Trinity, Father, Son, and Holy Spirit. Of the Son we now hear that he is "of one Being with the Father," showing the intimate connection between Father and Son. When we come to the third segment, we read that the Holy Spirit "proceeds from the Father (and the Son), who with the Father and the Son is worshiped and glorified." This would imply an intimate connection between Father, Son, and Holy Spirit. Yet there is no mention of the three being one, affirming the notion of the Triune God. Evidently, when of the Nicene Creed was formulated, the foremost concern was the unity of God the Father with Jesus Christ. Of course, the Holy Spirit as the Lord and the giver of life was closely associated with Father and Son. The faith "in one Lord, Jesus Christ," however, seems to put the Holy Spirit, "the Lord, the giver of life," in second place, since Jesus Christ is the one Lord (see Phil 2:11).

A third ancient creed, the so-called Athanasian Creed, most likely arose in southern Gaul, present-day France, during the fifth century;

it "reflects Augustinian and Ambrosian trinitarian theology."[4] Yet it has been named after Athanasius, the staunch defender of the divinity of Christ and the orthodox doctrine of the Trinity. Since the middle of the seventeenth century, however, the Athanasian authorship has been abandoned. While it gained popularity only in the West and today is largely forgotten by most Christians, it is decidedly Trinitarian. We read there: "We worship one God in trinity and the Trinity in unity, neither confusing the persons nor dividing the substance."[5] It emphasizes the Godhead and the Lordship of each of the persons of the Trinity, and it assures us that "there are not three gods but one God." Since it is rather lengthy and contains anathemas against heretical teachings, it is less a creed and more an affirmation of a particular theological confession of faith. Thus it concludes: "This is the Catholic faith; a person cannot be saved without believing this firmly and faithfully."

Where do we stand now on the issue of the Trinity? Should we side with Barth or with Schleiermacher? We noticed that the first two universally accepted creeds do not explicitly mention the Trinity. Yet they are also far from denying it. The Athanasian Creed, however, tells us that a person cannot be saved without firmly and faithfully believing in the Trinity. With that dictum we could already conclude our study without actually having started it. Yet Christians do not simply accept tradition, since that same tradition would also tell us that faith and reason cannot be substituted for each other, though they complement each other. In order to believe with a good conscience and not simply out of adherence to tradition, we must investigate the formation of the doctrine of the Trinity from its biblical roots to its present-day relevancy.

Since the doctrine of the Trinity did not fall down from heaven but has a long history during which it evolved, it is indispensable that we trace that development. We begin with the biblical sources, the foundation of our Christian faith, to see whether we find there any indications of the Trinity. We will then follow the Trinitarian development from the early church to the present. Covering nearly two thousand years of history, we could easily get lost in the intricacies of the available sources. But our intent is for a rather slender volume. We adduce only the most prominent voices in an exemplary fashion and avoid seemingly unnecessary investigations to make this text also readable

---

4. See Robert Kolb and Timothy J. Wengert, eds., *The Book of Concord: The Confessions of the Evangelical Lutheran Church* (Minneapolis: Fortress Press, 2000), 21.
5. For the text of the Athanasian Creed see ibid., 23–25.

for the nonspecialists. Having arrived on the present scene, we will restrict ourselves to the major voices, well knowing that this may not satisfy everyone. Yet brevity does not mean to sacrifice clarity. It is especially the question "How do we know?" that will guide us in our final deliberations.

1

Father, Son, and Holy Spirit in the Old Testament

Though we certainly do not encounter the Trinity in the Old Testament, we hear a frequent mentioning of the Spirit of God, for instance when the psalmist exclaims: "Do not take your holy spirit from me" (Ps 51:11). Similarly, during every Lenten season the suffering servant in Isaiah 52:53, who "was wounded for our transgression and crushed for our iniquities" (Isa 53:5), is interpreted as pointing to Jesus's suffering death at Golgotha. While there is no explicit mention of the Trinity in the Old Testament, the "persons" of the Trinity seem to be already present there. Therefore, an investigation into the Old Testament seems not unwarranted. Let us start with the Spirit.

The Holy Spirit in the Old Testament

The combination of "holy" (*qōdeš*) and "spirit" (*rûaḥ*) occurs in the Old Testament only twice, namely in Isa 63:10-11 and in the well-known passage in Psalm 51:13 ("Do not take your holy spirit from me"). Both passages belong to the postexilic period. In the Apocrypha and the Pseudepigrapha we find only a few references containing the combination of *holy* with *spirit*. In 2 Esdras 14:22, for example, we read that Ezra responds to Yahweh: "If then I have found favor with you, send the holy spirit upon me"; and according to Jubilees 1:21, Moses prays to God for his people, saying: "Create a pure heart and a holy spirit for them." This paucity of the term *Holy Spirit* does not mean that the term *spirit* is almost absent from the Old Testament; in fact, it occurs 378 times in the Hebrew texts and 11 times in the Aramaic passages. The Spirit has quite a few different meanings but is never a "member" of the Trinity. Already the Greek term *pneuma*, which is usually translated "spirit," denotes wind, breath, life, soul, spirit, and reason, to mention the most important usage. This is similar in the Old Testament to *rûaḥ*, the Hebrew equivalent to *pneuma*. It is the basic power of life that becomes visible in movement of the air and in humans with inhaling and exhaling.

The psalmist confesses: "By the word of the Lord the heavens were made, and all their hosts by the breath [*rûaḥ*] of his mouth" (Ps 33:6). In this parallelism *word* and *breath* are equated. When Jeremiah claims, "Their images are false, and there is no breath in them" (Jer 10:14), he is alluding here to the breath of life, which is missing in them, since the images or idols are dead objects. Yet *rûaḥ* can also mean anger, as we learn from Isaiah 33:11, where we read, "Your breath is a fire that will consume you." The same can be said about Yahweh, as we read in the song of Moses to the Lord: "At the blast of your nostrils the waters piled up" (Exod 15:8) so that the Israelites could escape from the pursuing Egyptians. As we see in Job 4:15, *rûaḥ* can denote a gentle breeze ("A spirit glided past my face"), but it also can be a "raging wind and tempest" (Ps 55:8).

The Spirit in Humans

Most important is the function of the spirit for us humans. As mentioned, idols have no spirit and therefore no life. God promises according to Ezekiel 37:5 that "I will cause breath to enter you, and you shall live," showing that the entering of the spirit into a human being enables that person to live. The "breath of life" is not confined to humans (see Gen 6:17), since all life has *rûaḥ*. This *rûaḥ* is no independent entity, because "the Lord, the God of the spirits of all flesh" (Num 27:16) is the one who "owns" the spirit. "When you [Lord] take away their breath [*rûaḥ*], they die and return to their dust" (Ps 104:29), the psalmist confesses to God. While we might infer from Ps 146:4 ("When their breath departs, they return to the earth") that ceasing to breathe and dying is a natural process, such reasoning was foreign to the Israelites. God gives the spirit, and he again takes it away. So we are reminded: "Both flesh and spirit are his" (Mal 2:15). And: "In his hand is the life of every living thing and the breath of every human being" (Job 12:10). Therefore we should take care that we do not lose our life by ungodly living.

Rûaḥ is also the seat of emotions, character, insight, and intelligence. We read, for instance, that the wives of Esau "made life bitter [mōrat rûaḥ] for Isaac and Rebekah" (Gen 26:35). The spirit can also be broken by sorrow (Prov 15:13) or be in anguish (Job 7:11). Rûaḥ can also denote "a hasty temper" (Prov 14:29), and the spirit can be "hardened" so that one acts "proudly" (Dan 5:20). This means that the whole range of emotions and traits of character, from unhappiness to jealousy and impatience, can be expressed with the term rûaḥ. We encounter the same range of meanings when we consider the cerebral functions of humanity. "It is the spirit in a mortal, the breath of the Almighty that makes for understanding" (Job 32:8). Similarly, we read in Daniel 6:3: "Daniel distinguished himself above all other presidents and satraps because an excellent spirit was in him." King Nebuchadnezzar concedes about Daniel that he "is endowed with the spirit of the holy gods" (Dan 4:8), since he knows the divine secrets. Yet even artistic skills are a result of the spirit, since Yahweh tells Moses: "You shall speak to all who have ability, whom I have endowed with skill [rûaḥ] that they make Aaron's vestments" (Exod 28:3). But one can also "err in the spirit" (Isa 29:24). And the Lord can even pour into the people "a spirit of confusion" (Isa 19:14). Humans are neither self-made nor independent in their faculties but ultimately depend on God for good and for bad.

Even the good traits in a human are expressive of rûaḥ. We read in Exodus 35:21: "They came, everyone whose heart was stirred, and everyone whose spirit was willing, and brought the Lord's offering." People can have a "lowly spirit" (Prov 16:19) or a "haughty spirit" (Prov 16:18), but a "broken spirit" is acceptable to God (Ps 51:17). And we read of "a generation whose heart was not steadfast, whose spirit was not faithful to God" (Ps 78:8). But how is God related to this rûaḥ?

Human Spirit and Divine Spirit

God is "the God of the spirits of all flesh" (Num 16:22), meaning that God is the author of all life. When Isaiah mentions that God created the whole world, he also includes humanity in it, saying that God "gives breath to the people upon it [i.e., the earth] and spirit to those who

3

walk in it" (Isa 42:5). Breath and spirit are equated here, since those who no longer breathe are dead and have no spirit in them. God is the one who gives the spirit so that people live, and God also preserves their spirit (see Job 10:12). When God takes away the breath of the people, they die (Ps 104:29), and then "the breath returns to God who gave it" (Eccles 12:7). This spirit in humans is not an independent entity that God gives, preserves, and in the end takes away. It is God's spirit that is active in living beings (see Ps 104:30). This spirit, "the breath of the Almighty," is not just an enlivening spirit. It also makes for understanding (Job 32:8) and can be imparted from one person to another through the laying on of hands (Deut 34:9).

The Function of the Spirit of God

The spirit of the Lord is a divine agent that introduces movement. Thus "the spirit of the Lord rushed on him [i.e., Samson], and he tore the lion apart" (Judg 14:6). It can also enable prophetic utterances, as we read in Num 11:25 in connection with the Sinai events: the Lord came down in the cloud and "took some of the spirit that was on [Moses] and put it on the seventy elders; and when the spirit rested upon them, they prophesied." The spirit of the Lord can also transfer people to a different location, as we read in the story of Elisha (2 Kgs 2:16). Even the charisma of a leader is dependent on "the spirit of the Lord" (Judg 3:10). But when the spirit of the Lord departs from a person, God can send "an evil spirit" that can torment that person, as we hear in the case of King Saul (1 Sam 16:14). Apart from this all-determining reality of God's spirit, there are other spirits that are also under God's control. There is, for example, "a lying spirit" that is put in the mouth of the prophets of King Ahab on the initiative of this spirit, but with Yahweh's command (1 Kgs 22:21–23). The whole spiritual world is under God's control.

Most important is the enlivening function of God's spirit; we hear: "I will put my spirit within you, and you shall live" (Ezek 37:14). God creates life and also the whole world through his spirit. Therefore we read in connection with the creation narrative that "a wind [*rûah*] from God swept over the face of the waters" (Gen 1:2). All mental faculties depend on the divine spirit, such as "ability, intelligence, and knowledge" (Exod 31:3). Similarly, we hear of Isaiah (48:16): "And now the Lord God has sent me and his spirit." It is not one's own ability but God's spirit that works in people to accomplish their work properly.

Therefore the psalmist prays: "Restore to me the joy of your salvation, and sustain me with a willing spirit" (Ps 51:12).

Such sentiment implies that there is judgment, as exemplified by Jerusalem when Isaiah writes: "The Lord has washed away the filth of the daughters of Zion and cleansed the bloodstains of Jerusalem from its midst by a spirit of judgment and by a spirit of burning" (Isa 4:4). It is again God's spirit through which judgment is administered. Yet judgment is not the ultimate function of the spirit. There will be restoration through God's spirit when "a spirit from on high is poured out on us ... then justice will dwell in the wilderness, and righteousness in the fruitful field." Then there will be "righteousness, quietness and trust forever" (Isa 32:15-17). Social justice, security, and happiness will prevail in the end through God's spirit. This eschatological vision is safeguarded by God when he promises: "I will put my spirit within you, and make you follow my statutes and be careful to observe my ordinances" (Ezek 36:27). God's spirit working in humans makes all the difference. In Joel 2:29 we even hear from Yahweh: "In those days, I will pour out my spirit." This signifies the beginning of the day of Yahweh. The eschatological fulfilment associated with prophetic utterances, dreams, and visions is brought about by Yahweh through his spirit.

God's spirit is active everywhere (Ps 139:7) and endures forever, since it is not like perishable flesh (see Isa 31:3). It needs no instruction and is incomparable in knowledge and might (Isa 40:13). As the mediator of creation, the divine *rûaḥ* is intimately related to the Lord God. But it can also be distinguished from God, as we gather from Ezekiel when God commands the spirit to put life back into "the slain that they may live" (Ezek 37:9). The spirit, therefore, can even be considered a person-like being. The *rûaḥ* Yahweh stands for his activity in history and creation, and thus it is always God who acts. "Therefore *rûaḥ* Yahweh can be synonymous for God's innermost being and for his presence."[1]

"In rabbinic theology 'spirit of God' and 'spirit of prophecy' are used almost synonymously."[2] The conclusion was that there is no holy spirit if there is no prophet. This led to the conviction that after the last prophets—Haggai, Zechariah, and Malachi—the spirit had abandoned Israel, if not already earlier with the destruction of the first temple. Since Ezra was the last inspired prophet, the normative period in

---

1. Friedrich Baumgärtel, "πνεῦμα, πνευματικός," in *TDNT* 6:367.
2. Victor H. Matthews, "Holy Spirit," in *ABD* 3:263.

which Yahweh's revelation to Israel occurred ended with him.[3] Only at the end time will the spirit return to God's people.

The Son (of God) in the Old Testament

When we read in Genesis 6:1-4 of "the sons of God" who had children with "the daughters of humans," these "sons" are at the most angelic beings or gods, in contrast to the Lord. Such references have little bearing on the issue of the Son of God as the other divine agent of the Trinity. Even the idea of a "council of the holy ones" in which the "Lord God of hosts" rules, meaning that the supreme God presides over a divine pantheon (see Ps 89:7-8), is of little relevance to our issue. At most it shows that the Old Testament writers felt free to adopt concepts prevalent in their religious environment. Yet the idea that Yahweh fathered other divine beings, common in the ancient Near East, was foreign to the Bible. Yahweh's divinity was not to be compromised by other divine beings. The situation was different in the case of a divine pantheon. It demonstrated Yahweh was the supreme God. Yahweh is occasionally shown to preside over a heavenly assembly, with which even Satan is associated. Again, Satan is subject to Yahweh and responsible to him, as we gather from the book of Job (Job 1:6-12).

Three times the king is called the "son of God." Yahweh commands Nathan to tell David: "I will be a father to him, and he shall be a son to me" (2 Sam 7:14). The analogy to divine kingship in the ancient Near East seems evident. We hear, for instance, that "from the very beginning of Egyptian history the king was identified in the written sources with Horus—'the Lofty One', the falcon-like sky-god." Later, "the king is no longer regarded simply as identical with the god of heaven and earth; nor is he any longer seen as his incarnation; he is simply the son of a divine father." Further, "the Egyptian king is simultaneously God and man," by being a visible incarnation of the deity.[4] "The Semitic rulers of Akkad (ca. 2350-2150 BCE) claimed divinity for themselves."[5] About the prince of Tyre (Syria) we hear God say through Ezekiel: "You have said, 'I am a god; I sit in the seat of the gods, in the heart of the seas,' yet you are but a mortal, and no god" (Ezek 28:2). Here it is clearly enunciated that mortals, even if they are princes or kings, are no gods.

---

3. This allowed for establishing the time frame of the Old Testament canon with its inspired writings.
4. Siegfried Morenz, *Egyptian Religion*, trans. Ann E. Keep (Ithaca, NY: Cornell University Press, 1984 [1976]), 34, 35, 40.
5. Jarl Fossum, "Son of God," in *ABD* 6:128.

Nobody is equal to God, and the foolish attempt to call oneself equal to God leads to one's personal demise.

The Davidic Kingship

When we read in Psalm 2:7—this royal psalm that was perhaps used on occasion of the coronation of a king—that Yahweh says: "You are my son; today I have begotten you. Ask of me, and I will make the nations your heritage, and the ends of the earth your possession," we should not be misled to think here of a biological act. It is rather a divine "adoption." "The king was 'born' from God when he was installed."[6] Making a covenant with David, God announces: "He shall cry to me, 'You are my Father, my God, and the Rock of my salvation!' I will make him the firstborn, the highest of the kings of the earth" (Ps 89:26-7). This has nothing to do with a biological connection but shows that the Davidic kingship is under the special protection of God. God will assist the king against other rulers and elevate his kingship above all others. Whether one perceives this as an adoption that coincided with the inauguration of the king or whether the king is only legitimized by Yahweh is relatively unimportant.[7] Decisive are two items: first, and most important, the king is not divine but stands under divine protection and receives a divine promise. Second, the divine promise given through Nathan, "Your house and your kingdom shall be made sure forever before me; your throne shall be established forever" (2 Sam 7:16), gave rise to the messianic expectations that culminated with Jesus of Nazareth.

It is not only the king who is under special protection of God, like a son is protected by his father. In the context of Israel's exodus from Egypt we read that Moses will tell the Pharaoh: "Thus says the Lord: Israel is my firstborn son. I said to you, 'Let my son go that he may worship me'" (Exod 4:22). Similarly, we read in the song of Moses concerning Israel: "O foolish and senseless people! Is not he your father, who created you, and who made you and established you?" (Deut 32:6). This relationship between father and son, between Yahweh and Israel, is not a natural connection, one that cannot be dissolved. But the Lord does not want to abandon those with whom he has made his covenant. He has called Israel out of Egypt and preferred it over all other nations.

---

6. Ibid.
7. Georg Fohrer, "υἱός," in *TDNT* 8:351, vehemently disclaims that this has anything to do with adoption, though his argumentation is not totally convincing.

Therefore, Yahweh is disappointed that it has "rebelled" against him and has "forsaken the Lord" (Isa 1:2–4). Nevertheless, he wants them to return to him. "Return, you faithless children, I will heal your faithlessness"; all the other sacred sites and rites amount to nothing, since "in the Lord our God is the salvation of Israel" (Jer 3:22–23). Implied in this call to return is a summons of repentance.

But a return was not that simple, because of Israel's attraction to its surrounding religious environment. Fertility rites were a central feature of Canaanite religion to secure the fecundity of flocks and people as well as crops. This was enticing for the Israelites. Instead of worshiping their God, they worshiped the local gods in high places (see 1 Kgs 3:2). "They kept sacrificing to the Baals, and offering incense to idols" (Hos 11:2). All sorts of calamities consequently befell Israel, which were perceived as God's judgment. But God did not abandon his chosen people. Yahweh announces amid these problems: "On that day I will raise up the booth of David that is fallen, and repair its breaches, and raise up its ruins, and rebuild it as in the days of old" (Amos 9:11). The Davidic-Solomonic empire will be resurrected to how it was in the days of David and Solomon. At the end of time the old situation will be reenacted. This feature has endured to this day with some Jewish faithful and still causes political discomfort among the surrounding nations. This "resurrection" to the grandeur of old will not occur at some predictable date but "on that day," the day of the eschatological fulfilment. When this will occur is not for Israel to decide. It is God's prerogative to set this date.

The Messiah as the Son of God

Christos, the Greek equivalent for the Hebrew word translated "messiah," is the title most frequently applied to Jesus of Nazareth in the New Testament. Most Christians therefore understand Jesus of Nazareth to be the Messiah and assume that this title originated from promises contained in the Old Testament. But in looking for explicit references in the Old Testament, we discover that there are hardly any messianic references that have eschatological significance.[8]

---

8. Hans-Peter Müller, *Ursprünge und Strukturen alttestamentlicher Eschatologie* (Berlin: Töpelmann, 1969), 212, points out very convincingly that in the total context of Old Testament eschatology the hope for a Messiah plays only an unimportant role. The Messiah belongs mostly on the side of the people who are redeemed by Yahweh, and only seldom is he conceived of as the actual bringer of salvation or even its mediator. In coming from the New Testament, however, we notice that there the Messiah is usually understood as an eschatological figure, as a redeemer sent by and representing God and as one who initiates the end time and brings salvation to the people.

The Significance of the Term *Messiah*

The term *Messiah*, or "anointed one," can refer to the high priest (Lev 4:5), but usually it denotes the king of Israel (2 Sam 1:16), who was anointed when he was designated king. Yet the expected king of the final time, of the eschaton, is never called the Messiah.[9] The only exception is Isaiah 45:1, where a foreigner, Persian King Cyrus the Great (590/580–529 BCE), is called the messiah to whom God speaks. This reference demonstrates the high expectations that were connected with the Cyrus Edict, which permitted the exiles to return to Jerusalem. But the Old Testament writers are not aware of a person called the Messiah who is to bring eschatological salvation. The eschatological fulfillment is too closely connected with God as the actor in history to be mediated by a messianic figure.

Though the title "Messiah" is not used in the Old Testament in an eschatological context, the hope is already present for a God-provided figure who will usher in the eschaton. This figure seems to have originated from a retrospective glorification of David and from the promise that was given to him through Nathan (2 Sam 7:12–15).

Main Sources for the Concept of a Messiah

The messianic figure who is expected to bring about eschatological salvation is usually associated with the house of David. The blessing Jacob gave to Judah (Gen 49:8–12) can be considered as the oldest of these "messianic" expectations. The one who is supposed to come is described as one who will bring about and live in an age of "paradisaical abundance."[10] He will bind his foal to the vine, and he will wash his garments in wine. The oracle of Balaam (Num 24:15–19) talks with a nationalistic and political tint about the star that will come forth out of Jacob and have dominion over the neighboring nations. The restoration of the fallen "booth of David," as indicated in the book of Amos, seems to go along similar lines (Amos 9:11–15). This restoration

---

9. See A. S. van der Woude, "Messias," in *Biblisch-Historisches Handwörterbuch*, ed. Bo Reicke and Leonhard Rost, 4 vols. (Göttingen: Vandenhoeck & Ruprecht, 1962–1979), 2:1197. For the following see also Hugo Gressmann, *Der Messias* (Göttingen: Vandenhoeck & Ruprecht, 1929), 1. Though the king was understood as viceroy and mandatory of Yahweh himself, as expressed in the royal psalms, the office of the king did not seem to exert much influence on the development of the idea of the Messiah. See Gerhard von Rad, *Old Testament Theology*, vol. 1, *The Theology of Israel's Historical Traditions*, trans. D. M. G. Stalker (Edinburgh: Oliver & Boyd, 1962), 318–20.
10. Gerhard von Rad, *Genesis: A Commentary*, trans. J. H. Marks (Philadelphia: Westminster, 1961), 425, who, however, does not call it a "messianic" passage.

is expected as a dominion of Israel over all the nations. In recapitulating an idealized past as "the days of old" (Amos 9:11) the messianic time is described as a time of prosperity and peace ("The mountains shall drip sweet wine, and ... my people Israel ... shall rebuild the ruined cities and inhabit them" [Amos 9:13-14a]).

In Isaiah's proclamation the messianic references are expanded beyond the scope of the immediate national and historical reality (Isa 7:10-17; 9:1-7; 11:1-8). Many exegetes hesitate to consider Isaiah 7:10-17 a messianic reference, since the birth of a child with the name Immanuel by a young woman could easily refer to Isaiah's own wife.[11] As Brevard Childs (1923-2007), however, cautions: "The reader is simply not given information regarding the identity of the maiden." But the other two announcements, Isaiah 9:1-6 and 11:1-8, clearly have messianic character. In the midst of the darkness of destruction a light is emerging (Isa 9:1-6). The Lord has broken the yoke that Assyria had imposed on Israel, and now his anointed will be enthroned. The child who was conceived and the son who was given is not a child in the physical sense but the anointed one who becomes the son of Yahweh through his enthronement (see Ps 2:7). His names, "Wonderful Counselor, Mighty God, Everlasting Father, Prince of Peace," indicate that his reign will be one of justice and of peace. In Isaiah 11:1-8 the messianic peace is emphasized even more in stating that the "spirit of the Lord" will rest on the Messiah, and his reign now encompasses all of nature. Finally, Micah proclaims that from Bethlehem, the village of David, the messianic ruler will come forth, "whose origin is from of old" (Mic 5:1-5). The return of the Israelites to their homes is presupposed, and the messianic peace and the magnitude of the kingdom are stressed.[12]

Toward the end of the Old Testament era, Haggai and Zechariah appear. For them the destruction of the Israelite nation and the return

---

11. See Georg Fohrer, *Messiasfrage und Bibelverständnis* (Tübingen: Mohr, 1957), 11-14, who treats there all pertinent messianic references. See also Gerhard von Rad, *Old Testament Theology*, vol. 2, *The Theology of Israel's Prophetic Traditions*, trans. D. M. G. Stalker (New York: Harper & Row, 1965), 173-74, who gives a good survey of the discussion on Isa 7:10-17, and Brevard S. Childs, *Isaiah* (Louisville, KY: Westminster John Knox, 2001), 66.

12. We certainly agree with Georg Fohrer, "Die Struktur der alttestamentlichen Eschatologie," in *Studien zur alttestamentlichen Prophetie (1949-1965)* (Berlin: Töpelmann, 1967), 45-46, when he says that the eschatological prophecy of the Old Testament usually does not refer to the end of the world or of history. It views the eschatological events as taking place within the framework of the nations, where political events or other historical incidents provide the starting point. But Fohrer also points out that nature and the cosmos are often included in these views. Especially toward the later parts of the Old Testament, the tendency is clearly universalistic in comprising the totality of the world and history.

from exile are past events. They are aware that these events did not usher in the messianic kingdom. Since God was present earlier in his temple in Jerusalem, they emphasize the importance of rebuilding the temple as the prerequisite for the coming of Yahweh and of his kingdom (Hag 1:7–8; Zech 4:9). It is not enough to reoccupy the promised land, but it is necessary to reinstitute the place of worship as the cultic center of Israel and to be ready for the eschatological advent of Yahweh. Both prophets see themselves at the beginning of the time of salvation. The building of the temple initiates the time of salvation, the messianic prosperity starts (Hag 2:19), and everybody will live in messianic peace (Zech 8:12). Both see in Zerubbabel the anointed of the Lord the coming Messiah (Hag 2:20–23; Zech 4:6–10).

But their high expectations end in disappointment. Zerubbabel is never enthroned, and the hope for the fulfillment of the Davidic promise has to be revised again. The exulting words, "Lo, your king comes to you; triumphant and victorious is he, humble and riding on a donkey, on a colt, the foal of a donkey" (Zech 9:9) are too early. One generation before Zechariah, Deutero-Isaiah judged the situation much more realistically in the songs of the Servant of Yahweh. Confronted with the stubbornness and unbelief of his people, he realizes that true deliverance and fulfillment of salvation can only be brought about through the vicarious suffering of the true Servant of Yahweh. "We have all turned to our own way, and the Lord has laid on him the iniquity of us all" (Isa 53:6). Though the messianic element of the victorious king is not lacking in Deutero-Isaiah's description of the suffering servant, the author ultimately did not dare to identify him with a historic figure. The understanding that the bringer of salvation could not be identified with a figure of present or past history but will be a figure acting in and through history was more clearly conceived in the time of apocalyptic.

Expansion of the Messianic Hopes in the Apocalyptic Period

During the time of apocalyptic, a different role was attributed to the Messiah. In the apocalyptic visions of Daniel, God is still the ruler of the world. God brings about the cosmic and political changes and initiates the eschatological time of salvation. In the apocalyptic books of 1 Enoch, 2 Esdras, and 2 Baruch, the Messiah enjoys a more independent position. He himself destroys the enemies and brings about the salvation of Israel. Together with his independence there is an increasing emphasis on his preexistence. He who existed before all worlds comes in the end time from heaven to initiate the time of salvation. To some degree this is already prefigured in the "Son of Man" imagery of Daniel 7. There the Son of Man (be he a corporate or an individual figure) signifies the final victory of God's power and greatness over the anti-God powers.[13] As a messianic figure, he ushers in the final triumph of God's people in God's kingdom in God's appointed time.[14]

While the prophets conceived of the enemies of Israel also as God's enemies who will either be converted or destroyed in the end time, in the apocalyptic period all anti-God powers were included in this picture. If God is to have dominion over the world, all powers have to succumb. For instance, according to 1 Enoch, God smites the gentiles in their final assault against Israel. Thereafter he sets up his throne, and the coming of the messianic kingdom is preceded by "the day of the great judgment," in which not only wicked people "but also Azazel, demons and fallen angels will be punished or destroyed."[15] All the gentiles will become righteous and worship God, and Jerusalem with its holy temple will be the center of the kingdom. While in 1 Enoch the kingdom is established on this earth, the tendency is to idealize this kingdom. Thus Jerusalem as its center is not the old Jerusalem but a new Jerusalem, which is either conceived as a purification of the old (1 Enoch 6–36) or as a replacement of it (1 Enoch 83–90).[16]

In the Similitudes of Enoch this view is expanded. The kingdom is now seen to be established not only on a transformed earth but also in a transformed heaven. In the Testament of Moses, a book that probably originated when Jesus was still in his teens, this tendency goes even further. We are told that God's kingdom "will appear throughout his whole creation" (Testament of Moses 10:1). The whole conception of

---

13. See D. S. Russell, *The Method and Message of Jewish Apocalyptic: 200 BC–AD 100* (London: SCM, 1964), 327.
14. H. H. Rowley, *The Relevance of Apocalyptic: A Study of Jewish and Christian Apocalypses from Daniel to the Revelation*, rev. ed. (New York: Association, 1963), 29-30, mentions that "no member of the Davidic house headed the rising against Antiochus Epiphanes, and it would have been a sheer lack of realism to import a Davidic Messiah into the visions. . . . On the other hand, the alleged thought of a Levitical Messiah had certainly not yet arisen." Rowley also gives good treatment to the question of whether the Son of Man in Daniel can be interpreted as the Messiah and comes to the conclusion that "there is no evidence that the Son of Man was identified with the Messiah until the time of Jesus" (32). Though literally speaking Rowley is right, the Son of Man figure in Daniel 7 certainly cannot be regarded as totally unmessianic. We rather follow here von Rad, *Old Testament Theology*, 2:312, who says that "there can be no doubt that the son of man described in Dan. VII. 13 is initially presented as a Messianic figure in the wider sense of the term."
15. Russell, *Method and Message of Jewish Apocalyptic*, 287.
16. See ibid., 290.

the coming events of the end is no longer confined within nationalistic or this-worldly expectations. It is supramundane, and the kingdom is viewed as a kingdom of heaven.

Gerhard von Rad leaves open the question of whether the apocalyptic view of history is a detrimental alienation from the belief in Yahweh or "a breakthrough to new theological horizons."[17] This breakthrough, we must assert, has occurred in Jesus of Nazareth. The apocalyptic dimension of the kingdom of God was the center of his message. Yet before we move to the New Testament, we must take note that in some intertestamental literature God refers to the Messiah as "my son." For instance, in 4 Ezra 7:28-29 we read about a temporary messianic kingdom and the end of the world: "For my son the Messiah shall be revealed with those who are with him, and those who remain shall rejoice four hundred years. And after these years my son the Messiah shall die." German New Testament scholar Eduard Lohse (1924–2015), however, cautions that in postbiblical Judaism one was careful not to associate the sonship with a biological relationship and therefore used the metaphor "son of God only in quotations of messianic promises."[18] He even doubts that in the apocalyptic literature there are any references to the messianic title "Son of God." While the Greek original in the quotation above can be referring to a servant as well as son, American New Testament scholar Jarl Fossum observes that the idea "of the king as God's 'servant' was associated with that of his divine sonship."[19]

While 4 Ezra is certainly post-CE, in the Testament of Levi, which dates back to the first century BCE, Levi is told by God that "you shall announce the one who is about to redeem Israel" (Testament of Levi 2:10). Later Levi is promised that he will "become a son" to God, a "minister and priest in his presence" (Testament of Levi 4:2). To that effect he is installed as the priestly Messiah but also receives the royal insignia of crown and scepter (Testament of Levi 8). We are reminded here of the early Old Testament notion that the high-priestly office really belonged to the king. When the kingship ceased to exist, many of the royal functions were transferred to the high priest. We notice this, for instance, when Zechariah is told by the Lord to make a crown of silver and gold and place it on the head of the high priest Joshua (Zech 6:11).

We have seen that the Davidic kingship seemed to play a pivotal role

---

17. Ibid., 322.
18. Lohse, "υἱός," 8:360.
19. Fossum, "Son of God," 6:129.

in the concept of the son of God. While all of Israel and also individuals can be called son(s) of God, this kingship seemed to have an enduring effect and entailed a messianic promise that directed the attention to an end-time fulfillment with the Messiah as God's son to usher in the kingdom. Though the sonship was more metaphoric and was never conceived of as biological, it shows the close connection between God and this special figure of God's son or of his Messiah.

What have we learned from this survey about the Trinity in the Old Testament and those writings that join up to the New Testament times? Jesuit scholar Edmund J. Fortman (1901–90), who called himself "a firm believer in the Triune God,"[20] presents a comprehensive historical investigation of the doctrine of the Trinity. Yet even he confesses in conclusion to his survey of the Old Testament: "The Old Testament writings about God neither express nor imply any idea of or belief in a plurality or trinity of persons within the one Godhead. Even to see in them suggestions or foreshadowings or 'veiled signs' of the trinity of persons, is to go beyond the words and intent of the sacred writers."[21] Indeed, while all three entities of the Trinity are present, God as Father, the Son of God, and the Spirit, their meanings do not lead up to anything resembling the Trinity. The spirit of Yahweh is a creative power, a spirit of judgment of life and a charismatic and prophetic spirit. Apart from the spirit as a human and worldly phenomenon, the spirit is always Yahweh's spirit without any intent of a personification of that spirit. When Yahweh calls himself father, it is especially in relation to Israel. Whether collectively understood or represented by its king, Israel can be called "son" in this context. The title "Messiah" is usually connected with the king of Israel. Yet the expected king of the end time is never called the Messiah. There the expectation lies in the Messiah as the Son of God. What, then, is the story of the New Testament sources that seem to be formative for the doctrine of the Trinity?

---

20. Edmund J. Fortman, *The Triune God: A Historical Study of the Doctrine of the Trinity* (Philadelphia: Westminster, 1972), xv.
21. Ibid., 9.

2

Father, Son, and Holy Spirit in the New Testament

When we look at the New Testament sources, we notice at once that it is no longer Yahweh or the Lord God who occupies center stage but Jesus of Nazareth. In the Gospels the divine Sonship of Jesus plays a leading role. Mark, as the oldest Gospel, "presents the baptism in the sense of an appointment to an office and a bestowal of the Spirit at the beginning of Jesus's ministry. At the same time, however, the evangelist is aware of the conception of a perversion in being by the Spirit of God," so German New Testament scholar Ferdinand Hahn (1926–2015).[1] This means that Jesus was appointed to his office as the bringer of salvation and was filled with the Holy Spirit.

While Jesus is understood as the *bringer of salvation*, very little attention is given to the way he is related to the Lord God as the *sender of salvation*. There is one interesting phenomenon connected with this new situation. In the Septuagint, the Greek translation of the Old Testament, the term *kyrios*, that is, "Lord," is generally used to render the Hebrew term *Yahweh* into Greek. In the New Testament the term *kyrios* is still used for God in quotations and allusions to the Old Testament (see Mark 1:3) and in pronounced references to God, for example when

---

1. Ferdinand Hahn, *Titles of Jesus in Christology: Their History in Early Christianity*, trans. Harold Knight and George Ogg (Cambridge, UK: James Clarke, 2002 [1969]), 305.

Jesus says to God, "I thank you, Father, Lord of heaven and earth" (Matt 11:25) and when he speaks of "the Lord of the harvest" (Matt 9:38), implying that God is the Lord of the whole history of the world. Similarly, Paul talks about "the blessed and only Sovereign, the King of kings and Lord of lords" (1 Tim 6:15). But generally Jesus Christ is called the *kyrios*, and God is referred to with the generic term *theos*, meaning "God."

Jesus as the Lord

Best known is the hymn in Philippians 2:6–11, which concludes: "and every tongue should confess that Jesus Christ is Lord, to the glory of God the Father." Jesus Christ is *kyrios*, and the Father is *theos*. God gives Christ "the name that is above every name," which is, of course, the name for God, and consequently "every knee should bend, in heaven and on earth and under the earth." Jesus is pronounced here *kyrios* "to the glory of God the Father." German New Testament scholar Werner Foerster (1897–1975) concludes: "The name of *kyrios* implies a position equal to that of God."[2] Equally important is that God the Father recedes, so to speak, into the background, since he loses distinctiveness through the generic term *theos*, while Jesus Christ as *kyrios* comes to the fore. His name is a proper name, and one can easily associate with him a certain figure, Jesus of Nazareth.

Being the *kyrios* is closely connected with Jesus's exaltation, meaning his resurrection. Thus we read in Romans 10:9: "If you confess with your lips that Jesus is Lord and believe in your heart that God raised him from the dead, you will be saved." The two items belong together: that Jesus is Lord and that God raised him from the dead. Not just the exalted One is called *kyrios* but also the Jesus who walked on this earth. In the Hellenistic environment of nascent Christianity, there were many lords and many gods. But for Christians there is just one God and one Lord, as Paul explains to the Christians in Corinth: "Though there may be so-called gods in heaven or on earth—as in fact there are many gods and lords—yet for us there is one God, the Father, from whom are all things and for whom we exist, and one Lord, Jesus Christ, through whom are all things and through whom we exist" (1 Cor 8:5–6). It is interesting that Jesus Christ is also introduced here as the one "through whom are all things." He is the mediator of creation. But if this is true, his roots must go far back. Another interesting

---

2. Werner Foerster, "κύριος," in *TDNT* 3:1089.

facet is that in the same letter Paul uses the Aramaic term *Maranatha* ("our Lord, come") and closes his letter with the phrase "the grace of our Lord Jesus be with you" (1 Cor 16:22-23). This would indicate that the designation of Jesus as Lord is very old and was already used by the Aramaic-speaking Christians in Palestine. Eduard Lohse points out that this term meaning "our Lord, come" refers back to Psalm 110:1.[3]

Psalm 110 is quoted by Peter in his sermon in Acts 2, where he tells his fellow Jews that God raised Jesus from the dead and "exalted [him] at the right hand of God," having received "from the Father the promise of the Holy Spirit" (Acts 2:33). Through the resurrection Jesus becomes exalted, and this makes possible the pouring out of the Holy Spirit at Pentecost. This spirit who has been active in Israel can now be poured out by Jesus onto Christians. Having quoted Psalm 110:1, Peter continues, "Therefore let the entire house of Israel know with certainty that God has made him both Lord and Messiah, this Jesus whom you crucified" (Acts 2:36). Sitting at the right hand of God means equal dignity with God, a fact that is also expressed by sitting in the presence of God. Through the resurrection and exaltation, God has made Jesus to be the Messiah. It is not David who has poured out the Spirit but Jesus, since David has never been raised up into heaven to God's right hand, as occurred with Jesus.[4]

The hymn of praise in Colossians 1:15-20 regarding "our Lord Jesus Christ" (Col 1:3) has numerous connections to Paul's letters.[5] Jesus is "the image of the invisible God" (Col 1:15), his manifestation and representative, since an actual picture of God cannot be produced. In Jesus we can approach and experience God. He is "the firstborn of all creation." This implies both a chronological priority and one of significance. In Israel the firstborn had preference over all the other siblings (see Ps 89:27). We owe all of creation, including our own existence, to Jesus Christ, since "in him all things in heaven and on earth were created" (Col 1:16). Jewish philosopher Philo of Alexandria (15/10 BCE-40 CE) wrote in his *On the Special Laws*: "The image of God is the Word, by which all the world was made."[6] In Colossians the divine word through which God created the world is identified with Christ. In him, through

---

3. Eduard Lohse, *Der Brief an die Römer* (Göttingen: Vandenhoeck & Ruprecht, 2003), 296, in his excursus *"Kyrios Jesus."*
4. See Jacob Jervell, *Die Apostelgeschichte* (Göttingen: Vandenhoeck & Ruprecht, 1998), 150, in his comments on Acts 2:36.
5. For details see Ulrich Luz, in J. Becker and U. Luz, *Die Briefe an die Galater, Epheser und Kolosser* (Göttingen: Vandenhoeck & Ruprecht, 1998), in his commentary on Colossians, 200.
6. Philo, *On the Special Laws* 1.16.81.

him, and for him all things were created. Christ is, so to speak, the architect by whom the plan for the world took shape. He is also the force through which the world came into being, and he is the goal toward which the whole creation is directed. Therefore nothing can exist outside or beyond Christ. He is also the one who holds together the whole created order. Philo reasons very similarly, saying: "For the word of the living God being the bond of every thing, as has been said before, holds all things together, and binds all the parts, and prevents them from being loosened or separated."[7] We will notice that in the prologue of the Gospel of John the word or the *logos*, meaning Christ, is the indispensable force in creation.

Again we note the difference that Christ makes when we read that he is "the firstborn from the dead" (Col 1:18). According to apocalyptic thinking, if Jesus was resurrected, then the end-time resurrection will surely follow, since his resurrection necessitates a subsequent resurrection. Jesus is "the first fruits of those who have died" (1 Cor 15:20), and this "first" has significance, since the future resurrection of the faithful is rooted in Christ's resurrection. This "first" can be traced in many New Testament sources, such as Revelation 1:5; Acts 26:23; and so on. But in this hymn of praise we also hear that "in him the fullness of God was pleased to dwell" (Col 1:19). The Godhead freely decided to dwell in Christ, and he became the place where God "dwells." This has nothing to do with Baptism, where the Holy Spirit descended on Jesus, but relates to the incarnation, similar to John 1:14: "The Word became flesh and lived among us, and we have seen his glory, the glory as of a father's only son."

But the divine fullness does not only dwell in Jesus. It pleased God to reconcile to him through Christ all things in the whole cosmos. Through Christ's death the forgiveness of sins has become a reality, since in Christ God reconciled the world with himself. The peace that issues from the reconciliation is not confined to this earth but extends even to heaven, meaning to the cosmic powers. Most people at that time were convinced of many different cosmic powers, as we can see in the multitude of deities that received veneration. But they will all be brought down by Christ. How can this be asserted facing a world that in the first century CE was no more peaceful and reconciled than it is today? Everything hinges on the resurrection of Christ and the confidence that results from it. Since the early Christians had personally

---

7. Philo, *On Flight and Finding* 20.112.

experienced that Christ was indeed resurrected, this experience gave them the confidence that, contrary to all evidence, the present world had no permanence. Christ would fulfill what had begun with his resurrection, the creation of a new world. Christ is then indeed the Lord. Through him God interacts with the world in his salvific and governing activity.

Jesus Stands in the Place of God

Only rarely was Jesus called *kyrios* during his days on earth, though it nevertheless makes sense to trace this term back to Jesus. The actual connection with the *kyrios* was important. Bishop Eusebius of Caesarea (260/264–339/340) writes in his *Ecclesiastical History* that some aristocratic families kept their genealogical records. Among them were those called "*desponsyni* [belonging to the master] so called because of their relation to the Savior's family."[8] Jesus must have been well known as *kyrios* or "master" through these families. Yet for missionary purpose in a Hellenistic world, the term *kyrios* was not so well suited. Therefore it was not often used in the Gospels.[9] Jesus used other means to show his close association with God.

The first remarkable feature is Jesus's conduct. German New Testament scholar Ernst Fuchs (1903–83), in "The Quest for the Historical Jesus" (1956), deals with the parables as a means of investigating Jesus's self-understanding. He asserts that "*Jesus's conduct* was itself the real framework of his proclamation." In this way "Jesus validates the will of God in exactly the same way as a man must do if he were in God's place."[10] God's will is exemplified by Jesus's own conduct. This implies that Jesus's conduct provided the actual context of his proclamation. Consequently, if conduct and speech point in the same direction, we have in all probability an original saying of Jesus. Jesus lived as one who dared to act as if he stood in God's place.

This can be seen best in his approach to the Old Testament law.

Jesus and the Law

Pharisaic-Rabbinic Judaism, which had gained control of the synagogue in Jesus's day, viewed the law "as a thoroughly performable sum

---

8. Eusebius, *Ecclesiastical History* 1.7.
9. This is the explanation given by Foerster, "κύριος," 1093.
10. Ernst Fuchs, "The Quest for the Historical Jesus," in *Studies of the Historical Jesus*, trans. Andrew Scobie (Naperville, IL: Alec R. Allenson, 1964), 21.

of commandments and prohibitions."[11] Altogether there were 248 commands, corresponding to the 248 members of the human body, and 365 prohibitions for the 365 days of the year.[12] The commandments were divided into easy and difficult ones, depending on how much (or little) energy or financial investment they required. Each of these commandments was interpreted by the rabbis through numerous stipulations called *halakah* ("the way"), which were recorded in the *mishna* ("the tradition") in the second or third century. The prime concern of the Pharisees was to fulfill the demands of the Torah as interpreted by the Halakah.

Jesus had no intention of revolting against the Jewish law. Jesus said, "Whoever breaks one of the least of these commandments, and teaches others to do the same, will be called least in the kingdom of heaven; but whoever does them and teaches them will be called great in the kingdom of heaven" (Matt 5:19). With such an approach, he should have had nothing to fear from the Pharisees, the scribes, and the rabbis, who largely followed the rabbinic emphasis on the law. Yet the coexistence of the Torah and the Halakah caused problems for Jesus. He did not just opt for a more radical interpretation of the Torah, as, for instance, the Qumran community did, but drew a sharp distinction between the Torah and the Halakah. When he was challenged on the Halakah (Mark 7:5) he retorted that those who follow it "abandon the commandment of God and hold to human tradition" (Mark 7:8). He flatly rejected the Halakah as human precepts and human tradition, since it was implicitly designed to restrict the commandment of God in order to circumvent it (Mark 7:9).

While others countered such halakic abuses of the law with an even stricter interpretation of the Halakah, Jesus did not promulgate such "secondary" radicalism. Rather, he altered the relationship of the people to the law itself. We can see this best in Jesus's understanding of the Sabbath. When he intentionally violated the Sabbath law, he knew that he had attacked something constitutive of the Jewish way of life. While the Hellenistic world knew of many holidays, it did not have a special day of rest, as the Jewish people did. Yet Jesus pushed aside the

---

11. Leonhard Goppelt, *Theology of the New Testament*, trans. John E. Alsup (Grand Rapids: Eerdmans, 1981), 1:88. As Udo Schnelle, *Theology of the New Testament*, trans. M. Eugene Boring (Grand Rapids: Baker Academic, 2009), 134–38, points out, there was a multifaceted understanding of the law during the time of Jesus. Yet each position presupposed that the law could be fulfilled.
12. See Hermann L. Strack and Paul Billerbeck, *Kommentar zum Neuen Testament aus Talmud und Midrasch*, vol. 1, *Das Evangelium nach Matthäus*, 2nd ed. (Munich: C. H. Beck, 1966), 900–902, who provide numerous illustrations. We notice here that numbers were not left to chance but had significance beyond that for which they were used.

Halakah, claiming that "it had been developed only to reduce the area of human responsibility."[13] Jesus did not just question the interpretation of the commandment but the validity of the commandment itself. As he was going to heal someone on the Sabbath, he asked a rhetorical question: "Is it lawful to do good or to do harm on the Sabbath, to save life or to kill?" (Mark 3:4). This put the whole issue of keeping the Sabbath into a new light. It was no longer just a question of whether human life was at stake. He introduced the maxim "At all times and in all places conduct yourself in such a way that life is enhanced and not diminished." In principle Judaism would have agreed with this precept. Yet Jewish leaders held that it was illusory to enact this precept in everyday life. There the commandment (and its Halakah) limited the responsibility of the people to God. Jesus, however, expressed a total and unlimited demand. In healing the sick person he suspended the Sabbath commandment while showing that through this action God's unrestricted intention of enhancing life had been accomplished. The Jews had only one choice: either to align themselves with Jesus and therewith agree to this suspension of the law, the very foundation of their faith, or to adhere to the law and to eliminate its suspender.

Jesus's attitude towards the law culminates in the so-called antitheses of the Sermon on the Mount (Matt 5:21–48). He contrasted the halakic "You have heard that it was said to those in ancient times" with his own "but I say to you." He does not establish a new Halakah, but with an emphatic "I" Jesus authoritatively sets his command, that is, the will of God, in opposition to the traditional understanding of the divine will. Jesus makes it clear that he does not abolish the law. "Do not think that I have come to abolish the law or the prophets; I have come not to abolish but to fulfill" (Matt 5:17). But "the law and the prophets were in effect until John came" (Luke 16:16). Here it becomes clear that with Jesus's proclamation of God's will, his listeners experience a new and final disclosure of the divine will. As we heard from Ernst Fuchs, Jesus "dares to affirm the will of God as though he himself stood in God's place."[14] Jesus did not abolish the commandment concerning the Sabbath or any other commandment (Matt 5:18). They were given by God for our life on earth, which is threatened by sinfulness and evil. Decisive, however, was that Jesus pointed to what stood behind the law, the God who wills the preservation and enhancement of life. Since in Jesus's life and mission God is present, his proclamation of God's will

---

13. Goppelt, *Theology of the New Testament*, 1:93. See ibid., 93–94 for the following.
14. Fuchs, "Quest for the Historical Jesus," 21.

is of utmost importance for people who want to enter the kingdom of God. Therefore he told them: "Unless your righteousness exceeds that of the scribes and the Pharisees, you will never enter the kingdom of heaven" (Matt 5:20). Jesus's authoritative explication of God's will is part of God's eschatological saving activity, which had begun in Jesus. This means that Jesus understood himself as executing God's will.

Jesus Allows *Proskynēsis*

Since Jesus saw himself in line with God, it is not surprising that he allows prostration (*proskynēsis*) before him. *Prostration* is the technical term for venerating deities; it dates far back in the history of religion in the Mediterranean region. Homer, who lived in the seventh or eighth century BCE, tells of Odysseus that "he kissed the earth, and lifting up his hands prayed to the nymphs" as a sign of veneration after he had been rescued from the sea.[15] In the Septuagint too *proskynēsis* refers predominantly to adoration of the true God or of idols. We hear, for instance, in the context of the Ten Commandments concerning anything that is on earth, in heaven, or beneath the earth: "You shall not bow down [*proskyneo*] to them or worship them; for I am the Lord your God" (Exod 20:5). For the Israelites as well as for Christians, *proskynēsis* is reserved for God alone.

We read in the story of the wise men that when they entered the house and saw the child "they knelt down [*proskynēsis*] and paid him homage" (Matt 2:11). Of course, as a newborn baby Jesus could not have rejected such adoration that was reserved for God alone. The situation is different when, later in his life, such adoration was directed to him as an adult, for instance when "a leper came to him, and knelt before him" (Matt 8:2). People seem to sense that Jesus is at least a divine agent, and therefore they respond with *proskynēsis*. When the disciples execute *proskynēsis*, they usually seem to have an understanding of who Jesus really is, such as when he walks on water, to which they respond with *proskynēsis*, saying, "Truly you are the Son of God" (Matt 14:33). But then the story goes even further.

Jesus Identifies Himself with God

Jesus identified himself in such a way with God as to claim that he was

---

15. Homer, *Odyssey* 13.412–413, trans. Robert Fitzgerald, 273, swcta.net/moore/files/2014/08/The-Odyssey-Greek-Translation.pdf, accessed April 7, 2016.

the final self-disclosure of God; his confession of such led to his conviction as a heretic. But how did he express this? In his trial before the Sanhedrin, the question is put to Jesus: "Are you the Christ, the Son of the Blessed One?" (Mark 14:61). Based on Jesus's answer to this question, the high priest concludes that Jesus has committed blasphemy. But what was contained in Jesus's answer that would lead to such a devastating reaction? Jesus seemingly recites only Jewish eschatological expectations from the Old Testament when he answers: "I am; and 'you will see the Son of Man seated at the right hand of the Power,' and 'coming with the clouds of heaven'" (Mark 14:62).

The issue becomes clear when we consider the Old Testament use of the opening phrase in Jesus's answer, "I am" (*egō eimi*). In the Septuagint we find this phrase several times, most prominently in Deutero-Isaiah, rendering the Hebrew 'anî hû', meaning "I [am] He," into Greek. In Deutero-Isaiah the phrase 'anî hû' is a solemn statement or assertion that is always attributed to Yahweh (e.g., Isa 41:4; 43:10; 46:4). Over against claims made by other gods, this phrase asserts polemically "I am He," that Yahweh is he, that is, the Lord of history. It also seems to be a concise abbreviation of the longer form of divine self-predication, especially of "I am Yahweh." While the 'anî hû' formula as divine self-predication of Yahweh occurs outside Deutero-Isaiah only in Deuteronomy 32:39, the self-predication "I am Yahweh" is rather widespread in the Old Testament. As German New Testament scholar Ethelbert Stauffer (1902-79) has pointed out, there is also some evidence that the 'anî hû' was used liturgically in the worship of the Jerusalem temple, since the Levites presumably sang the Song of Moses, containing Deuteronomy 32:39, on the Sabbath of the Feast of Tabernacles.[16] The use of 'anî hû' lived on in the worship service of the temple and of the synagogues and was even known to the Qumran community.

At a few decisive places in the Gospels, Jesus uses the term *egō eimi* in a way analogous to the Old Testament theophany formula. For instance, according to Mark 13:6, Jesus says: "Many will come in my name and say, 'I am he!' and they will lead many astray." In Matthew this theophanic self-predication is expanded into an explicitly christological statement that reads "saying, 'I am the Messiah!'" (Matt 24:5).

Returning to the answer that Jesus gave the high priest in Mark 14:62, we must admit that it could be interpreted without reference

---

16. So Ethelbert Stauffer, *Jesus and His Story*, trans. Richard and Clara Winston (New York: Alfred A. Knopf, 1960), 179.

to the Old Testament revelational phrase 'anî hû' or to any of its variations. It could simply have been a solemn way of saying "yes," as Matthew interprets it in Matthew 26:64. Philip B. Harner, for instance, arrives at the conclusion that "it is not likely that we can understand the *ego eimi* of Mark 14:62 and Luke 22:70 in an absolute sense."[17] This is surprising, however, considering that the corollary evidence seems to lead in the opposite direction, namely that the *egō eimi* in Mark 14:62 is indeed used in an absolute sense as a divine self-predication. The matter becomes clearer if we look at the usage of *egō eimi* in other passages in Mark. The phrase appears first in Mark 6:50, at the conclusion of the account of the miracle of the walking on water, where Jesus tells his disciples: "Take heart, it is I; do not be afraid." Here the phrase functions almost in a titular sense and as a revelational phrase. In Mark 13:6 Jesus warned his disciples, "Many will come in my name, saying, 'I am he!' and they will lead many astray." Again *egō eimi* is used as a formula of revelation or identification, since its misappropriation leads the believer astray.

We may conclude that Jesus's use of the *egō eimi* in Mark 14:62 is more than a simple affirmation. He uses a revelational phrase to disclose himself and identify himself with God. As the words following the *egō eimi* show, the messianic secret is lifted, and Jesus unashamedly admits his divine sonship: "In Mk. 14:62 therefore Jesus is making an explicit Messianic claim, the Messianic Secret is being formally disclosed."[18] Since the messianic secret was carefully hidden in Mark, we may wonder whether Jesus's response does not reflect the theology of the evangelist more than Jesus's own words. We might be overestimating the historical value of this passage if we do not concede the possibility that this passage has been carefully edited to reflect the eschatological hopes of the nascent church.

There is yet another way of determining the historical probability of the *egō eimi* response of Jesus at his trial. As Ernst Fuchs has pointed out, Jesus emphasizes in his proclamation the will of God in such a way that only someone who stood in God's place could do.[19] For instance, in his parables Jesus does not simply tell us how God acts but tells us that God acts the way Jesus does. Luke writes that the Pharisees and scribes remark, "this fellow welcomes sinners and eats with them" (Luke 15:2).

---

17. Philip H. Harner, *The "I Am" of the Fourth Gospel* (Philadelphia: Fortress Press, Facet Books, 1970), 34.
18. Norman Perrin, "The High Priest's Question and Jesus's Answer (Mark 14:61-62)," in *The Passion in Mark: Studies on Mark 14-16*, ed. Werner H. Kelber (Philadelphia: Fortress Press, 1976), 82.
19. For the following see Fuchs, "Quest for the Historical Jesus," 20–21.

In response to this remark, Jesus tells them parables of God's concern for the lost and sinful, implying that God acts like Jesus. Mark 14:62 would then indicate that at the end of his career Jesus not only acted as if he stood in God's place, but he actually did act in God's place by using the revelational formula *egō eimi*. In all likelihood *egō eimi* was Jesus's own response to the high priest. Since Jesus did not conform to the prevalent messianic expectations but nevertheless made claims that could only be understood in messianic terms, the high priests and most other people at that time conclude that Jesus has committed blasphemy.

Another similarly misunderstood theophanic self-predication occurs in Jesus's reply to the Samaritan woman. She says to him in the traditional messianic expectation, "'I know that Messiah is coming' (who is called Christ). 'When he comes, he will proclaim all things to us.'" Jesus corrects her, saying, "I am he, the one who is speaking to you" (John 4:25-26). He reveals himself as the full self-disclosure of God. But the woman does not understand him. She is too enmeshed in the traditional pattern of messianic thinking.

The overall impression that Jesus of Nazareth left was of one who had assumed an authority unlike anyone before him. He considers himself empowered to go beyond the law and point to its real meaning. He claims to stand in God's place as one who conveys God and God's will to his people. He emphasizes that God's will will exalt him as judge and savior of all. Yet there is still another term we need to consider if we want to assess the relationship between God (the Father) and Jesus.

God as Father

In the Old Testament we read that Israel is God's son and "You [Israelites] are children [sons] of the Lord your God" (Deut 14:1). In Judaism, then, to address God as father became quite popular. Small wonder that Jesus too addresses God as Father. As Joachim Jeremias (1900-1979) notes, "there is an increasing tendency to insert the designation of God as Father into Jesus's words."[20] Having critically examined the 170 uses of "Father" for God in the mouth of Jesus as recorded in the Gospels, Jeremias states that when Jesus speaks of "your Father" he speaks only to his disciples and nobody else beyond the Twelve. Therefore, "'your Father' is one of the core words in the didache of

---

20. Joachim Jeremias, *Abba. Studien zur neutestamentlichen Theologie und Zeitgeschichte* (Göttingen: Vandenhoeck & Ruprecht, 1966), 34.

the disciples."[21] God shows himself as their father in forgiving them; God treats them with mercy and care and provides for their salvation. There are also sayings in which Jesus refers to God as "my Father." Jeremias analyzes carefully Matthew 11:27 ("All things have been handed over to me by my Father, and no one knows the Father except the Son and anyone to whom the Son chooses to reveal him") and comes to the conclusion that this is a central assertion of Jesus concerning his mission. Jesus claims "to be in a singular way the recipient and mediator of the knowledge of God, a claim which has numerous parallels in the Gospels."[22] All these passages express the singular revelation and authority given to Jesus. Yet he did not talk about this very often, only to his disciples. His authority is founded in the disclosure of God to him, just like a father talks to his son. It is not surprising that this usage has no parallels in rabbinic literature.

It is most interesting that when Jesus addresses God as Father he uses the Aramaic *Abba*. For example, at Gethsemane Jesus prays to God: "Abba, Father, for you all things are possible" (Mark 14:36), inquiring whether he must succumb to capture, trial, and death. Paul even tells us that this term was used in Christian congregations in addressing God, something that seems strange, since they usually conducted their services in Greek. So we read in Romans 8:15: "When we cry, 'Abba! Father!' is that very Spirit bearing witness with our spirit that we are children of God." Evidently they followed the example set by Jesus himself. Since there is not a single text in Jewish literature in which God is addressed as "Abba," this usage is unique to Jesus. Why would he do this?

Abba is actually Aramaic baby talk. It was used in postbiblical times, as Bishop John Chrysostom (347-407) tells us: "'Abba, Father,' which name is a special sign of true-born children to their fathers."[23] In the days of Jesus *Abba* was no longer baby talk but the address of grown-up children to their father. When Jesus addresses God with *Abba*, this not just a sign of intimacy between Jesus and God but, as we gather from the Gethsemane episode, shows the total obedience of the Son to the Father ("yet not what I want but what you want"). As Jeremias notes, Jesus never talks about "our Father" when he talks with the disciples about their relationship with God but distinguishes between "my

---

21. Ibid., 46.
22. Ibid., 53.
23. Chrysostom, *The Epistle to the Romans* (Homily 15) (NPNF[1] 11:442), in reference to Romans 8:15; and see also Jeremias, *Abba*, 61, who refers here also to other church fathers indicating the usage of *Abba* in postbiblical Antioch.

Father" and "your Father."[24] "According to Mt. [Matthew] Jesus taught His disciples to pray: 'Our Father.' But in the Synoptics, even in traces of the earliest sources, we never find that He associated Himself with the disciples in this 'our.' Thus 'my' expresses a relationship to God which cannot be transferred."[25] By using *Abba* Jesus expresses the certainty that the Father has given him full knowledge of God, and therefore he can disclose God to his disciples. Since the disciples are allowed and even taught to use the term *Abba* in the Lord's Prayer, they can participate in his relationship with God. Yet this address is reserved for God and should not be used in everyday language, as Jesus enjoins his disciples (see Matt 23:9).

We can now conclude that Jesus had a unique relationship to God, knowing him intimately, representing him, and acting in his place.[26] Since he was also truly human, we can appropriately call him the human face of God. But what about the Holy Spirit?

The Spirit of God

In Judaism one encounters a more independent spirit, which is shown by personal attributes that are accorded to him.[27] The spirit speaks, is in sorrow, comforts, and rejoices, to name just a few of his ways of interacting with humanity. Yet the Spirit is God's and is sent by God. Having the spirit is a sign of God's grace and of being in contact with God.

God's Spirit at Work in Jesus

In the New Testament Jesus is seen as having God's Spirit in order to perform miraculous healings (Matt 12:16–18). This is interpreted as fulfillment of the Old Testament prophecies. In the story of Jesus's temptation, the Spirit "drove him out into the wilderness" (Mark 1:12), indicating the irresistible power of God's Spirit. At Jesus's Baptism, the Spirit descends on him, and a voice from heaven is heard (Mark 1:10–11). Jesus is the messianic figure on whom the Spirit rests. Yet already his conception was the work of the Holy Spirit (Matt 1:18–20).

---

24. See Jeremias, *Abba*, 64.
25. So rightly Gottlob Schrenk, "*Pater: D. Father in the New Testament*," in *TDNT* 5:988.
26. Craig A. Evans, "Jesus's Self-Designation 'The Son of Man,'" in *The Trinity: An Interdisciplinary Symposium on the Trinity*, ed. Stephen T. Davis et al. (Oxford: Oxford University Press, 1999), 46, rightly concludes: "The belief in the deity of Jesus appears to be rooted in his teaching and activities and not simply in post-Easter ideas."
27. See for the following Erik Sjöberg, "*Ruah*," in *TDNT* 6:387.

God's creative power brings forth Jesus. When he starts his teaching ministry in Nazareth he quotes Isaiah 61:1-2, saying: "The Spirit of the Lord is upon me, because he has anointed me to bring good news to the poor," and concludes: "Today this Scripture has been fulfilled in your hearing" (Luke 4:18-21). From the very beginning Jesus is in full possession of the Holy Spirit, not just since Baptism or the beginning of his ministry but from his conception. Similar to Moses, Jesus can then impart the Spirit to the Christian community.

After his resurrection Jesus gives the Holy Spirit to his followers. He announces this impartation by saying: "I am sending upon you what my Father has promised" (Luke 24:49); they "will be baptized with the Holy Spirit" (Acts 1:5). There is no actual Baptism for his followers but an outpouring of the Holy Spirit on them. This event is described in very graphic details: "And suddenly from heaven there came a sound like the rush of a violent wind, and it filled the entire house where they were sitting. Divided tongues, as of fire, appeared among them, and a tongue rested on each of them" (Acts 2:2-3). The strong sound and the fire reminds us of the appearance of God at Mount Sinai (Exod 19:16-18). The advent of the Spirit is audible and visible. He rests on each of them, and they are filled with the Spirit. Now they begin to speak "in other languages," though it remains undetermined whether this means speaking in tongues or actually in other languages to communicate the gospel with the Jews who have come from different countries. Since the Spirit gives the ability to perform unusual deeds, it could actually refer to speaking in other languages. Especially in the Acts of the Apostles, we notice that the apostles are under the guidance of the Holy Spirit. For instance, the Spirit speaks to Peter (Acts 10:19), he sets Barnabas and Paul apart for the work to which "he called them" (Acts 13:2), and Peter and John lay their hands on people in Samaria so that "they received the Holy Spirit" (Acts 8:17).

The Spirit and Baptism

Usually the Holy Spirit is imparted in Baptism. This is not surprising since we read in the command of the risen Lord: "Go therefore and make disciples of all nations, baptizing them in the name of the Father and of the Son and of the Holy Spirit" (Matt 28:19). Father, Son, and Holy Spirit appear here next to one another, and Baptism is administered in their name. This contrasts to other New Testament passages in which we read of Baptism "in the name of Jesus Christ" (Acts 2:38; 19:5).

Matthew gives no explanation whether or how the Son and the Spirit are coeternal with the Father and therefore would form a Trinity. "The essential point is that the one encountered in Jesus as the Son of God and in the Spirit-led church as the people of God is not some subordinate deity, but the one true God."[28] Yet Baptism administered without at least calling on the name of Jesus is a Baptism without the Spirit, as we see with the followers of John the Baptist who do not have the Holy Spirit (Acts 19:1–7).

We hear already from John the Baptist that he baptizes "with water for repentance," but after him someone is coming who "will baptize with the Holy Spirit and with fire" (Matt 3:11; see also John 1:33). Though we have some indications that Jesus baptized (see John 3:22–4:1), the Gospel of John makes it clear that "it was not Jesus himself but his disciples who baptized" (John 4:2). This sounds like a later correction to make sure that Jesus was not "an imitator of John the Baptist."[29] In addition, we are told in the Acts of the Apostles that with John's baptism the gift of the Holy Spirit is not yet conveyed. Only when they are baptized "in the name of the Lord Jesus" and Paul lays his hands on them does "the Holy Spirit came upon them" (Acts 19:5–6). Yet New Testament scholar Robert W. Wall (1947–) in his commentary on this episode cautions us that we should "not presume a formal relationship between Christian baptism and the reception of the Holy Spirit."[30] In Acts of the Apostles Christian baptism can be administered without any reference to the reception of the Spirit (Acts 16:15), and the outpouring of the Spirit of prophecy, which in this episode is connected with Baptism, can occur prior to Baptism, as was the case with Paul himself (Acts 9:17), or after Baptism, as with the above-mentioned Christians in Samaria (Acts 8:15–17), or there can be baptism with the reception of the Holy Spirit but without any mention of prophecy (Acts 2:38). There is not one instance in the New Testament that follows the sequence baptism, reception of the Holy Spirit, and prophecy. One thing is certain: that Christian Baptism, whether in the name of Father, Son, and Holy Spirit or just in the name of Jesus (Christ) is intimately connected with the Holy Spirit.

---

28. M. Eugene Boring, *The Gospel of Matthew*, in *NIB*, on Matthew 28:18–20.
29. So Gail R. O'Day, *The Gospel of John*, in *NIB*, on John 4:2.
30. Robert W. Wall, *The Acts of the Apostles*, in *NIB*, on Acts 19:5–7.

The Paraclete and Jesus

The Gospel of John does not talk explicitly about the Holy Spirit. Jesus, however, promises his disciples that his Father will give them "another Advocate" who will be with them forever. "This is the Spirit of truth whom the world cannot receive" (John 14:16–17). This mentioning of "other advocate," or *paraklētos* in Greek, seems to imply that Jesus himself is the paraclete or advocate of his disciples. This view is strengthened when we read in 1 John 2:1: "We have an advocate [*paraklētos*] with the Father, Jesus Christ the righteous." This Spirit will be in and with his disciples as Jesus now is in and with them (John 14:17–20). In the Spirit Jesus will come to his disciples (John 14:18), though he is not identical with the Spirit. He tells his disciples that once he is gone "I will send him to you" (John 16:7). But both Jesus and the Spirit are sent by God and proceed from him. They teach and witness to God and convict the world of its sins (John 16:8).

Only five times in the Johannine writings (John 14:16–26; 15:26; 16:7; 1 John 2:1) and nowhere else in the New Testament do we find this term *paraklētos*. Since the term is not self-explanatory, each time the paraclete is mentioned, his function is explained. We notice already in the Old Testament that important people such as Moses [Exod 32:11] and Amos [Amos 7:2] intercede to God for their people. The pseudepigraphic Testament of Judah states that "the spirit of truth testifies to all things and brings all accusations" [Testament of Judah 20:5]. This means there is an advocate who convicts people of their sins, something that is again picked up by John. This angel-like spirit convicts as the spirit of truth and furthers spiritual existence as the spirit of knowledge.[31] A plurality of good and evil spirits and a further development of a dualistic worldview was propagated especially in late Judaism and to some extent found its continuity in the New Testament.

When Jesus talks about a paraclete, we notice that the paraclete stands firm on his side as the one who witnesses to him and helps the disciples to remember Jesus's words and actions after he has been glorified. In convicting the world, the dualistic view emerges but is at once overcome, since "the ruler of this world has been condemned" (John 16:11). This shows God's righteousness, since in death Jesus goes to God and completes his work. Therefore we read in 1 John 2:1 that "we have an advocate with the Father, Jesus Christ the righteous." This would

---

31. See Eduard Schweitzer, "πνεῦμα," in *TDNT* 6:443–44.

mean that Jesus Christ himself can be the advocate or the paraclete. The sign of apparent defeat is actually the victory sign over a sinful world, since with his death Jesus has atoned for the sins of the whole world and can bring this to the attention of God the Father.

While the Spirit had already descended on Jesus at his baptism (John 1:34), the gift of the Spirit becomes a reality in believers' lives only after Jesus's death, resurrection, and ascension (John 20:22). Therefore the evangelist explains: "For as yet there was no Spirit, because Jesus was not yet glorified" (John 7:39). While the Spirit is already present, "Spirit as it is known in the life of the church did not yet exist, because the Spirit of God is redefined in the light of Jesus's death, resurrection, and ascension."[32] This "post-Jesus time" is exactly the period in which Paul reflects on the work of the Holy Spirit.

Being in the Spirit

When we read, "Now the Lord is the Spirit, and where the Spirit of the Lord is, there is freedom. ... for this comes from the Lord, the Spirit" (2 Cor 3:17-18), we are unable to clearly discern who is meant by "Lord" (*kyrios*) and how this *kyrios* is related to the Spirit. More precisely, Paul writes of "the Spirit of God" and of "the Spirit that is from God" (1 Cor 2:11-12), indicating that there is also a "spirit of the world." Paul then tells the Christians in Rome: "The Spirit of God dwells in you. Anyone who does not have the Spirit of Christ does not belong to him" (Rom 8:9), intimating that the Spirit of God and the Spirit of Christ are the same. Paul continues: "If the Spirit of him who raised Jesus from the dead dwells in you, he who raised Christ from the dead will give life to your mortal bodies also through his Spirit that dwells in you" (Rom 8:11). The Holy Spirit is that divine power through which Jesus was raised to new life, and it is that divine gift that is imparted to believers. It is not a divine substance but that power that was promised in the Old Testament and that Christians now experience in God's present acts.

"It is God in the Spirit, who is present in Christ, who as Lord, establishes and enables the new life of the faithful."[33] When we look back at Romans 8:9-11, then, "Paul's primary interest is to affirm in as many ways as possible the divine presence with believers as that which defines them and gives them meaning" and not the relationship

---

32. So O'Day, *Gospel of John*, on John 7:39.
33. So Eduard Lohse, *Der Brief an die Römer* (Göttingen: Vandenhoeck & Ruprecht, 2003), 233, in his excursus on the Spirit.

between Father, Son, and Holy Spirit.[34] Since Christ is active in the Christian community, he can be identified with the Spirit, and since he is the Lord of the Spirit, he can be distinguished from the Spirit. We see the distinction between Christ and Spirit in Paul's argumentation concerning Christ's resurrection, where he writes: "'The first man, Adam, became a living being'; the last Adam became a life-giving spirit" (1 Cor 15:45). The resurrected and exalted Jesus Christ is present through the Spirit. Paul's primary interest is to affirm in different ways God's presence with believers as that which defines them and gives them new meaning in life. He affirms that "the ministry of the Spirit [will] come in glory" (2 Cor 3:8), since it is a ministry empowered by the Spirit. Behind it stands "the Spirit of the living God" (2 Cor 3:3).

The life of a person is decided by relying either on the flesh, by which Paul means worldly standards, or on the Spirit. Paul writes: "If you sow on the Spirit, you will reap eternal life from the Spirit" (Gal 6:8). The work and power of the Spirit is therefore eschatologically structured, leading to life eternal. It is a decision to "live by the Spirit" (Gal 5:16) and to be "led by the Spirit" (Gal 6:18). In so doing we escape the ways of this world and reap the fruit of the Spirit, meaning a life in tune with God.

Traces of the Trinity?

Yet what is the relation of the Spirit in terms of the Trinity? Paul uses a triadic formula in a letter, saying, "The grace of our Lord Jesus Christ, the love of God, and the communion of the Holy Spirit be with all of you" (2 Cor 13:13), and he mentions in one breath the same Spirit, the same Lord, and the same God (1 Cor 12:4-6). But these references do not express a Trinitarian relationship between Father, Son, and Holy Spirit. The exalted Christ is present in the Spirit, and the faithful are living in the Spirit. The Spirit is intimately related to the Father and to the Son as God's gift and empowerment in the end time. But there is no personal unity of the three. Paul and with him the whole New Testament was not interested in such an issue. For him it was decisive that God was acting in the risen Christ through the power of his Spirit for the benefit of the faithful. God as the sender of salvation had acted through Jesus as the bringer of salvation and continued to be present in his Spirit, dispensed through the risen Christ. The early Christian community was so excited about salvation being offered through God's gra-

---

34. So J. Paul Sampley, *The Second Letter to the Corinthians*, in *NIB*, in his comments on 2 Corinthians 3.

ciousness that questions about the relationship between Father, Son, and Holy Spirit were deemed futile.

But such questions soon arose, as we can see in the Johannine Comma (comma meaning here a short clause), which may date back to the second or third century. In 1 John 5:7-8 we read: "There are three that testify: the Spirit and the water and the blood, and these three agree." In addition to the Spirit as witness to salvation is Jesus, whereby the water may stand for his Baptism and the blood for his death. But in the later amended version the text reads: "There are three that testify in heaven, the Father, the Word, and the Holy Spirit, and these three are one. And there are three that testify on earth, the Spirit and the water and the blood, and these three agree." The heavenly witnesses and the witnesses on earth agree with each other. Moreover, the Father, Son, and Holy Spirit are pronounced as one. Yet such considerations go beyond the New Testament witness and belong to the affirmations of the early church.

What do we find, then, in the New Testament concerning the Trinity? Certainly, God the Father gains prominence, especially in Jesus's own words. Jesus considers himself the Son over against God as his Father. He even claims oneness with God. Yet what about the Holy Spirit? Edmund Fortman states the issue squarely: "The New Testament writers do not witness to the Holy Spirit as fully and clearly as they do to the Son."[35] The Spirit is still God's empowering Spirit, through whom—or rather through which—Jesus conducts his ministry, through which Jesus is resurrected from the dead, and through which God in Jesus Christ continues to be present until today. In the Gospel of John the paraclete assumes person-like features. But is he really the Holy Spirit if Jesus Christ is also called the paraclete?[36] There is no explicit reference in the New Testament that in one God there are three coequal divine persons.

In the Pauline writings the Spirit has a certain independent status. The Spirit leads to the Father, for he teaches believers to say "Abba"

---

35. Edmund J. Fortman, *The Triune God: A Historical Study of the Doctrine of the Trinity* (Philadelphia: Westminster, 1972), 32.
36. Ben Witherington III, "The Trinity in the Johannine Literature," in the massive and commendable *Oxford Handbook of the Trinity*, ed. Gilles Emery and Matthew Levering (Oxford: Oxford University Press, 2011), 77, seems to be too optimistic when he writes with regard to the Gospel of John and the Johannine Letters: "While most Trinitarian discussion in the NT is implicit at best, here it begins to become more explicit because we begin to get rather clear-cut divisions of labor in regard to what Father, Son, and Spirit do, even though they all testify to the same truth." The division of labor is not that clear cut, especially when we consider that Jesus talks about another paraclete and then he himself is called paraclete. Now, who is who?

(Rom 8:15), he makes intercession for the saints before God, and he even searches out the depth of God (1 Cor 2:10). While this does not allot to the Spirit the status of an independent person, he is still far off in personal terms. The Spirit comes from God and is closely related to Jesus Christ in his works. When we come to the Gospel of John, there is a unity of the essential being between Father and Son, a unity that is realized in the unity of their will and work. *"John advocates an exclusive monotheism in the binitarian form: the worship of the one God is extended to the Son."*[37] Out of the fullness of the unity of Father and Son the Father and/or the Son sends the Spirit, whose origin is oriented entirely to the Father and the Son. There is no mutual indwelling of the Spirit in either Father or Son. Therefore the claim by German New Testament scholar Udo Schnelle (1939–) that "Johannine thinking is trinitarian thinking!" is slightly exaggerated.[38] Wherever we look in the New Testament, there are a few triadic formulas in which Father, Son, and Holy Spirit are mentioned, but the three are not reflected on in and for themselves but rather in terms of their roles and functions in the divine plan of salvation. That this salvation was finally accomplished through Jesus, the human face of God, and by the power of the Spirit of God was of utmost importance for the New Testament writers. Everything else was relegated to second place.

---

37. Udo Schnelle, *Theology of the New Testament*, trans. M. Eugene Boring (Grand Rapids: Baker Academic, 2009), 711.
38. Ibid., 712.

3

The Early Church and the Emerging Trinitarian Reflections

The Apostles' Creed, which dates back to the second century, starts with the affirmation of God the Father, the Creator of heaven and earth. This monotheistic faith, "grounded in the religion of Israel, loomed large in the minds of the earliest fathers; though not reflective theologians, they were fully conscious that it marked the dividing line between the Church and paganism."[1] Yet addressing God as Father raised the issue of his relation to the Son. As we have seen, however, Jesus never told his listeners about his relation to his Father except that he acted as if he stood in God's place. This "implicit" Christology was then changed after Easter into an explicit Christology by the Christian community. But why did it not it suffice to say that God the Father was the sender of salvation and Jesus Christ its bringer? Why did the question become who Jesus himself was, and why was his relation to the Father so important? This becomes at once clear if we consider the context of the time. We will see that these questions are by no means just speculative questions but are of truly existential import.

---

1. J. N. D. Kelly, *Early Christian Doctrines* (New York: Harper & Row, 1978), 83.

Existential Questions and Experimental Answers

In the Hellenistic context demigods abounded. Quite often these semi-divine emissaries came to the help of humans. But they were subject to the laws of this world and its finitude, and their help could at most be of a temporary nature. If Jesus Christ can provide lasting salvation, then, in the minds of people in a first-century Hellenistic environment, he must be truly divine. This option, however, posed the danger of polytheism. Would not the true divinity of Christ impair the Jewish monotheism out of which most Christians initially came? If there was more than one God, these "gods" would have to fight for supremacy among each other, or each of them would have only a limited sphere of influence. Considerations like these influenced the so-called Trinitarian controversy, actually a misnomer for these discussions, since the concept of the Holy Spirit was only given ancillary attention.

The subsequent christological controversy again confronted some of the following truly existential questions: If Jesus had not really assumed human nature, as was commonly believed at the time, could he have actually redeemed humanity, since he would have been so removed from it? Yet if he had taken on human nature, did this not threaten his divinity, from which salvation would necessarily have come? But even if both "natures" were maintained, how could they ever be joined to form one being? Would not a savior composed of two "natures" almost resemble a monster, totally unlike a truly divine or truly human being? One can easily imagine that questions like these defied easy answers or simple solutions. In addition, there was no ready-made terminology that one could use, since strict monotheism combined with a totally divine savior would have been a novelty in a world that was either monotheistic (Judaism) or polytheistic (Hellenism) but not both.

Then there was the divine Spirit. It had been interchangeably attributed to either Father or Son. Again, the exact nature of the relation between God and Spirit or Christ and Spirit or even between all three was not yet in focus. Of course, Christians always abhorred the idea that they venerated more than one God. But how could the two or three divine entities be subsumed under one deity? In writing about the creation, Bishop Theophilus of Antioch (ca. 183) says: "In like manner also the three days which were before the luminaries, are types of the Trinity [*triados*], of God, and His Word, and His wisdom."[2] This term *triados* seems to be the first use of a term resembling *Trinity*, yet without defining exactly what is meant by this term. The actual term *Trinity* was introduced by Tertullian (after 150–after 220), who wrote both in Greek and Latin.³ He wrote an apology against Praxeas, of whom we know nothing except that he thought that the Father and the Son were so much the same that we could say that God the Father suffered on the cross. Tertullian points out that the biblical witness is different. We worship neither two nor three gods; rather, there is a unity of the Godhead "which derives the Trinity out of its own self."⁴ He is the first, as far as we know, to use the term *Trinity* in its present meaning, and he also reflects on the nature of the Trinitarian relationship.

But at the beginning there were rather simple statements about Jesus Christ that show the necessity of regarding him as fully divine. We read in 2 Clement 1:1-2: "We ought to think of Jesus Christ as we do of God, as the judge of the living and the dead. And we ought not to belittle the one who is our salvation, for when we belittle him, we also hope to receive but little."⁵ Jesus Christ is our Savior only if he is truly divine. But how is he related to God the Father in his divinity? To this Ignatius of Antioch (second century) responds: "There is only one physician, who is both flesh and spirit, born and unborn, God in man, true life in death, both from Mary and from God, first subject to suffering and then beyond it, Jesus Christ our Lord" (Ignatius, *To the Ephesians* 7.2).⁶ Here we are again confronted with the assertion of the true divinity of Christ, but now with more intensive reflection, indicating two ways of looking at Christ, the human and the divine. How the two are related is not yet enunciated. Here the first eminent theologian of the early church, Origen of Alexandria (ca. 185–ca. 253), puts forth a decisive elaboration. That a clarification was needed is evident by Justin Martyr's (ca. 100–ca. 165) designation of Christ simply as "another God and Lord subject to the Maker of all things."⁷ No wonder his Jewish opponent objected to such unadulterated polytheism.

To avert the danger of pluralism within the divinity, monarchianism, meaning "one primordial power," was advanced. But whether in the dynamistic form, which saw an impersonal divine power active

---

2. Theophilus, *To Autolycus* 2.15 (*ANF* 2:100–101).
3. So also Stephen M. Hildebrand, "The Trinity in the Ante-Nicene Fathers," in *Oxford Handbook of the Trinity*, ed. Gilles Emery and Matthew Levering (Oxford: Oxford University Press, 2011), 106, without citing the source.
4. Tertullian, *Against Praxeas* 3 (*ANF* 3:599).
5. Ichael W. Holmes, trans. and ed., *The Apostolic Fathers in English*, 3rd ed. (Grand Rapids: Baker Academic, 2006), 77.
6. Ibid., 98.
7. Justin Martyr, *Dialogue with Trypho* 56 (*ANF* 1:223).

in the human being Jesus, or in the modalistic variety, which argued that the Son and the Spirit are simply modes of the appearance of the one God, monarchianists claimed "that the Savior was merely human," an assertion to which Eusebius of Caesarea (ca. 260–ca. 340) rightly objected.[8] While the proponents of monarchism "saved" monotheism, they sacrificed the divinity of Christ to do so. More clarity was introduced by Irenaeus (ca. 130–202), who wrote:

> Therefore the Father is Lord, and the Son is Lord, and the Father is God and the Son is God; for He who is born of God is God. And thus God is shown to be one according to the essence of His being and power; but at the same time, as the administrator of the economy of our redemption, He is both Father and Son: since the Father of all is invisible and inaccessible to creatures, it is through the Son that those who are to approach God must have access to the Father.[9]

Irenaeus of Lyons (in present-day France) avoids a divine pluralism and emphasizes the unity of God. In talking about the economy of redemption, he introduces a salvation-historical approach, but that nearly leads him to a modalistic concept of the relation between Father and Son, as if they were merely appearances of the one God. It is also noteworthy that the Spirit is not mentioned here, though Irenaeus does mention him at other points.

Irenaeus affirms, for instance, the preexistence of both Son and Spirit, saying: "The Word, namely the Son, was always with the Father; and that Wisdom also, which is the Spirit, was present with Him, anterior to all creation." But there is only one God, "who by the Word and Wisdom created and arranged all things."[10] Wisdom is equated here with the Holy Spirit, and the Word of God with the Son. They are the two agents or "effective means" through whom God works. Concerning the creation of humanity, we read that the first human being "was formed after the likeness of God, and molded by His hands, that is, by the Son and Holy Spirit."[11] Everything is made and ordered through the Son and the Holy Spirit. Therefore God needs no angels to assist him concerning the creation and in maintaining the world. Irenaeus continues: "For His *offspring* and His *similitude* do minister to Him in every respect; that is, the Son and the Holy Spirit, the Word and Wisdom."[12]

---

8. Eusebius, *The History of the Church*, a new trans. with commentary by Paul L. Maier (Grand Rapids: Kregel, 1999), 201.
9. Irenaeus, *Demonstration of the Apostolic Preaching* 47 (ACW 16:78).
10. Irenaeus, *Against Heresies* 4.20.3, 4.20.4 (ANF 1:488).
11. Ibid., 4.preface.4 (ANF 1:463).

The Son is now called the offspring and the Spirit the similitude. The terminology is still in flux, and even the issue of equality between the three divine entities is not addressed. In contrast to later controversies, even a possible subordination of Word and Wisdom (Son and Spirit) to God the Father, which the wording implies, is of no interest to Irenaeus. All-decisive is the issue of monotheism, that there is just one God. This is seen again in his *Demonstration of the Apostolic Preaching*, where he writes: "Thus God is shown to be one according to the essence of His being and power," even though "as the administrator of the economy of our redemption, He is both Father and Son."[13] We could interpret this as a modalistic statement. But for Irenaeus such implications are irrelevant as long as the unity of the Godhead is maintained. This should make us think, in light of the fact that present-day theology theological reflections are begun with the affirmation of the Triune God instead of arguing, as Irenaeus and many theologians of early Christendom did, from the salvation-historical process of God the Father working in and through Christ.

In conclusion, we note that Irenaeus, though concerned with the unity of Father, Son, and Holy Spirit, did not provide a doctrine of the Trinity that would deal with intra-Trinitarian relations as we would encounter them later. Yet, as Irenaeus admits, we should leave some questions in the hands of God. "If any one, therefore, says to us, 'How then was the Son produced by the Father?' we reply to him, that no man understands that production, or generation, or calling, or revelation, or by whatever name one may describe His generation, which is in fact altogether indescribable."[14] This intellectual modesty that he expressed against gnostic speculations remained unheeded. One wanted to know the secrets of the Godhead if for no other reason than that one feared with the semblance of a subordination of the Son under the Father that the full Godhead of the Son would be compromised. If the Son did not fully participate in the being of the Father, how could he provide salvation? As in the pagan environment, demigods had only limited salvific potential.

Origen of Alexandria, one of the most prolific and erudite theologians of the early church, opened the door for further speculative work when he wrote that the apostles stated with utmost clearness those points that they deemed necessary to everyone. "On other subjects

---

12. Ibid., 4.7.4 (*ANF* 1:470).
13. Irenaeus, *Demonstration of the Apostolic Preaching* 47 (*ACW* 16:78).
14. Irenaeus, *Against Heresies* 2.28.6 (*ANF* 1:401).

they merely stated the fact that things were so, keeping silence as to the manner or origin of their existence; clearly in order that the more zealous of their successors, who should be lovers of wisdom, might have a subject of exercise on which to display the fruit of their talents."[15] Indeed, there was a lot of experimenting, especially with the issue of how to relate Father, Son, and Holy Spirit.

Late in the second century Theodotus of Byzantium, also known as Theodotus the Tanner, introduced an idea that was sometimes called "dynamic monarchianism" or "adoptionism." According to Hippolytus of Rome (ca. 170–235), who was presumably a student of Irenaeus and rival bishop of Rome and who attacked Pope Callixtus I and his successors for excessive laxity, Theodotus claimed that Jesus was a (mere) man, born of the virgin Mary, and

> at his baptism in [the] Jordan received Christ, who came from above and descended (upon him) in form of a dove. And this was the reason, (according to Theodotus) why (miraculous) powers did not operate within him prior to the manifestation in him of that Spirit which descended, (and) which proclaims him to be the Christ. But (among the followers of Theodotus) some are disposed (to think) that never was this man made God, (even) at the descent of the Sprit; whereas others (maintain that he was made God) after the resurrection from the dead.[16]

This is how Theodotus understood the relationship between God the Father and the Son, and it comes as no surprise that Bishop Victor of Rome (d. 199) excommunicated him. Yet his argument was based on Matthew 3:16, where the Spirit descends on Jesus at baptism. The exaltation of Christ on his resurrection is clearly affirmed by Paul in Philippians 2:9–11. The main concern in the position of Theodotus, however, was a strict monotheism, which could be attained through this kind of adoptionism. Yet the church reacted very strongly, not because the emphasis in Theodotus's position was on the human side of Jesus Christ but because this idea implied that Jesus became the Son of God only by being connected with the Christ. Neglected were Jesus's conception through the Spirit and his birth, or, in Johannine terminology, that the Word (*Logos*) became flesh (John 1:14).

The emphasis on the one divine monarchy came in many different gowns but always left open some questions that could not be satisfactorily answered by referring to the New Testament witness and for which

---

15. Origen, *First Principles* preface.3 (ANF 4:239).
16. Hippolytus, *Refutation of All Heresies* 7.23 (ANF 5:115).

there was no universally accepted terminology. Hippolytus relates, for instance, that the followers of the presbyter Noetus of Smyrna (ca. 230), who was condemned in Rome for heresy, claimed: "I acknowledge Christ to be God, He is the Father Himself, if He is indeed God; and Christ suffered, being Himself God; and consequently the Father suffered, for He was the Father Himself."[17] We encounter with Noetus the idea that the Father in the mode of incarnation becomes the Son and consequently suffers death. This kind of modalism preserved the singularity of just one God and was therefore also called monarchianism (see above). The followers of Noetus in turn charged Hippolytus that he advocated two Gods, the Father and the Son. Hippolytus responded by pointing to the New Testament witness, saying that when Jesus said, "'I and the Father *are one*,' let him attend to the fact, and understand that He did not say, 'I and the Father *am one*, but *are one*.' For the word *are* is not said of one person, but it refers to *two persons*, and one power."[18] This means there is just one Godhead but two persons in that Godhead. Since the Father is the one from whom everything comes and also the Son, the issue is still one of equality in being. Is the Son, so to speak, derived from the Father, or is he of the same being?

It was especially Dionysius, a student of Origen and bishop of Alexandria from 248 until his death in 265, who came under heavy attack by representatives of monarchianism. They claimed that Dionysius separated the Father from the Son. But for him the title "Father" denoted the common bond between Father and Son. The Spirit too, he claims, "cannot be parted either from Him that sent or from Him that conveyed Him." Then he continues: "Thus then we extend the Monad indivisibly into the Triad, and conversely gather together the Triad without diminuation into the Monad."[19] But he also rejects the charge, "namely, that I denied Christ to be of one essence with God. For even if I argue that I have not found this word (*homoousion*) nor read it anywhere in the Holy Scriptures, yet my subsequent reasonings, which they have suppressed, do not discord with its meaning."[20] For him the term *homoousios*—"of the same being"—means nothing but "belonging to the same nature or species," such as parent and child or seed and plant. The term was not yet a sign of orthodoxy, as we see with Paul of Samosata (200–275), bishop of Antioch (260–268).

---

17. Hippolytus, *Against the Heresy of Noetus* 2 (ANF 5:224).
18. Ibid., 7 (ANF 5:226).
19. So Athanasius, *On the Opinion of Dionysius* 17 (NPNF[2] 4:182), who quotes Dionysius.
20. Ibid., 18 (NPNF[2] 4:183).

In 268 seventy bishops, priests, and deacons assembled in Antioch for a synod meeting and deposed Paul for corruption on a grand scale and because of his monarchianist tendencies. There they also rejected the term *homoousios*. Whether he really amassed a huge fortune "through lawless deeds, plundering churches, and blackmailing the brethren," as the assembly of Antioch in a letter to the bishops of Rome and Alexandria alleged, is difficult to determine. There may also have been envy involved. When they made the accusation against him that "he will not confess that the Son of God descended from heaven," they most likely noticed that he denied that the divine Logos had his own *hypostasis*, or reality.[21] For Paul there was only one single *hypostasis*, or reality, which belonged to the one Godhead. Therefore the synod was correct in rejecting the notion of *homoousios*, since in this context it would have meant that there is just one divine being but not also three equal entities.

Basil the Great (329/30–379), bishop of Caesarea Mazaca in Cappadocia (in modern-day Turkey), commented on the decision of the council: "They maintained that the homoousion set forth the idea both of essence and of what is derived from it, so that the essence, when divided, confers the title of co-essential on the parts into which it is divided." But then he added: "Even at that time there were men who asserted the Son to have been brought into being out of the non-existent, the term homoousion was adopted, to extirpate this impiety. For the conjunction of the Son with the Father is without time and without interval."[22] Basil wrote at a time when the *homoousion* belonged to the accepted theology, and he explained that *homoousion* was once understood as one substance that was underlying Father, Son, and Spirit. Such thinking was, of course, utterly wrong. But he also mentioned that even at that time the term *homoousion* was used by some to reject the idea that at one time the Son was not yet. The right understanding of the *homoousion*, however, according to Basil and according to the subsequent discussion, affirmed the eternal procession of the Son from the Father. It was especially Origen in the East and Tertullian in the West who steered the discussion in the direction that Basil matter-of-factly conveys, which paved the way for an acceptable proposition.

---

21. See Maier, *Eusebius: The Church History*, 277, and see Michael Schlusser, "Paulus von Samosata," in *TRE* 26:160–62.
22. Basil the Great, *Letter* 52.1–2 (NPNF[2] 8:155).

The Contributions of Origen and Tertullian

Origen was born in Alexandria, Egypt. His father was executed in 202 during persecution of Christians under Emperor Septimus Severus (193–211).[23] Origen grew up as the eldest of seven children and started out as a teacher of literature to sustain the family, which had become impoverished due to the death of their father. Origen's studies were furthered by a wealthy lady who treated him as her own child and took him into her home. He was only eighteen when he started giving catechetical instructions, and several of his students suffered martyrdom.[24] He was under surveillance and frequently changed his living quarters. Yet he sold his books of ancient literature and concentrated on studying the Bible. Soon he led a catechetical school and, taking Matthew 19:12 literally, castrated himself and led an ascetic life. During another violent persecution Origen left Egypt, went to Caesarea, and also visited Rome; after a brief return to Alexandria, he spent the rest of his life in Caesarea. Of his New Testament commentaries the most significant is that on the Gospel of John. But especially well-known are the four volumes *On First Principles*, the first Christian dogmatics. It opens with a long exposition on the Trinity, which is recapitulated at the end of the work. "Father, Son, and Holy Spirit are not considered apart from the economy of the creation and redemption."[25] His fame spread so far that Mamaea, the mother of Emperor Septimus Severus, "was determined to get an interview with him and test his universally esteemed theological prowess. She was staying in Antioch at the time and sent a military escort to bring him to her. He visited with her for some time, showing her many things that redounded to the glory of the Lord and the virtue of the divine teaching."[26] In the persecution of Christians under Emperor Decius (249–251), Origen was imprisoned and severely tortured but survived, though he died a few years later from the effects of the torture. He was a most productive theologian and composed several hundred works.

Although he exerted influence on other controversies, most important are his reflections on the Trinity. We read in his commentary on the Gospel of John: "We, however, are persuaded that there are three hypostases, the Father, the Son, and the Holy Spirit, and we

---

23. For information on Origen's life see Maier, *Eusebius: The Church History*, 208.
24. See Rowan Williams, "Origenes/Origenismus," in *TRE* 25:398.
25. So Stephen M. Hildebrand, "The Trinity in the Ante-Nicene Fathers," in *Oxford Handbook of the Trinity*, 103.
26. Maier, *Eusebius: The Church History*, 224.

believe that only the Father is unbegotten. We admit, as more pious and as true, that the Holy Spirit is the most honored of all things made through the Word, and that he is [first] in rank of all the things that were made by the Father through Christ."[27] We have three hypostases of the Godhead, but only one, the Father, is unbegotten. Nevertheless, the Word "does not *come to be* 'in the beginning' from not being 'in the beginning,' nor does he pass from not being 'with God' to coming to be 'with God,' for before all time and eternity 'the Word was in the beginning,' and 'the Word was with God.'"[28] This means that the Word (Christ) was always with God the Father and was coeternal with him. Since "the Son also may have all things which the Father possesses," he is also God and omnipotent.[29] And yet Origen can call him a "'second' God."[30] This does not imply for him that there are two Gods, but he notes that in the Gospel of John that God the Father is called "the God" whereas the Word is simply called "God."[31] Still, he says of Christ that "the holy Scriptures know Him to be the most ancient of all the works of creation."[32] The Greek word *demiurgema* used here by Origen means a "created being."[33] While Origen showed the interconnectedness of the Son with the created order, this order comprises the initial spiritual world as well as our present fallen world. The Son is dependent on the divine will, yet not as something or someone other over against the Father but his concrete manifestation. To understand the Son as someone or something created, as was the later charge against Origen, misses the point. For him the Creator and the created are not that vastly separated, as they were later thought to be. The Greek mind-set in which Origen grew up and lived emphasized oneness and wholeness instead of distinct separateness. This means the Father and the Son are basically one, but they are of different rank. What, then, is the position of the Spirit?

In his commentary on John, Origen is very clear when he writes: "The Holy Spirit is the most honored of all things made through the Word, and he is [first] in rank of all things which have been made by the Father through Christ." He continues: "The Holy Spirit seems to have need of the Son ministering to his hypostasis, not only for it to

---

27. Origen, *Commentary on the Gospel according to John* 2.75, trans. Ronald E. Heine (FC 80:114).
28. Ibid., 2.9 (FC 80:97).
29. Origen, *First Principles* 1.2.10 (ANF 4:250).
30. Origen, *Against Celsus* 5.39 (ANF 4:561).
31. Origen, *Commentary on the Gospel according to John* 2.14–15 (FC 80:98).
32. Origen, *Against Celsus* 5.37 (ANF 4:560).
33. For the following see Williams, "Origenes/Origenismus," 25:409.

exist, but also for it to be wise, and rational, and just." The gifts given to the saints from God are administered by Christ but subsist "in accordance with the Holy Spirit."[34] Nevertheless, Origen identifies the Spirit of God in the Old Testament with the Holy Spirit of the New Testament accounts, such as in Genesis 1:2.[35] Just like the Son, the Spirit is also from the beginning, since "nothing in the Trinity can be called greater or less."[36] This assurance of all three being equal in the Trinity stands in contrast to the impression that the Spirit is certainly below Father and Son and that the Son is below the Father, since "the fullness of unoriginated Godhead is concentrated in the Father, Who alone is 'the fountain-head of deity.'"[37]

There are three divine hypostases. They are equal with regard to their divinity but not according to order or to the persons. There they are distinctly graduated and therefore not totally equal.[38] This is understandable when we consider their actual evolvement, the Son from the Father, and the Spirit from the Father and/through the Son. Origen would not concede a dissimilarity between Father and Son, since he knew the term "of one being" (*homoousios*).[39] It meant the same spiritual substance and the same will but not the sameness in power. As persons, they are different. The Son is God, but as the image of God the Father. In other words, the Son is God, highly to be praised, but viewed from the standpoint of the eternal God, the Son is the first one in a whole chain of emanations.

There are two problems immediately apparent in Origen's christological proposal. On the one hand, if the oneness of Father and Son is emphasized too much, it is difficult to distinguish between the two; on the other hand, if the subordination of the Son under the Father is emphasized too much, the Savior becomes a semi-God. While Origen held oneness and subordination in dialectic tension, his successors did not exhibit the same skill. The resulting problems were either of the right-wing Origenist type, which shortchanged the independence of the Son, or of the left-wing Origenist type, which minimized the Godhead of Christ. Both approaches advanced beyond the older economic type of relation between Father and Son, which suggested a successive

---

34. Origen, *Commentary on the Gospel according to John* 2.75–77 (FC 80:114).
35. See Origen, *First Principles* 1.3.3 (ANF 4:252).
36. Ibid., 1.3.7 (ANF 4:255).
37. Kelly, *Early Christian Doctrines*, 131.
38. So Adolf Martin Ritter, "Dogma und Lehre in der Alten Kirche," in *Handbuch der Dogmen- und Theologiegeschichte*, ed. Carl Andresen (Göttingen: Vandenhoeck & Ruprecht, 1982), 1:130.
39. Further see Reinhold Seeberg, *Lehrbuch der Dogmengeschichte*, 6th ed. (Darmstadt: Wissenschaftliche Buchgesellschaft, 1965), 1:510–12.

THE TRINITY

(i.e., economic) disclosure of persons in the Trinity and which understood the Trinity as a reference to God's eternal being.

While Origen worked in the East and used the Greek language as his medium of communication, Tertullian worked in the West and wrote in Latin. He was a first-generation Christian who lived between 198 and 220 in Carthage (present-day Libya) as an independent Christian writer and thinker. He acquired a general knowledge of philosophy, jurisprudence, and medicine in Rome and had an excellent command of Latin. We can name him as the first representative of Latin theology. Since the wealthy ship owner Marcion of Sinope (ca. 85–ca. 160), in present-day Turkey, was an important leader in early Christianity who rejected the Old Testament God, Tertullian wrote five books against him to show that the God of the Old Testament is no other than the gracious God of the New Testament and the Father of Jesus Christ. Since "God is the great Supreme, existing in eternity, unbegotten, unmade, without beginning, without end," such a God is not "if He is not one."[40] There cannot be a duality of Gods, as Marcion asserted, a creator God and a redeemer God.

Having defended the oneness of God against Marcion, Tertullian then defended the Trinity against Praxeas, a theologian from Asia Minor and contemporary of Tertullian. Praxeas emphasized the unity of the Godhead so much that he thought that the Father and the Son are basically the same so that the Father suffered on the cross. For Tertullian this patripassianism—the idea that God the Father suffered on the cross—was basically wrong, since we must distinguish between Father, Son, and Holy Spirit. The Trinity constitutes the difference between the Jewish faith and Christianity. Tertullian explains: "God was pleased to renew His covenant with man in such a way that His Unity might be believed in, after a new manner, through the Son and the Spirit, in order that God might now be known openly, in His proper Names and Persons, who in ancient times was not plainly understood, though declared through the Son and the Spirit."[41] The Trinity is not a novelty that was introduced by the Christians; it was just not plainly understood before. While Tertullian does not want to collapse the Trinity into one divine monarchy, he also does not want to separate the three into some kind of polytheism. He asserts: "The Father is one, and the Son one, and the Spirit one, and They are distinct from Each Other." Yet this does not "imply a separation among the Father, and the Son,

---

40. Tertullian, *Against Marcion* 1.3 (ANF 3:273).
41. Tertullian, *Against Praxeas* 31 (ANF 3:627).

and the Spirit.... It is not by way of diversity that the Son differs from the Father, but by distribution: it is not by division that He is different, but by distinction; because the Father is not the same as the Son, since they differ from the other in the mode of their being. For the Father is the entire substance, but the Son is a derivation and portion of the whole." Tertullian emphasizes here the salvation-economic aspect of the Trinity when he continues: the Father "showed a third degree in the Paraclete, as we believe the second degree is in the Son, by reason of the order observed in the *Economy*."[42] These gradations correspond to the divine plan of salvation so that the Father has the whole divine substance in its totality, while the Son is derived from that. Yet there is a unity insofar as the Father works in the world through the Son, and both work through the Spirit.

Tertullian sums up the issues, writing that the difference of Father, Son, and Holy Spirit lies "on the ground of Personality, not of Substance—in the way of distinction, not of division. But although I must everywhere hold one only substance in three coherent and inseparable (Persons), yet I am bound to acknowledge, from the necessity of the case, that He who issues a command is different from Him who executes it."[43] As we will see later, there are three persons but just one divine substance. Similar to Origen, Tertullian showed a clear tendency to subordinate the Son under the Father, and the Holy Spirit under both Father and Son. We will notice some of these issues again as we approach the Council of Nicea. But the journey there was difficult, since the subordination of the Son under the Father could always diminish the full divinity of the Son.

The Difficult Road to Nicea

The catchword for Nicea was *homoousios*, suggesting the Son is of the same being as the Father. Yet this term was far from being acceptable to everyone. As mentioned above, at the Synod of Antioch in 268 this term was rejected. The reason was that there was unease about the Son being a mere Word (*logos*) or an impersonal divine property instead of an existing hypostasis beside the Father. Evidently the *ousia* ("being") was perceived as being identical with hypostasis ("essence of underlying reality"). The big, unresolved issue was still how to express the unity of the Trinity and distinguish at the same time between the three

---

42. Ibid., 9 (*ANF* 3:603–4).
43. Ibid., 12 (*ANF* 3:607).

persons. This was the vexing question because the Greek language was good in showing the unity of being, which was also favored by Platonic thought, but not in indicating the difference of the three entities of the Trinity. The term *person* (*persona*) was a Latin concept, and the dominant theological language was still Greek. Yet there was a significant change.

During the lifetime of Origen, Christians were often persecuted in the Roman Empire. With the Edict of Milan in 313, issued by Constantine (272–337) and his coruler Licinius (ca. 263–325), the Christian faith was tolerated in the Roman Empire, and once Constantine became the sole ruler of the empire he made himself the patron of the Christian faith. He supported the church financially, had an extraordinary number of basilicas built, granted privileges (e.g., exemption from certain taxes) to clergy, promoted Christians to high-ranking offices, returned property confiscated during the Great Persecution of Diocletian, and endowed the church with land and other wealth. Though the Christian faith was not yet the official religion of the empire, Constantine felt that he was responsible for the unity of the faith. When the Council of Nicea was called by the emperor, its decisions became state law. Being declared outside the right faith had not just ecclesial but also worldly consequences. One could be exiled or punished by the state for not believing the right things. Theological deliberations became more and more serious matters for both the church and the state. This was especially the case with regard to the relationship between God the Father and the Son. Discussions on the subject abounded.

The Concern of Arius

Arius (ca. 260–336) was born into a Christian family in Libya. Having studied in Antioch, he settled in Alexandria and was deacon and then presbyter at the church of the Baucalis, the oldest church in Alexandria. He was entrusted with the task of explaining the Bible in catechesis and preaching, and he had a good reputation. Yet under Bishop Alexander (312–328), who initially patronized him, the presbyter Arius became more and more independent, which galled the bishop. Moreover, he preached "that the Son of God was made out of that which had no prior existence, that there was a period of time in which he did not exist; that, as possessing free will, he was capable of vice and virtue, and that he was created and made."[44] Only reluctantly did the bishop oppose his presbyter. But this made the dissension worse, and soon it was no longer just a local affair.

In 320 Arius wrote a letter to his bishop, Alexander, in which he outlined his faith. He even claimed that he had learned this faith from his bishop, namely that

> we know one God—alone unbegotten, alone everlasting, alone without beginning, alone true, alone possessing immortality, alone wise, alone good, . . . who begot an only-begotten Son before eternal times, through whom he made the ages and everything. . . . There are three *hypostases*. God being the cause of all is without beginning, most alone; but the Son, begotten by the Father, created and founded before the ages, was not before he was begotten.[45]

Arius affirmed his belief in the one God who is the uncreated principle of all things. This implied for Arius that the Son must have been created, and therefore he could not have been before he was created. Since an eternal procession of the Son from the Father jibes with the Father being the uncreated principle of all things, there was a beginning of the Son before the time of the world. The eternal procession of the Son is rejected, since it can be understood as an emanation from the Godhead. This notion is for Arius too close to Greek mythology and to gnostic ideas. Arius even asserted that "'God was not always a Father;' but 'once God was alone, and not yet a Father, but afterwards He became a Father.'"[46] God created the Son and created through him the world. This means that the mediator of creation is part of the created world. Christ, "'as others, is God only in name.' And, whereas all beings are foreign and different from God in essence, so too is 'the Word alien and unlike in all things to the Father's essence and propriety.'" It comes as no surprise that Arius declares "that 'the Word is not the very God;' 'though He is called God, yet He is not very God,' but 'by participation of grace, He, as others; is God only in name.'"[47] Christ is not God in the full sense but is accorded this title only through God's grace. Nevertheless, Arius affirms the Trinity, saying, "there is a Triad, not in equal glories. Not intermingling with each other are their subsistences. One more glorious than the other in their glories unto immen-

---

44. According to Sozomen, *Ecclesiastical History* 1.15 (NPNF[2] 2:251).
45. Arius, "Letter to Alexander of Alexandria," in *The Trinitarian Controversy*, trans. and ed. William G. Rusch (Philadelphia: Fortress Press, 1980), 31–32.
46. Extracts of the *Thalia of Arius* in Athanasius, *Orations against the Arians* 1.2.5 (NPNF[2] 4:308).
47. Extracts of the *Thalia of Arius* in Athanasius, *Orations against the Arians* 1.2.6 (NPNF[2] 4:309).

sity."⁴⁸ We notice again the strict separation of the three entities and their considerable differences. It is a Trinity in name but not in reality.

Arius intended to safeguard monotheism by conceding only one uncreated principle. As Athanasius shows, however, if the Arians named Christ "God from regard for the Scriptures, they must of necessity say that there are two Gods, one Creator, the other creature, and must serve two Lords, one Unoriginate, and the other originate and a creature."⁴⁹ Arius falls exactly into the polytheistic trap from which he wanted to escape. It was certainly not ignorance of Scripture but the philosophic insistence on one uncreated principle from which everything else was to be deduced. Philosophy and logic gained the upper hand, and therefore church historian Reinhold Seeberg (1859–1935) justifiably states: "Therefore the christology of Arius has become the worst christology which we know."⁵⁰ Yet Arius was not alone in his emphasis on this strict monotheism. With his *Thalia,* which literally means "abundance," "good cheer," or "banquet," he disseminated his concepts. It was written in verse, in order to aid memorization and popular distribution of his ideas. He had many followers among both bishops and laity, not just in Egypt but also in Palestine and Syria. Evidently the notion of one supreme God and one divine mediator, Jesus Christ, was more persuasive than a Trinity composed of three equal entities. On the other hand, people also knew about divine mediators from Greek mythology. They could offer help, yet only in a limited sense. The one who had claimed "I and the Father are one," however, extended unlimited grace. Therefore others did not follow Arius. The first of those was his bishop, Alexander.

The Arian Controversy

Alexander first heard of Arius's views in a meeting with presbyters. When he noticed that these views were disseminated in many provinces and cities, "he convened a council of many prelates; and excommunicated Arius and the abettors of his heresy."⁵¹ At the synod in 320, thirty-six presbyters and forty-four deacons, including Athanasius of Alexandria, agreed to a condemnation of Arianism and signed a document to that effect. The aforementioned letter to his bishop that

---

48. Extracts of the *Thalia of Arius* in Athanasius, *On the Councils of Ariminum and Seleucia* 2.15 (NPNF² 4:457).
49. Athanasius, *Orations against the Arians* 3.25.16 (NPNF² 4:402).
50. Seeberg, *Lehrbuch der Dogmengeschichte*, 2:27.
51. According to Socrates, *Ecclesiastical History* 1.6 (NPNF² 2:3).

Arius had composed did not sit well with Alexander, especially since the bishop himself was supposed to have been the source of Arius's ideas. But Arius remained successful in spreading his new belief and made the prospect of a formal schism a very real one. When the situation threatened to get out of hand, Alexander called a general council of the entire church in 321. The council gathered no fewer than one hundred participants. At this council Arius continued to argue his earlier position, that the Son could not be coeternal with the Father, and even went on to say that in substance the Son was not similar to the Father. The assembled council then placed Arius under anathema until such time when he recanted his positions.

Alexander sent letters to other bishops to inform them about this decision and asked for their approval. One of these letters is preserved in the *Ecclesiastical History* of Socrates (ca. 380–ca. 440), who worked as lawyer in Constantinople and wrote a seven-volume church history, and another in the *Ecclesiastical History* of Theodoret of Cyrus (ca. 393–ca. 458/466), an influential theologian and bishop of Cyrus. We can gather from these letters that Alexander understood the arguments of Arius and refuted them especially with reference to the Gospel of John. For instance, they raised the question of how Arius could claim that Christ is mutable and susceptible of change if Christ says "I and the Father are one." Or how could Arius reckon Christ to be one of the things made when we read that "all things were made by him"? Alexander further declares "that the Son is immutable and unchangeable, all-sufficient and perfect, like the Father, lacking only His 'unbegotten.'" He is "the only-begotten Son of God, begotten not out of that which is not, but of the Father, Who is; yet not after the manner of material bodies, by severance or emanation."[52] Alexander emphasizes the difference between Father and Son in the difference between begotten and unbegotten, and at the same time their sameness.

But the ideas of Arius continued to prove attractive to others. Arius left for Palestine and received support from a number of bishops, among them Eusebius of Nicomedia (d. 341). Nicomedia, the metropolis of Bithynia (in present-day Turkey), was the residence of Emperor Licinius, whose wife, Constantia, a half-sister of Emperor Constantine, was an admirer of Eusebius. When Constantine defeated Licinius and became the sole emperor in 325, the scales tipped against Arius. The emperor felt that as *pontifex maximus*, the high priest of Christendom,

---

52. According to Theodoret, *Ecclesiastical History* 1.3 (NPNF[2] 3:39).

he was personally responsible to God for the unity of the faith. He sent a letter to both Alexander and Arius, first mentioning that the bishop inquired as to what his presbyters thought of "a certain inexplicable passage of the written Word." Then the emperor mentions to Arius that he "rashly gave expression to a view of the matter such as ought either never to have been conceived, or when suggested to your mind, it became you to bury it in silence." And now the emperor concludes that through this dispute "the most holy people being rent into two factions, have departed from the harmony of the common body." Constantine then suggests: "Now, I say these things, not as compelling you all to see exactly alike on this very insignificant subject of controversy, whatever it may be; since the dignity of the communion may be preserved unaffected, and the same fellowship with all be retained, even though there should exist among you some dissimilarity of sentiment on unimportant matters." Constantine felt personally responsible for the unity of faith, and therefore he urged for peace and reconciliation. He felt, however, that the actual controversy was a petty argument over unintelligible minutiae that "few are capable either of adequately expounding, or even accurately understanding."[53] He may have been correct. Yet even the personal delivery of this letter by Bishop Hosius of Cordoba (ca. 256–357/58) from Spain, whom the emperor held in high esteem, did not change the atmosphere.

Arius and his many followers had become a serious problem to the unity of the church and to the unity of the empire. Shortly after receiving the message from Constantine, Alexander requested another general council of the diocese, which seems to have confirmed its agreement with the profession of faith Alexander had earlier circulated. It was an agreement to the use of the theological term *consubstantial*. It also reaffirmed the excommunication of Arius. Arius himself formally complained to the emperor over his treatment by Alexander. In response, Constantine commanded Arius to plead his case before an ecumenical council of the church, to be held at Nicea (present-day Iznik in Turkey), which was close to the emperor's residence in Nicomedia. On his way back to Constantine's residence in Nicomedia, Hosius stopped in Antioch, where he called together a synod that was to decide who should fill the vacant bishop's seat there. The synod did not confine itself to the election process but also pursued the issue of the so-called Arian heresy.[54] This synod, in the winter of 324/325, was

---

53. See Socrates, *Ecclesiastical History* 1.7 (NPNF[2] 2:6–7).

rather modest in tone and put forward a creed that affirmed the faith in one God and in one Lord Jesus, who was "not begotten from nothing but from the Father" and "who always is and not at a prior time was not."[55] This creed decisively rejected the Arian proposal. Yet the idea of the full unity with God was not touched on. By that time Constantine was already planning to convene a council of the whole empire at Nicea.

The First Council of Nicea (325)

The council was opened probably on June 14, 325, the first ecumenical council ever convened by an emperor. Approximately 318 bishops gathered there, mostly from the East. Hosius of Cordoba was also present, and two presbyters who represented the bishop of Rome. The emperor himself presided over the council and also entered the discussion when he deemed it necessary. It was opened by the emperor in the central building of the palace. Not all of the participants were well-versed theologians. A bishop, most likely Eusebius of Nicomedia, in whose province the council took place, opened the council with a brief eulogy to the emperor before he himself addressed the assembly in Latin, expressing his desires to "see you all united in one judgment, and that common spirit of peace and concord prevailing amongst you all, which becomes you, as consecrated to the service of God, to commend to others."[56] The assembly can be divided into three groups: the Arians, including Eusebius of Nicomedia; the followers of Origen, including Eusebius of Caesarea; and the anti-Arians, including Alexander of Alexandria. The discussions took place in Greek. Yet we do not know exactly how the discussions proceeded. We are only informed that, except for five bishops, all agreed to the dogmatic decisions. Several of the dissenters, among them Eusebius of Nicomedia, afterwards changed their minds and agreed with the dogmatic decisions of the council. Arius was anathematized and prohibited "from entering into Alexandria. At the same time an edict of the emperor sent Arius himself into exile" together with his followers.[57]

Eusebius of Caesarea also had a difficult time agreeing with the deci-

---

54. See for details Adolf Martin Ritter, "Dogma und Lehre in der Alten Kirche," in *Handbuch der Dogmen- und Theologiegeschichte*, ed. Carl Andresen (Göttingen: Vandenhoeck & Ruprecht 1982), 1:164.
55. "The Synodal Letter of the Council of Antioch, (A.D. 325)," in William Rusch, *The Trinitarian Controversy* (Philadelphia: Fortress Press, 1980), 47.
56. Eusebius, *Life of Constantine* 3.12 (NPNF^2 1:523).
57. Socrates, *Ecclesiastical History* 1.8 (NPNF^2 2:10).

THE TRINITY

sions of the council. But then he sent a letter to his church with the creed of Nicea and explained his standpoint. Having quoted the creed, Eusebius writes:

> When these articles of faith were proposed, there seemed to be no ground of opposition: nay, our most pious emperor himself was the first to admit that they were perfectly correct, and that he himself entertained the sentiments contained in them; exhorting all present to give them their assent, and subscribe to these very articles, thus agreeing in an unanimous profession of them, with the insertion, however, of that single word "homoousios" (consubstantial), an expression which the emperor himself explained, as not indicating corporeal affections or properties, and consequently that the Son did not subsist from the Father either by division or abscission: for, said he, a nature which is immaterial and incorporeal cannot possibly be subject to any corporeal affection; hence our conception of such things can only be in divine and mysterious terms.[58]

The term *homoousios*, which was accepted at Nicea, had the function of showing that the Son or the Logos was fully and truly divine. No longer was there any affirmation of three hypostases, as Origen's followers preferred. Yet the *homoousios* could easily be interpreted as talking just about one hypostasis, namely the divine. This was even more so since the decision at Nicea rejected the idea that the Son "is of other substance [hypostasis] or essence [ousia] than the Father."[59] Is there then only one hypostasis, the one of the Father? While the creed sanctioned by the emperor and his conciliatory approach unified the church, the discussions were not ended, and neither were the disagreements.

On June 19, 325, the council accepted the creed, and a month later the council concluded with a big celebration. The creed dwelt extensively on Jesus Christ and read:

> We believe in one God, the Father Almighty, Maker of all things visible and invisible:—and in one Lord Jesus Christ, the Son of God, the only-begotten of the Father, that is of the substance of the Father; God of God, Light of light, true God of true God; begotten not made, consubstantial [*homoousios*] with the Father; by whom all things were made both which are in heaven and on earth; who for the sake of us men, and on account of our salvation, descended, became incarnate, was made man, suffered, rose again the third day, and ascended into the heavens, and will come to judge the living and the dead. [We] also [believe] in the Holy Spirit.[60]

58. Ibid., 1.8 (*NPNF*[2] 2:11).
59. Ibid.
60. Ibid.

We notice here that the Holy Spirit is most briefly mentioned. Above all the emperor wanted peace and not excommunications. There seems to have been another synod meeting in 327 at which Arius was allowed to return to Alexandria, and his followers were rehabilitated. Those, however, who maintained the orthodox interpretation of Nicea lost the grace of the emperor and their positions.[61] The emperor seemed to have not abandoned the decisions of Nicea but wanted universal agreement to these decisions and the restitution of unity. We must remember that he had called the disagreements between Alexander and Arius "petty" and "unintelligible."

---

61. See Ritter, "Dogma und Lehre in der Alten Kirche," 1:171.

4

The Struggle over the Decision of Nicea

For the participants at the Council of Nicea, the issues to be settled were far from petty. They seemed to be issues of life and death and stirred up not just theologians but often the whole population of Christians. Especially through a rapid succession of emperors who either supported one side or the other, the decision of Nicea was often threatened. There was, however, one theologian, Athanasius (ca. 298–373), who unwaveringly stood up for that decision and who often felt the consequences when he was either sent into exile or fled to escape his persecutors.

Athanasius, the Defender of the *Homoousios*

In Alexandria Athanasius had become the successor of the deceased bishop Alexander. Once Constantine was convinced that Arius had agreed to the decision of Nicea he told Athanasius in no uncertain terms to readmit Arius into the church, saying: "For if I learn that you have hindered or excluded any who claim to be admitted into communion with the Church, I will immediately send some one who shall depose you by my command, and shall remove you from your place." And yet Athanasius wrote and endeavored to convince the emperor that this anti-Christian heresy had no communion with the church. Evidently the emperor realized that he could not so easily depose Athanasius and therefore assured him "that he was a man of God."[1] Arius was then again anathematized by the emperor, and his writings were to be condemned to the flames. But nothing came of this. Those leaning toward Arius gained the upper hand, and the emperor, sensing the orthodox Athanasius was actually the troublemaker, called a synod meeting at Tyre in 335 and had him deposed and eventually exiled to Treveri, the imperial residence on the Mosel River. The charge against him, however, was not theological: he had allegedly threatened to stop the grain ships to Constantinople that regularly left Alexandria every autumn![2] Arius was then reinstituted by the same synod into the church, though he had died a year earlier.

When Constantine died in 337, his empire was divided among Constantine II (337–340), Constans (337–350), and Constantius II (337–361). This division of the empire also did away with a unified church. Though Athanasius returned to Alexandria after a little more than a year in Treveri, his stay in Alexandria was brief and full of problems. Eusebius of Nicomedia had convinced Emperor Constantius that the restoration of the bishops exiled in 337, especially that of Athanasius, was against all ecclesial law. The emperor sent a letter of complaint to Athanasius but did little else. The unrest in Alexandria got out of hand once the opposing party ended up appointing a new bishop to succeed Athanasius. Since his persecutors pursued him even at night, he had to escape from Alexandria and made his way to Rome, where he stayed from 339 to 346.

Athanasius's stay in the West, first in Treveri and then in Rome, may have had a decisive influence on him.[3] While he hardly used the term *homoousios* before 350 and even made use of *homoios* ("like" or "similar"), he became a staunch defender of the *homoousios*. While this may have been the result of his attempt to prevent the emperor from undoing the decision of Nicea, something else may also have had an important influence on Athanasius. In the West he learned the Latin nomenclature of *unius substantiae* ("of one substance") concerning Father and Son and equated it with the *homoousios*. It might even be that the influence of Hosius of Cordoba led to the adoption of the *homoousios* at Nicea

---

1. Athanasius, *Orations against the Arians* 59, 62 (NPNF[2] 4:132–33).
2. See Adolf Martin Ritter, "Dogma und Lehre in der Alten Kirche," in *Handbuch der Dogmen- und Theologiegeschichte*, ed. Carl Andresen (Göttingen: Vandenhoeck & Ruprecht, 1982), 1:173n31.
3. For the following see ibid., 1:181.

and all its subsequent problems. It was a term thought out in Latin (*unius substantae*) but expressed in Greek (*homoousios*).

At the instigation of Pope Julius I, the Roman emperors Constans and Constantius II called a council at Serdica (now Sofia, the capital of Bulgaria) in 342 to resolve the increasing tensions between the Christian East and West. Both Athanasius and Marcell of Ancyra had been deposed from their bishop's seats, since they had vehemently opposed Arianism and had sought refuge in Rome. Yet the Eastern bishops, under the leadership of Eusebius of Nicomedia, thought that the West had acted wrongly, since the bishops from the East (Athanasius and others), who had been excommunicated, were accepted. The Western party alleged that the Eastern bishops had fallen away from the decisions of Nicea and had become Arians. The bishops from the East in turn refused to sit together with their Western counterparts and were also weary of Rome seeming to have the final say. Finally, the two factions excommunicated each other. The Eastern party withdrew, and the Western faction drew up a strong anti-Arian statement, which was favored by Emperor Constans. He also urged Constantius II to restore the exiled bishops. The latter canceled his severe measures against the Nicene party and in a public letter forebode any further persecution of the Athanasians in Alexandria. Finally, "when Gregory [the bishop who was selected to replace Athanasius] died about ten months later, he [emperor Constantius II] sends for Athanasius with every mark of honor, writing to him no less than three times a very friendly letter, in which he exhorted him to take courage and come."[4] Athanasius then returned to Alexandria in 346.

When emperor Constans was assassinated in 350 by dissatisfied soldiers, his brother Constantius II became the sole ruler of the empire. This also brought a change in his approach toward the Arians. Constantius II wanted to unify the church by turning away from Nicea, since this creed did not bring unanimity to the church or to the empire. Therefore he forbade the term *ousia* ("essence") and also the term *homoousios* ("same essence") and replaced it with *homoios* ("like" or "similar"), saying in a creed of 559: "But whereas the term 'essence,' has been adopted by the Fathers in simplicity, and gives offence as being misconceived by the people, and is not contained in the Scriptures, it has seemed good to remove it, that it be never in any case used of God again, because the divine Scriptures nowhere use it of

---

4. Athansius, *History of the Arians* 21 (NPNF[2] 4:277).

Father and Son. But we say that the Son is like the Father in all things, as also the Holy Scripture say and teach."[5] But the banishment of the *homoousios* did not bring lasting peace either, especially after the emperor died in 361. It strengthened the Arian wing of the church but also brought together those who did not want to have the Nicene Creed annulled. Already in 356 the situation for Athanasius had become so dangerous that he had to escape from the city and most likely hid himself in the cell of one of the monks in the Nitrian desert, where he was safe and also close enough to be kept informed of the events in the church. How disliked he had become by the Emperor Constantius II became clear a year earlier from a conversation with Pope Liberius, a fearless supporter of Athanasius, in which the emperor declares about Athanasius: "Not one of the victories which I have gained, not even excepting those over Magnentius and Silvanus, equals the ejection of this vile man from the government of the Church."[6]

With Julian Apostata as emperor (361–363), the old Roman religion was supposed to be reinstituted, and therefore the church was to be free from government involvement. All the bishops banished by Constantius II were called back from exile, including Athanasius. In 362 he called together a council in Alexandria that set the tone for other councils to be held: the *homoios* was rejected, and Nicea was reaffirmed. The instigators of Arianism, of course, could not be accepted back into the church. But those who had formerly compromised themselves and now repented were received back. As Jerome (ca. 347–420) tells us: "The West assented to this decision, and it was through this conclusion, which the necessities of the times demanded, that the world was snatched from the jaws of Satan."[7] Athanasius was not out for revenge but sought reconciliation and church unity. Emperor Julian did not like such a strengthening of the church. The emperor wanted to ban him from the city and from all of Egypt, so Athanasius reacted quickly on his own and left Alexandria in 362 once more so that the ban could not be handed to him. He also deluded his pursuers and "returned secretly to Alexandria; and there he remained concealed until the persecution was at an end."[8] Yet the danger was not completely over. Once more in 365 Athanasius had to flee under the reign of Emperor Valens (328–378). But he was recalled the following spring when a revolt in

---

5. As quoted by Athanasius, *On the Councils of Ariminum and Seleucia* 8 (NPNF[2] 4:454).
6. Theodoret, *Ecclesiastical History* 2.13 (NPNF[2] 3:78).
7. Jerome, *The Dialogue against the Luciferians* 20 (NPNF[2] 6:330).
8. Socrates, *Ecclesiastical History* 3.14 (NPNF[2] 2:86).

the empire had broken out and the emperor needed all the support he could get, including that of Athanasius. From that point until his death in 373, Athanasius could finally live in relative peace.

What made Athanasius such a defender of the *homoousios*, or rather such an enemy of the Arians, who asserted that there is an ontological distinction between God the Father and the Son? Again we must remember that for him salvation was at stake: demigods or heroes abounded in Greek mythology. They were often helpful in many respects, but sooner or later their power of influence came to an end. They were not in total control. Only a supreme God who was in total control could change our fate and save us. According to Athanasius, if Jesus Christ was not like this one supreme God but just in the slightest way different from him, then our salvation was in jeopardy. Jesus Christ had to be fully God. And this true God came to us through the incarnation. Athanasius was very much concerned about the Godhead of Christ. But he also paid attention to the Spirit, since through him we can become one with God the Father, as Athanasius affirms:

> For since the Word is in the Father, and the Spirit is given from the Word, He wills that we should receive the Spirit, that, when we receive It, thus having the Spirit of the Word which is in the Father, we too may be found on account of the Spirit to become One in the Word, and through Him in the Father.... It is the Spirit then which is in God, and not we viewed in our own selves; and as we are sons and gods because of the Word in us, so we shall be in the Son and in the Father, and we shall be accounted to have become one in Son and in Father, because that Spirit is in us, which is in the Word which is in the Father.[9]

In typically Eastern fashion, the Spirit is given from the Son (the Word), who is in the Father. Athanasius therefore can affirm with Nicea the Holy Triad and the one Godhead, in contrast to the Arians, who thought of the Holy Spirit as being a creature who "came into being as a thing made by the Son."[10] Yet Athanasius alone could not bring the church at large to agree to the decision of Nicea. As we have noted, he was not just the unyielding defender of the *homoousios* but also conciliatory toward those who advocated the *homoiousios*. He wrote:

> Those, however, who accept everything else that was defined at Nicaea, and doubt only about the Coessential [*homoousios*], must not be treated as

---

9. Athanasius, *Orations against the Arians* 3.25 (NPNF[2] 4:407).
10. So Athanasius, *Letter 56: To Jovian* (NPNF[2] 4:567-68).

enemies; nor do we here attack them as Ariomaniacs, nor as opponents of the Fathers, but we discuss the matter with them as brothers with brothers, who mean what we mean, and dispute only about the word. For, confessing that the Son is from the essence of the Father, and not from other subsistence, and that He is not a creature nor work, but His genuine and natural offspring, and that He is eternally with the Father as being His Word and Wisdom, they are not far from accepting even the phrase "Coessential."[11]

Such a positive acknowledgement of the position of those who advocated the *homoios*, but at the same time a clear condemnation of the idea that the Son was a creature, opened the way for an alliance against the actual Arians, or better neo-Arians.

Approaching the Trinitarian Settlement in Constantinople

The neo-Arian movement gained special prominence through Aetios of Antioch (d. 367), who worked as a goldsmith in Antioch to support his widowed mother, studied philosophy, and later became a deacon. He and his disciple Eunomius (d. ca. 395) claimed that God is unbegotten and therefore totally unequal with the Son. According to Gregory of Nyssa (ca. 331/40–ca. 395) who occupied the bishop seat in Nyssa (in present-day south-central Turkey), Eunomius avoided using the term *Father* in order that the Son might not be included in the eternity of the Father. He also avoided the term *Son* so that there would be no natural affinity between the Son and the Father.[12] Similarly, he avoided using the term *Holy Spirit*, since the word *holy* is also used for God the Father and would move the Spirit too close to Father and Son. So, for Eunomius, instead of a Triune God there is total dissimilarity of Father, Son, and Spirit.

Up to this point the Holy Spirit had received little attention even by, for example, Athanasius. But with the neo-Arian party the so-called Pneumatomachians (i.e., combaters against the Spirit) came to the fore, claiming that the Holy Spirit should not be given equal rank with the Father and the Son. They also said that the Holy Spirit was a creation of the Son and a servant to both Father and Son.[13] The founder of this movement was Macedonius—thus their name the Macedonians—who was introduced into the See of Constantinople by the

---

11. Athanasius, *On the Councils of Ariminum and Seleucia* 41(NPNF² 4:472).
12. Gregory of Nyssa, *Against Eunomius* 2.14 (NPNF² 5:128).
13. See Basil, *Letter to the Church of Antioch* 140.2 (NPNF² 8:204).

Arians in 342 and enthroned there by Emperor Constantius II. He was deposed by the same emperor in 360 for having caused too much bloodshed and died in 364. As the church historian Socrates relates: "Such were the exploits of Macedonius on behalf of Christianity, consisting of murders, battles, incarceration, and civil wars."[14] As the many examples of such misdeeds cited by Socrates show, theological disputes often became actual wars having little to do with the spirit of the founder of Christianity.

Such an extremist position only furthered the attempt to achieve an understanding between those who rallied around Athanasius and those who advocated the *homoiousios*. Yet in the back of their minds was still the position of Sabellius, a priest presumably from Libya in North Africa. He lived most likely around the year 200 in Rome, and we know about him only through those who condemned his modalist teachings. He taught that God was single and indivisible, with Father, Son, and Holy Spirit being three modes or manifestations of the one divine Person. Athanasius claimed that Sabellius taught "that the Same becomes at one time Father, at another His own Son."[15] A Sabellian modalist would say that the one God "successively" revealed himself to humanity through time as the Father in creation, the Son in redemption, and the Spirit in sanctification and regeneration. Basil the Great, the older brother of Gregory of Nyssa and since 370 bishop of Caesarea and metropolitan of Cappadocia, explains the position of Sabellius and his followers more precisely, saying that Sabellius "affirms that God is one by hypostasis, but is described by Scripture in different Persons, according to the requirements of each individual case; sometimes under the name of Father, when there is occasion for this Person; sometimes under the name of Son when there is a descent to human interests or any of the operations of the oeconomy [of salvation]; and sometimes under the Person of the Spirit when the occasion demands such phraseology."[16]

Basil then explains his own position, saying

> that *ousia* has the same relation to hypostasis as the common has to the particular. Every one of us both shares in existence by the common term of essence (*ousia*) and by his own properties is such a one and such a one. In the same manner, in the matter in question, the term *ousia* is common, like goodness, or Godhead, or any similar attribute; while hyposta-

---

14. Socrates, *Ecclesiastical History* 2.38 (NPNF² 2:67).
15. Athanasius, *Orations against the Arians* 3.4 (NPNF² 4:395).
16. Basil, *Letter to Count Terentius* (Letter 214) (NPNF² 8:254).

sis is contemplated in the special property of Fatherhood, Sonship, or the power to sanctify. If then they describe the Persons as being without hypostasis, the statement is per se absurd; but if they concede that the Persons exist in real hypostasis, as they acknowledge, let them so reckon them that the principle of the *homoousion* may be preserved in the unity of the Godhead and that the doctrine preached may be the recognition of true religion, of Father, Son, and Holy Ghost, in the perfect and complete hypostasis of each of the Persons named.[17]

There is only one essence (*ousia*) that signifies the Godhead, but there are three special properties (hypostases). All three share in common the one essence, but the individual hypostasis is peculiar to each one. Basil's friend Gregory of Nazianzus (329/330–390), who became patriarch of Constantinople, defines as the special property of the Father the "unbegottenness," the special property of the Son the "generation" from the Father, and the special property of the Spirit the "procession" from the Father, according to John 15:26.[18] Different from what Eunomius taught, unbegottenness, generation, and procession are not part of the essence of God but show how the essence manifests itself in the three persons. "The Three are One in Godhead, and the One Three in properties."[19] Gregory makes it clear that though we call the Father first, the Son second, and the Holy Spirit third, there is no deficiency or subjection of essence. According to their common essence, all three are equal, while in peculiarity they are different but again not unequal. There is just one nature and one dignity of the Godhead.

The three Cappadocians (also called the Cappadocian Fathers, named after the Cappadocian region in present-day Turkey)—Basil the Great, his younger brother Gregory of Nyssa, and Gregory of Nazianzus—pursued to a greater extent the issue of the Trinity, including the differentiation between the three persons. In his *Fifth Theological Oration* Gregory of Nazianzus elaborates on the doctrine of the Trinity and poses the question of whether one should even inquire into the Holy Spirit, since he is "this strange God of Whom Scripture is silent."[20] His answer is in the affirmative and is well argued, with ample scriptural references. He admits that "the Old Testament proclaimed the Father openly and the Son more obscurely. The New manifested the Son, and suggested the Deity of the Spirit. Now the Spirit Himself dwells among

---

17. Ibid.
18. Gregory Nazianzen, *The Fifth Theological Oration: On the Holy Spirit* 8 (NPNF[2] 7:320).
19. Ibid., 9 (NPNF[2] 7:320).
20. Ibid., 1 (NPNF[2] 7:318).

us, and supplies us with a clear demonstration of Himself."[21] Then Gregory proceeds to show how the Spirit was involved in the ministry of Jesus. This moves him to argue that we should "worship God the Father, God the Son, and God the Holy Ghost, Three Persons, One Godhead, undivided in honor and glory and substance and kingdom."[22]

Once the full deity of the Spirit is asserted, the question of tritheism emerges: Are there now actually three gods? Gregory responds in this way: "When then we look at the Godhead, or the First Cause, or the Monarchia, that which we conceive is One; but when we look at the Persons in Whom the Godhead dwells, and at Those Who timelessly and with equal glory have their Being from the First Cause—there are Three Whom we worship."[23] There is a unity of the Godhead, which is differentiated in three persons. There is not simply a numerical distinction or one by name among the persons of the Trinity, but one that highlights the respective peculiarities of the persons.[24] Gregory is candid enough to admit that though he has looked everywhere for analogies, he has been unable "to discover anything on earth with which to compare the nature of the Godhead."[25] The Triune God is so unique that it has no comparison.

While the Holy Spirit so far had almost been a peripheral issue, Basil the Great wrote in 375 a whole book *On the Holy Spirit*. The reason for this was that the so-called Macedonians or Pneumatomachians denied the divinity of the Spirit. Basil argues for a new form of the doxology, which he rephrases: "Glory to God the Father with the Son, together with the Holy Spirit."[26] Some Macedonians preferred the wording "glory to the Father through the Son in the Holy Spirit," since they claimed that this shows the essential difference between Father, Son, and Holy Spirit. But Basil demonstrated that his doxology affirms the Spirit's equality with the Father and the Son in power and dignity. The church is able to participate in the saving work of Christ through the Spirit, since that Spirit is "the giver of life," as will be suggested by the Council of Constantinople. The Spirit is said to renew the image of God

---

21. Ibid., 26 (*NPNF*[2] 7:326).
22. Ibid., 28 (*NPNF*[2] 7:327).
23. Ibid., 14 (*NPNF*[2] 7:322).
24. Gregory explains concerning the relationship between and the properties of the persons: "The very fact of being Unbegotten or Begotten, or Proceeding has given the name of Father to the First, of the Son to the Second, and of the Third, Him of Whom we are speaking, of the Holy Ghost that the distinction of the Three Persons may be preserved in the one nature and dignity of the Godhead." Ibid., 9 (*NPNF*[2] 7:320).
25. Ibid., 31 (*NPNF*[2] 7:328).
26. See Basil the Great, *On the Holy Spirit* 1–2 (*NPNF*[2] 8:3–4), where he claims he was attacked because of this wording.

in believers by revealing the glory of the Son, who is the image of the invisible God. Since the Spirit connects believers with the Son and the Father in their redemptive work, it was important that the Spirit also be accorded true divinity.

The three Cappadocians decisively shaped the doctrine of the Trinity, at least for the Eastern Church, and unified those who to some degree could accept the decision of the Council of Nicea. By affirming the unity of the essence while admitting the distinction but not a difference in the respective hypostasis or person of the Trinity, they went beyond inequality of the persons, which Origen and his followers preferred. There was one Godhead with one will and one working, one being and one glory. This Godhead is of eternal nature and in a unified way is active as Father through the Son in the Spirit. But now it was necessary to consider Christology officially in the context of the Trinity. This came rather quickly with the ascent of Theodosius.

Emperor Valens (328–378) died in battle with the Goths, and Theodosius the Great (347–395) ascended to the throne of the eastern empire. On February 27, 380, he issued the Edict of Thessalonica, which states:

> It is our desire that all the various nations which are subject to our Clemency and Moderation, should continue to profess that religion which was delivered to the Romans by the divine Apostle Peter, as it has been preserved by faithful tradition, and which is now professed by the Pontiff Damasus and by Peter, Bishop of Alexandria, a man of apostolic holiness. According to the apostolic teaching and the doctrine of the Gospel, let us believe in the one deity of the Father, the Son and the Holy Spirit, in equal majesty and in a holy Trinity.[27]

The suggestion is that whoever follows this creed is a catholic Christian, and all others are heretics and will undergo divine and worldly judgment. The church was of prime concern to the emperor, and Nicene Christianity had become the state religion.

The Decision of Constantinople (381)

The emperor then called together a council at Constantinople, which again consisted mainly of bishops from the eastern empire. Among other items, the council reaffirmed the Nicene Creed and expanded it with reference to the Holy Spirit. Now it affirmed that the Spirit was

---

27. Codex Theodosianus 16.1.2, www.sevencouncils.com/an-orthodox-journey/the-edict-of-thessalonica, accessed April 8, 2016.

involved in the incarnational process by saying that Jesus Christ "was incarnate from the Holy Spirit and the Virgin Mary." Also the Holy Spirit is referred to as "the Lord and life-giver, who proceeds from the Father, who with the Father and the Son is together worshipped and together glorified, who spoke through the prophets." Most of these insertions reflect scriptural precedents: "incarnate from the Holy Spirit" in Luke 1:25, the Holy Spirit as "Lord" in 2 Corinthians 3:17, as life giver in John 6:63, and as "proceeding from the Father" in John 15:26. The phrase "who with the Father and the Son is together worshipped and together glorified," however, is not expressly mentioned in Scripture. We find a resemblance to this phrase when Athanasius says that the Spirit "is glorified with the Father and the Son."[28] Also, a letter sent by Basil states that "the Son is confessed to be of one substance with the Father, and the Holy Ghost is ranked and worshiped as of equal honor."[29] Though the Nicene-Constantinopolitan Creed essentially claims the *homoousia* of the Spirit, it scrupulously avoids the term so as not to alienate those who did not want to elevate the Spirit to the status of God.[30] With regard to the created beings and the Creator, the Holy Spirit is undoubtedly on the side of the latter, but the creed avoided speaking of the Godhead of the Spirit and his unity of being with Father and Son.

In the Nicene Creed we read that Jesus Christ is "of one substance with the Father," but it does not say such of the Holy Spirit. The enlarged third article in the creed from Constantinople now reads that "and [we believe] in the Holy Spirit, the Lord, the giver of life, who proceeds from the Father, who in unity with the Father and the Son is worshiped and glorified, who has spoken through the prophets. [We believe] in one holy catholic and apostolic Church. We acknowledge one baptism for the forgiveness of sins. We look for the resurrection of the dead and the life of the world to come." Concerning Jesus Christ we now read that he "was incarnate of the Holy Spirit and the virgin Mary."

Though we customarily now speak of the Nicene-Constantinopolitan Creed, we hardly hear of it until the Council of Chalcedon (451), and except for minor variations it is already contained in the *Ancoratus* ("the well-anchored person"), one of the earliest works of Epiphanius

---

28. Athanasius, *Letters to Serapion Concerning the Holy Spirit* 1.31, in Khaled Anatolios, *Athanasius* (London: Routledge, 2004), 230.
29. Basil the Great, *Letter* 90.2 (*NPNF*[2] 8:176).
30. See the extensive comments by J. N. D. Kelly, *Early Christian Creeds*, 3rd ed. (London: Longman, 1972), 342-43.

(310/320–403), bishop of Salamis. Nevertheless, we know, also in the light of the preceding controversies, that the synod members affirmed the faith of Nicea and, through the influence of the Cappadocian Fathers, also wanted to strengthen the position of the Holy Spirit. This is exactly what this creed accomplished.

The following year Emperor Theodosius summoned another synod in Constantinople, while simultaneously another synod met in Rome, with Pope Damasus presiding. From the meeting in Constantinople a synodical letter was sent to the synod in Rome, which showed that in Constantinople they were steadfast in the Nicene faith by writing:

> This is the faith which ought to be sufficient for you, for us, for all who wrest not the word of the true faith; for it is the ancient faith; it is the faith of our baptism; it is the faith that teaches us to believe in the name of the Father, of the Son, and of the Holy Ghost: According to this faith there is one Godhead, Power and Substance of the Father, of the Son, and of the Holy Ghost; the dignity being equal, and the majesty being equal in three perfect essences [*hypostases*] and three perfect persons.[31]

The letter also included the canons of the synod of Antioch (341) and the tome of the preceding synod in Constantinople. This showed that in both East and West the Nicene faith had supervened, especially since Theodosius sanctioned this faith by law and rejected Arianism as heretical.

A Parting of Ways

Officially the Arian version of how to think about Father, Son, and Holy Spirit was rejected. This meant the unity of the Christian faith was preserved. The terms with which Christians confessed the doctrine of the Trinity both in the East and in the West became in many ways settled from the fifth century onward. But there was still the division of language, Greek and Latin, though Greek was slowly making way for Latin as the new lingua franca, the common language of the Roman Empire. We should also not forget that the decisive steps with regard to the Trinity were made in the East under the influence of Greek terminology and Greek thought patterns. Even the Western representation at Nicea and Constantinople was rather sparse. It is true that the West had affirmed the decisions of these councils, but many Germanic

---

31. Council of Constantinople, AD 382, *The Synodical Letter* (NPNF² 14:189); and Theodoret, *Ecclesiastical History* 5.9 (NPNF² 3:138).

tribes, notably the Goths and the Vandals, had adopted Arianism and only from the sixth century onward were they converted to the faith of Nicea. The Third Council of Toledo in 589 marks the change of the Visigoths, who ruled southern France and then Spain, from the Arian to the Nicene faith. But this council also affirmed in canon 2 the *filioque*, in an anti-Arian move, to tie the Spirit closer to Father and Son. Eventually this unilateral change of the creed became a point of contention between East and West. But we are getting ahead of the story. Therefore we turn once more to the East, where Trinitarian thinking soon became standardized by John of Damascus.

John of Damascus

John of Damascus (675/76–749?), a monk and polymath whose fields of interest and contribution included law, theology, philosophy, and music, was not an original theologian but rendered the orthodox faith in a way that still today is exemplary for the East. He starts out with the assertion "that God is One, that is to say, one essence [*ousia*]; and that He is known, and has His being in three subsistences, in Father, I say, and Son and Holy Spirit; and that the Father and the Son and the Holy Spirit are one in all respects, except in that of not being begotten, that of being begotten, and that of procession."[32] One reason he does not start with the Trinity but with the belief in one God and then works himself up to the Word, the Son of God, and then to the Holy Spirit is that he depends very much on the *Catechetical Oration* of Gregory of Nyssa.[33]

Once John has established that there is a God and this God is one and not many, he then gives a "reasoned proof" that this one and only God is not Wordless. For there was never a time when God was not Word. Then he continues to show that "the Word must also possess Spirit."[34] The one God, who is the fountain of all that is, is of "one essence, one divinity, one power, one will, one energy, one beginning, one authority, one dominion, one sovereignty, made known in three perfect subsistences and adored with one adoration, believed in and ministered to by all rational creation, united without confusion and divided without separation."[35]

---

32. John of Damascus, *An Exact Exposition of the Orthodox Faith* 1.2 (NPNF[2] 9:1–2).
33. See Andrew Louth, "Late Patristic Developments on the Trinity in the East," in *Oxford Handbook of the Trinity*, ed. Gilles Emery and Matthew Levering (Oxford: Oxford University Press, 2011), 147, who also points out this dependence on Gregory of Nyssa.
34. John of Damascus, *An Exact Exposition of the Orthodox Faith* 1.7 (NPNF[2] 9:5).

The three subsistences or hypostases are not like three persons, since in terms of their external efficacy they are indistinguishable. But they are internally distinguished. John explains:

> So then in the first sense of the word the three absolutely divine subsistences of the Holy Godhead agree: for they exist as one in essence and uncreated. But with the second signification it is quite otherwise. For the Father alone is ingenerate, no other subsistence having given Him being. And the Son alone is generate, for He was begotten of the Father's essence without beginning and without time. And only the Holy Spirit proceedeth from the Father's essence, not having been generated but simply proceeding.[36]

John then admits that the nature of the generation and of the procession is quite beyond our comprehension. Yet according to John, Fatherhood, Sonship, and Procession are no human constructs but are communicated to us by the Godhead; they are the result of God's self-disclosure. Though Father, Son, and Holy Spirit are equals, John is somewhat defensive, saying, "if we say that the Father is the origin of the Son and greater than the Son, we do not suggest any precedence in time or superiority in nature of the Father over the Son . . . or superiority in any other respect save causation."[37] While John rejects any subordination of the Son (and the Spirit) under the Father, the latter is the cause of both Son and Spirit, as John concedes. While affirming generation and procession and defending their difference, he admits that he is unable to understand their difference. This means we arrive at creedal affirmations that had lost their experiential anchor. But the West did not fare much better.

Hilary of Poitiers

Very little is known about Bishop Hilary of Poitiers (d. 367/68), who is sometimes called the Athanasius of the West. But he wrote a major treatise on the Trinity and was instrumental in bridging the gap between the Western theologians who favored the *homoousia* of Father and Son and the Eastern theologians who preferred the *homoiousia* of Father and Son. After the synod of Biterrae (present-day Béziers in southern France) in 356, he was sent into exile because of his insis-

---

35. Ibid., 1.8 (*NPNF*[2] 9:6).
36. Ibid., 1.8 (*NPNF*[2] 9:8).
37. Ibid.

tence on the decisions of Nicea and spent four years in what is now central Anatolia in Turkey. His twelve-book *De Trinitate* (*On the Trinity*), composed in 359/60, was mainly directed against the Arians and was concerned with the unity of the Son with the Father. He argues, for instance, that since "the Spirit of God is also the Spirit of Christ" and since "the Spirit of truth proceedeth from the Father and is sent from the Father by the Son," there is no subordination of the Son under the Father but a unity in nature.[38] Regardless of whether we hear of the Spirit of Christ or of the Spirit of God, there is just one Spirit. "Since what is of God is also of Christ, and what is of Christ is also of God, Christ cannot be anything different from what God is. Christ, therefore, is God, one Spirit with God."[39]

While Hilary attempts to show with ample Scripture references and logic the oneness and essential equality of Father, Son, and Holy Spirit, in the end he concedes the insufficiency of humans to comprehend the Trinity. He writes:

> But I cannot describe Him, Whose pleas for me I cannot describe. As in the revelation that Thy Only-begotten was born of Thee before times eternal, when we cease to struggle with ambiguities of language and difficulties of thought, the one certainty of His birth remains; so I hold fast in my consciousness the truth that Thy Holy Spirit is from Thee and through Him, although I cannot by my intellect comprehend it.[40]

Finally he can do nothing but to affirm the faith in the Triune God, the faith into which he was baptized. Realizing the difficulties in expressing with words "the mystery of the Trinity," he could be open to mediate between those who affirm the *homoousia* of Father and Son as well as those who would only want to concede the *homoiousia*. Yet logical thinking was not completely abandoned. As the Only-begotten from the Father, the Son has the same substance as the Father, while differing from the Father by being the Son.[41] Hilary could therewith assert the similarity of Father and Son as well as their equality, sharing the same essence or substance. Since this substance was not thought of as some prior substance in which they shared but the substance of the Father, he held on to the full divinity of the Son, affirming with Athanasius the Nicene Creed and its essential oneness of Father and Son.

---

38. Hilary of Poitiers, *On the Trinity* 8.20–21 (NPNF[2] 9:143).
39. Ibid., 8.27 (NPNF[2] 9:145).
40. Ibid., 12.56 (NPNF[2] 9:233).
41. See Hilary of Poitiers, *On the Councils* 81.84 (NPNF[2] 9:25–26), where he explains the meaning of the *homoousion* at the Council of Nicea.

Augustine

Augustine (354–430), bishop of Hippo Regius (present-day Annaba in Algeria), was one of the most influential church fathers of the Western church. In his massive work *On the Trinity* he attempts to show "that the Trinity is the one and only and true God, and also how the Father, the Son, and the Holy Spirit are rightly said, believed, understood, to be of one and the same substance or essence."[42] He wants to do this "according to the authority of the Holy Scriptures" and with convincing logic. Revelation and reason are the two instruments by which he wants to lay out the doctrine of the Trinity. Most important for Augustine is the unity of the one God but also the Trinity.

The one God presents a unity, "because the will of the Father and the Son is one, and their working indivisible ... the Holy Spirit certainly not being thence excluded," as Augustine talks about the incarnation.[43] Though we name the individual persons of the Trinity when we speak of the incarnation, life, death, and resurrection of Christ, nevertheless "the Father, and the Son, and the Holy Spirit, as they are indivisible, so work indivisibly."[44] We distinguish in the Trinity three persons, but we cannot talk about the Trinity in a plural sense, since the divine substance is one. This divinity makes up their unity, as Augustine explains: "The effect of the same substance in Father and Son and Holy Spirit is, that whatsoever is said of each in respect to themselves, is to be taken of them, not in the plural in sum, but in the singular. For as the Father is God, and the Son is God, and the Holy Spirit is God, which no one doubts to be said in respect to substance, yet we do not say that the very supreme Trinity itself is three Gods, but one God."[45] There is not qualitative differentiation in the Godhead, since "nothing may hinder us from confessing the absolute equality of the Father, Son, and Holy Spirit."[46] Having said this, he compares the three persons of the Trinity to human qualities: "It is I that remember, I that understand, I that love, who am neither memory, nor understanding, nor love, but who have them. These things, then, can be said by a single person, which has these three, but is not these three. But in the simplicity of that Highest Nature, which is God, although there is one God, there are three persons, the Father, the Son, and the Holy Spirit."[47] Father,

---

42. Augustine, *On the Trinity* 1.2.4 (*NPNF*[1] 3:19).
43. Ibid., 2.5.9 (*NPNF*[1] 3:41).
44. Ibid., 1.4.7 (*NPNF*[1] 3:20).
45. Ibid., 5.8.9 (*NPNF*[1] 3:91).
46. Ibid., 6.9.10 (*NPNF*[1] 3:102).

Son, and Holy Spirit are not three distinct persons who fall under a certain species, such as divine, but each divine person is identical with the other, or rather with the whole divine substance. Therefore, Augustine states, "The Father, the Son, and the Holy Spirit together is not a greater essence than the Father alone or the Son alone; but these three substances or persons, if they must be so called, together are equal to each singly: which the natural man does not comprehend."[48] Similar to Hilary, Augustine admits the insufficiency of the human intellect to understand the Trinity. Though the Trinity is beyond human comprehension, he, just as many others before and after him, did not desist from reflecting on the Trinity.

Augustine emphasized the unity of God while allowing for the individual activities of the persons of the Godhead, such as the suffering, death, and resurrection of Christ, or the forgiving of sins through the Holy Spirit yet in cooperation with the Father and the Son, or the creation of the world through the Father, yet again in cooperation with the other two persons. But he also concedes that the Trinity and the workings through the individual persons are beyond human comprehension. The scriptural references notwithstanding, the Trinity is not simply deduced from Scripture; it is "a speculative construct."

From tradition Augustine inherited the notion of the three persons of the one Godhead. As we have seen, he does not agree to a qualitative or quantitative distinction between them. Augustine rules out that a distinction came about by accident, "because both the being called the Father, and the being called the Son, is eternal and unchangeable to them." Yet the distinction between Father and Son cannot be according to substance, since their substance is the same and is not different. The distinction must be "according to relation, which relation, however, is not accident, because it is not changeable."[49] The three persons are not in themselves something different, but only in their relation to one another and to the world. This relation is unchangeable and therewith eternal. Therefore the one God we encounter is never just the Father, or just the Son, or just the Holy Spirit. In the one being of God, the other two relations are always implied, even if we encounter just one. The three persons are the undivided Godhead, yet each from a different perspective, for instance, the Father by begetting, the Son by

---

47. Ibid., 15.22.42 (*NPNF*[1] 3:222).
48. Ibid., 7.6.11 (*NPNF*[1] 3:113).
49. Ibid., 5.5.6 (*NPNF*[1] 3:89).

being begotten. With the Spirit it is somewhat more difficult, since the Holy Spirit is

> a certain unutterable communion of the Father and the Son; and on that account, perhaps, He is so called, because the same name is suitable to both the Father and the Son. For He Himself is called specially that which they are called in common; because both the Father is a spirit and the Son a spirit, both the Father is holy and the Son holy. In order, therefore, that the communion of both may be signified from a name which is suitable to both, the Holy Spirit is called the gift of both.[50]

All three are at work in relation to the world. Yet the Holy Spirit comes from both Father and Son. Here something is enunciated that later on will officially split Christendom into an Eastern and a Western church. It is centered on the different perception of how the Holy Spirit comes forth: in the East it was said to have been from the Father through the Son, in the West from the Father and the Son. But more later about this issue referred to as the *filioque*, that is, "and the Son."

Since Augustine wrote in Latin, the Greek terms *ousia* and *hypostasis* were of little use to him. He explains that the Greek writers

> use also the word hypostasis; but they intend to put a difference, I know not what, between *ousia* and hypostasis: so that most of ourselves who treat these things in the Greek language, are accustomed to say *mian ousian, treis hypostaseis*, or, in Latin, one essence, three substances. But because with us the usage has already obtained, that by essence we understand the same thing which is understood by substance; we do not dare to say one essence, three substances, but one essence or substance and three persons.[51]

While emphasizing the relational character of the Trinity, the term *person* certainly fits better than the impersonal *hypostasis*. Augustine admits the poverty of human language to express appropriately the being and activity of the Trinity. We need to speak about it in the face of "the errors of the heretics," and "it must be devoutly believed, as most certainly known from the Scriptures."[52] Yet there is human weakness to utter in speech these things. Augustine expresses a certain uneasiness with talking about three persons, though he feels bound to it by Scripture and tradition.

---

50. Ibid., 5.11.12 (*NPNF*[1] 3:93).
51. Ibid., 5.8–9.10 (*NPNF*[1] 3:92).
52. Ibid., 7.5.9 (*NPNF*[1] 3:110).

In order to illustrate the relations suggested in the Trinity, Augustine uses different metaphors, some taken from the human mind or psyche. The reason he resorts to the human mind is that humans are created in the image of God, "and His image must be found in it."[53] The human mind mirrors for Augustine something of the relations suggested by the divine Trinity. For instance, he uses the concept of love: there is myself, and that which I love, and love itself. "For I do not love, except I love a lover; for there is not love where nothing is loved. Therefore there are three things—he who loves, and that which is loved, and love." Then he uses the metaphor of the mind and love, saying: "There are two things, the mind and the love of it, when it loves itself; so there are two things, the mind and the knowledge of it, when it knows itself. Therefore the mind itself, and the love of it, and the knowledge of it, are three things, and these three are one; and when they are perfect they are equal."[54] Another triad that Augustine uses to illustrate the Trinity is memory, understanding, and will. He writes: "My will also embraces my whole understanding and my whole memory, whilst I use the whole that I understand and remember. And, therefore, while all are mutually comprehended by each, and as wholes, each as a whole is equal to each as a whole, and each as a whole at the same time to all as wholes; and these three are one, one life, one mind, one essence."[55]

Augustine ends his work on the Trinity addressing God: "O Lord, our God, we believe in Thee, the Father and the Son and the Holy Spirit. For the Truth would not say, Go, baptize all nations in the name of the Father and of the Son and of the Holy Spirit; unless Thou wast a Trinity."[56] Then he asks to be set free from the multitude of speech, well knowing that his attempt to "describe" the Trinity is futile. We hear nothing here of three persons but of the "one God, God the Trinity."

While the errors concerning perception of the Trinity are rejected, the positive elaboration of the doctrine is still not accomplished. Reinhold Seeberg (1859-1935) therefore concludes: "The whole procedure is a freely suspended speculation which moves in the heights of the immanent life of the Godhead bare of any relationship to the reality of divine revelation. It is therefore ultimately just a logical exercise in which persons are vaporized to relations and the threefoldness is in

---

53. Ibid., 14.8.11 (*NPNF*[1] 3:189).
54. Ibid., 9.2.2–4.4 (*NPNF*[1] 3:126–27).
55. Ibid., 10.11.18 (*NPNF*[1] 3:143).
56. Ibid., 15.28.51 (*NPNF*[1] 3:227).

the end nothing but the perception of the one God under various viewpoints."[57] Though this evaluation may be somewhat exaggerated, two items remain clear for Augustine: there is a unity of the one God, and there are three divine entities, Father, Son, and Holy Spirit. This is also warranted by the New Testament witness.

The *Filioque*

As mentioned above, Augustine considered the Spirit as proceeding from the Father and the Son. Yet this was contrary to the Nicene Creed, expanded in 381 in Constantinople, which states that the Holy Spirit proceeds from the Father. Tertullian already earlier mentioned that on the one hand "I believe the Spirit *to proceed* from no other source than from the Father through the Son," and yet on the other hand that "the Spirit indeed is third from God and the Son."[58] This means that as a Western theologian he saw no contradiction in affirming the traditional conception that the Spirit proceeds from the Father through the Son, and the idea that the Spirit is a third from Father and Son. When we come to Bishop Ambrose of Milan (ca. 340–397), who was influential on Augustine, we read: "The Holy Spirit also, when He proceeds from the Father and the Son, is not separated from the Father nor separated from the Son."[59] The Athanasian Creed again affirms the procession of the Spirit from the Father and the Son.

The reason the West insisted on the *filioque*, the procession of the Spirit from the Father and the Son, becomes clear when we read in Ratramnus (d. ca. 868), a Benedictine monk in the abbey of Corbie in France, that the Greek theologians represent Arianism in matters of the Holy Spirit by "making levels in the Godhead" and "want the Holy Spirit to be inferior to the Father and the Son."[60] We remember that in 381 the *homoousia* of the Spirit was not affirmed, while the West evidently favored such a move, as we can see from the *filioque*. Orthodox theologians maintained the original wording of the Nicene Creed as agreed on in 381, while Rome reluctantly agreed to the *filioque*. This change in the creed was first introduced by Charlemagne (747/48–814) at a local synod of Aachen in 809 for his empire and finally accepted since 1014 by Rome for liturgical use. As the practice of chanting the

---

57. Reinhold Seeberg, *Lehrbuch der Dogmengeschichte*, 6th ed. (Darmstadt: Wissenschaftliche Buchgesellschaft, 1965), 2:162–63.
58. Tertullian, *Against Praxeas* 4, 8 (ANF 3:599, 603).
59. Ambrose, *On the Holy Trinity* 1.11.120 (NPNF[1] 10:109).
60. Ratramnus, *Against Greek Opposition* 1.3 (PL 121:220).

Latin creed at Mass spread in the West, the *filioque* became a part of the liturgy. This practice was adopted in Charlemagne's court in 798 and spread throughout his empire. This led to the alienation of the East from the West, since the Orthodox Church claimed that one cannot unilaterally change a creed that was adopted by the whole church. There was still another matter, as Patriarch Photios I of Constantinople (ca. 810–893/94) explains: if the Spirit proceeds from the Father and the Son, then this leads to two divine principles, and the unity of the Godhead is dissolved in favor of a twofoldness. Photios called this a return to "atheism," since it repeated the unholy "dogma of polytheism."[61]

The different arguments of Photios against the *filioque* provided enough ammunition against the West that in 1054 it finally came to a break between East and West and the excommunication of each by the other. A large part of the dissension was due to the rivalry between Rome and Constantinople and the assertion of the primacy of Rome over the whole church. Nevertheless, the disagreement over the *filioque* has played an important role until the present. The Second Council of Lyons pronounced in 1274: "We condemn and disprove those who presume to deny that the Holy Spirit proceeds eternally from Father and Son."[62] Yet the Roman Catholic Church has in recent times moved beyond this condemnation. The Vatican Declaration *Dominus Iesus* of 2000 no longer mentions the *filioque*, and in commemoration of the fifteen hundredth anniversary of the Council of Constantinople in 1981, Pope John Paul II (1920–2005) made the *filioque* in the Roman liturgy optional. But now we have jumped ahead of the story.

---

61. Photius, *Mystagogy of the Holy Spirit* 11 (PG 102:291). See also the extensive treatment of the *filioque* by Jaroslav Pelikan, *The Christian Tradition*, vol. 2, *The Spirit of Eastern Christendom (600-1700)* (Chicago: University of Chicago Press, 1974), 183–200.
62. Heinrich Denzinger, *Compendium of Creeds, Definitions, and Declarations on Matters of Faith and Morals*, ed. Peter Hünermann, 43rd ed. (San Francisco: Ignatius Press, 2012), 282.

5

Developments in the Middle Ages and in the Reformation Period

The New Testament focused on Jesus as the bringer of salvation. When we come to the early church, the question arose as to how Jesus Christ, bringer of salvation, is related to the sender, the one God. This immediately raised two questions: Was Jesus really equal to God so that he could bring lasting salvation? If so, would this not jeopardize the faith in one God? This meant that both in the New Testament and in the early church the issues that were later connected with the Trinity were basically existential issues. But this changed in the high Middle Ages.

Scholastic Intellectualism

While in the early church the issue of who was Jesus Christ in relation to God the Father was of existential significance, the issue slowly became more speculative. This tendency became even stronger through scholastic intellectualism. Theology became a learned discipline, often in the university context, and its students wanted to defend its tenets in a reasoned discourse on par with that of other learned disciplines.

Richard of St. Victor

During the high Middle Ages, which largely coincided with the rule of scholastic thinking, the influence of reason on the doctrine of the Trinity was still strongly felt. This was especially true for Richard of St. Victor (d. 1173), who hailed from the British Isles and joined the school of the Abbey of St. Victor outside Paris. His scholastic masterpiece *On the Trinity* is one of the most significant medieval works on the dogma of the Trinity. As Ruben Angelici, translator of *On the Trinity*, tells us: "This masterpiece awakened profound admiration in Richard's contemporaries. Latin codices of the *De Trinitate* are found scattered throughout Europe, and the work held a key place of influence at least until the end of the sixteenth century."[1]

Richard's scholastic interest is at once evident when he writes: "Our intention in this work will be to adduce not only plausible reasons to support that which we believe, but rather necessary ones."[2] The reason is that he has heard and read about the Trinity, "but I do not remember having read anything on the evidences for these assertions."[3] Authorities abound, he says, but arguments are rare. Therefore he wants to demonstrate the truth of these doctrines.

Richard considers God as the highest substance, which can have no equal. Therefore that highest substance must be one. "Just like the omnipotent being can only be one, there can only be one God."[4] Since God is also the highest charity, the fullness of love implies a plurality of persons. This then necessitates three persons for the perfect divine goodness, happiness, and glory. His basic idea is that love is derived from a multiplicity of persons, since the lover needs a person toward whom love is directed, and that the lover is loved again by the loved one. But there must be a third person, since the Father needs a companion in his love to the Son, as conversely the Son needs someone who loves with him the Father. Richard concludes that two divine persons with equal desire and analogous motivation must necessarily require a third person: it is "impossible for the two persons of the divinity not be associated with a third one."[5] While Augustine used love

---

1. Ruben Angelici, *Richard of Saint Victor: On the Trinity*, Eng. trans. and commentary (Eugene, OR: Cascade Books, 2011), 5.
2. Richard of St. Victor, *On the Trinity* 1.4, in Angelici, *Richard of Saint Victor: On the Trinity*, 75.
3. Ibid., 1.5, in Angelici, *Richard of Saint Victor: On the Trinity*, 76.
4. Ibid., 1.25, in Angelici, *Richard of Saint Victor: On the Trinity*, 89.
5. Ibid., 3.2–4, 3.14, in Angelici, *Richard of Saint Victor: On the Trinity*, 129.

to illustrate the Trinity in a metaphoric way, for Richard this becomes a logical exercise and an intellectual demonstration.

Anselm of Canterbury

The same is true for Anselm of Canterbury (1033–1109), born in Aosta, northeastern Italy, who became abbot of the Benedictine Abbey of Bec in Normandy, France, and later on archbishop of Canterbury. In some ways it seems that Richard depended on Anselm in his rational logical deductions. Anselm also wanted to continue the line of thinking that Augustine used, but with a scholastic bent. In his *Monologion* he lays out the doctrine of God and the Trinity. God is the Supreme Being, who exists without beginning and end everywhere and in every place. God is also the Supreme Spirit, who "most truly begets and the Word is most truly begotten. Therefore, just as the first is clearly true, so must the second be completely certain. Hence, it is the distinguishing property of the Supreme Spirit most truly to beget and the distinguishing property of the Word most truly to be begotten."[6] The Supreme Spirit is then the Father, and the Word is the Son. Anselm considers their sameness and their difference and concludes: "With respect to the fact that the one is the Father and the other is the Son they are so different that the Father is never called the Son nor the Son called the Father; and with respect to their substance they are so identical that the essence of the Son is always in the Father and the essence of the Father is always in the Son."[7] Anselm also seems to imply a gradation from Father to Son when he ascribes to the Father understanding, knowledge, wisdom, and truth, and correspondingly to the Son understanding of understanding, knowledge of knowledge, wisdom of wisdom, and truth of truth, since the Son participates in the paternal substance.

Father and Son love themselves and each other in equal degree. This love proceeds from the Father and the Son equally, and it is not two but one love. "This Love is in every respect the very thing that the Father and the Son are."[8] Anselm concludes that this Love is then referred by its proper name, Spirit, a name that signifies the substance of the Father and the Son equally, and the Spirit is what the Father and the Son are, though he has his own existence from them. Anselm explains:

---

6. Anselm of Canterbury, *Monologion* 41, in *The Complete Philosophical and Theological Treatises of Anselm of Canterbury*, trans. Jasper Hopkins and Herbert Richardson (Minneapolis: Banning, 2000), 57.
7. Ibid., 43, in *Complete Philosophical and Theological Treatises*, 59.
8. Ibid., 55, in *Complete Philosophical and Theological Treatises*, 66.

"Just as the Son is the substance, wisdom, and strength of the Father in the sense that He has the same essence, wisdom, and strength as the Father, so their Spirit can also be understood to be the essence, wisdom, and strength of the Father and of the Son in that He has exactly the same [essence, wisdom, and strength] as they do."[9] While Anselm attributes to the Father memory, to the Son understanding, and to the Spirit love, he asserts that this Supreme Being is so perfect that none of the three needs one of the others to remember, understand, or love. The only difference between the three is that the Father is unbegotten, the Son is begotten, and the Spirit proceeds. Anselm admits that with regard to the Trinity, "the hiddenness of so sublime a matter seems to me to surpass the entire acute gaze of the human intellect." He claims "that anyone who is investigating an incomprehensible doctrine should be content if by rational inference he comes to recognize that this doctrine is most certainly true."[10]

Anselm is convinced that he has delivered compelling proof for the certitude of faith in the matter of the Trinity. But he is unable to speak of the three persons of the Trinity. For him the oneness of the substance is what really matters, as he concedes: "For although I can speak of a trinity because of the Father, the Son, and their Spirit, who are three, nevertheless I cannot in a single word name that by virtue of which they are three (as if I were to say '[a trinity] by virtue of three *persons*,' as I might say 'a oneness by virtue of one *substance*')."[11] This means that the doctrine of the Trinity is elevated to an axiomatic truth, but it lacks salvific relevance.

This fundamental principle of Trinitarian theology we find nearly verbatim in the Bull of Union with the Copts and the Ethiopians, *Cantate Domino*, of February 4, 1442:

> First, then, the holy Roman Church, founded on the words of our Lord and Savior, firmly believes, professes, and preaches one true God, almighty, immutable, and eternal, Father, Son, and Holy Spirit; one in essence, three in Persons; unbegotten Father, Son begotten from the Father, Holy Spirit proceeding from the Father and the Son; the Father is not the Son or the Holy Spirit, the Son is not the Father or the Holy Spirit, the Holy Spirit is not the Father or the Son; the Father is only the Father, the Son is only the Son, the Holy Spirit is only the Holy Spirit. The Father alone from his substance begot the Son; the Son alone is begotten of the Father alone;

---

9. Ibid., 58, in *Complete Philosophical and Theological Treatises*, 68–69.
10. Ibid., 64, in *Complete Philosophical and Theological Treatises*, 74.
11. Ibid., 79, in *Complete Philosophical and Theological Treatises*, 85.

the Holy Spirit alone proceeds at once from the Father and the Son. These three Persons are one God, not three gods, because there is one substance of the three, one essence, one nature, one Godhead, one immensity, one eternity, and everything [in them] is one where there is not opposition of relationship.[12]

Thomas Aquinas

While Anselm starts with the general notion of God and then proceeds to the Trinity, Thomas Aquinas (ca. 1225–1274) clearly distinguishes between the philosophical knowledge of God through reason and the knowledge of the Trinity through revelation when he writes: "It is impossible to attain to the knowledge of the Trinity by natural reason." He elaborates: "The creative power of God is common to the whole Trinity; and hence it belongs to the unity of the essence, and not to the distinction of the persons. Therefore, by natural reason we can know what belongs to the unity of the essence, but not what belongs to the distinction of the persons."[13] This is exactly what we also noticed with the approach of Anselm, who also focused on the essence but not on the persons.

When Aquinas discusses the Trinity, he shows that Scripture talks about God as to signify procession, not in terms of a bodily procession but of an intellectual one. For example, the intelligible word proceeds from the speaker, yet remains in that person.[14] There are two processions in God, the Son and the Holy Spirit. The first is the procession of the Word in God, which is generation, for the Son proceeds by way of intelligible action. Then there is another procession, the procession of love, which proceeds by the way of will. But this procession of love is not generation, because "what proceeds in God by way of love, does not proceed as begotten, or as son, but proceeds rather as spirit; which name expresses a certain vital movement and impulse."[15] Aquinas distinguishes here between the intellect, pertaining to the generation of the Son, and the will, pertaining to the procession of the Spirit. The procession that is not called generation is then termed spiration, the procession of the Spirit. Since only acts of intellect and will remain

---

12. Heinrich Denzinger, *Compendium of Creeds, Definitions, and Declarations on Matters of Faith and Morals*, ed. Peter Hünermann, 43rd ed. (San Francisco: Ignatius Press, 2012), 343.
13. Thomas Aquinas, *Summa Theologica* 1q32a1r.
14. See ibid., 1q27a1r.
15. Ibid., 1q27a4.

within the Godhead, Aquinas concludes that there are no other processions possible in God.

Then he asks whether there are real relations in the Godhead, meaning relations that refer to another. He writes: "When something proceeds from a principle of the same nature, then both the one proceeding and the source of procession, agree in the same order; and then they have real relations to each other."[16] Since the divine processions are of the same nature, they are real relations to one another. There are four real relations in the Godhead—paternity, filiation, spiration, and procession—through which the three persons in the Trinity are what they are. Aquinas sums up his deliberations, saying:

> Real relations in God can be understood only in regard to those actions according to which there are internal, and not external, processions in God. These processions are two only, as above explained (27, 5), one derived from the action of the intellect, the procession of the Word; and the other from the action of the will, the procession of love. In respect of each of these processions two opposite relations arise; one of which is the relation of the person proceeding from the principle; the other is the relation of the principle Himself. The procession of the Word is called generation in the proper sense of the term, whereby it is applied to living things. Now the relation of the principle of generation in perfect living beings is called paternity; and the relation of the one proceeding from the principle is called filiation. But the procession of Love has no proper name of its own (27, 4); and so neither have the ensuing relations a proper name of their own. The relation of the principle of this procession is called spiration; and the relation of the person proceeding is called procession: although these two names belong to the processions or origins themselves, and not to the relations.[17]

The distinction of the persons is derived from their relations concerning their origin. The term *person*, according to Aquinas, signifies the relation directly and the essence indirectly. He explains by suggesting that, while the Godhead is God, the divine paternity is God the Father, who is a divine person. The same can be said for the divine filiation and the divine spiration. This means that there are three persons in the Godhead, since there are several realities subsisting in the one divine nature. But there cannot be more than three, since a real distinction between the divine relations can come only from relative opposition.

---

16. Ibid., 1q28a1.
17. Ibid., 1q28a4.

Aquinas then concludes that there can only be three persons in the Godhead, Father, Son, and Holy Spirit.[18]

While Aquinas often adduces the help of "the philosopher" Aristotle to advance his investigation, we hardly find any reference to Scripture. Yet he is adamant that it is impossible to attain the notion of the Trinity by natural reason. While the one God is the creative power, this God can be discerned by the creatures as their Creator; the persons of the Trinity, however, are beyond such causal inference.

When Aquinas considers the three persons in the Trinity, it is clear for him that since they have the same essence there is equality among them. Aquinas shows this with regard to the coeternity of Father, Son, and Spirit:

> The Father does not beget the Son by will, but by nature; and also that the Father's nature was perfect from eternity; and again that the action whereby the Father produces the Son is not successive, because thus the Son would be successively generated, and this generation would be material, and accompanied with movement; which is quite impossible. Therefore we conclude that the Son existed whensoever the Father existed and thus the Son is co-eternal with the Father, and likewise the Holy Ghost is co-eternal with both.[19]

There is no priority of one over the other, though there is some order whereby one is from the other, as Aquinas states, citing Augustine.[20] But they are equal in greatness and in power. When it comes to the mission of the persons of the Trinity, Aquinas considers that the Son was sent into the world by the Father, meaning that he began to exist visibly in the world by taking on our nature, though he was previously in the world, as Aquinas says with reference to John 1:1. And yet Aquinas rejects the implication that this would mean an inferiority of the sent person to the sender.[21] The explanation given by Aquinas that the Son had been everywhere beforehand and so there is not separation from the one omnipresent God is not very convincing.

The case is somewhat different with the Holy Spirit. Aquinas writes: "The Holy Ghost is possessed by man, and dwells within him, in the very gift itself of sanctifying grace. Hence the Holy Ghost Himself is given and sent."[22] The Holy Spirit does then affect the gifts that are

---

18. See ibid., 1q30a2.
19. Ibid., 1q42a2.
20. See ibid., 1q42a3.
21. See ibid., 1q43a1r1.
22. Ibid., 1q43a3.

connected with him, such as the power of prophesying and of working miracles. Sanctifying grace is given to us by the whole Trinity. To that effect Son and Spirit are sent to dwell in our soul. Though the Father too "dwells in us by grace, still it does not belong to Him to be from another, and consequently He is not sent."[23] Aquinas differentiates between Father on the one hand and Son and Spirit on the other. It is difficult to see here no gradation. Yet for Aquinas there is none.

What has Aquinas accomplished? He says: "Therefore, we must not attempt to prove what is of faith, except by authority alone, to those who receive the authority; while as regards others it suffices to prove that what faith teaches is not impossible."[24] We notice first his frequent reference to Augustine. This African theologian paved the way on which others traveled further. Then Aquinas also makes clear that the Trinity cannot be proved through reason. The starting point for his deliberations is revelation, even if he does not extensively quote Scripture. Nevertheless, his quotations of numerous sources show his familiarity with tradition, both that tradition that veered from the truth as expressed by ecclesial authority and that tradition represented by the church. As a teacher of the church, Aquinas honored the tradition of the church. But he was in no way a repristinator. For him it was important to show that what the church teaches is intellectually coherent and convincing. Therefore he attempted to prove the intelligibility of the Trinity. It is also not far from the truth to admit that "a speculative highpoint of the Augustinian psychological speculations on the Trinity is represented by Thomas Aquinas."[25]

Joachim of Fiore

While Joachim of Fiore (ca. 1135–1202) was perhaps the most important apocalyptic thinker of the Middle Ages, for us he is important for his concept of history. He saw in the unfolding of history a drama in three acts that corresponded to the three persons of the Trinity. Joachim was a Cistercian monk from Calabria in southern Italy, founder of the abbey San Giovanni in Fiore, and finally also of a new and stricter branch of the Cistercian order.[26] After long studies and meditations in the wilder-

---

23. Ibid., 1q43a5.
24. Ibid., 1q32a1.
25. So Hermann Stinglhammer, "*Trinität II: Mittelalter*," in TRE 34:103.
26. See for the following Bernard McGinn, *Visions of the End: Apocalyptic Traditions in the Middle Ages* (New York: Columbia University Press, 1979), 126–41, who calls Joachim "not only one of the most important apocalyptic authors of the Middle Ages, but one of the most significant theorists of history in the Western tradition" (126).

ness of the Calabrian mountains, he had some kind of revelation at a Pentecost celebration between 1190 and 1195 in which he discovered the meaning of the book of Revelation and the correspondence of the Old Testament with the New. In his *Exposition of the Apocalypse of John* he outlines the future stages of a providential development of history. He claims that each person of the Trinity is in a special way responsible for the advancement of history. Joachim writes: "The Father is a principle, the Son is a principle, the Holy Spirit is a principle—not three principles, but one principle. But because the faithful acknowledge that God is three Persons, he has willed to be three sorts of principles at three proper times of which the first belongs especially to the Father, the second to the Son, the third to the Holy Spirit."[27]

In analogy to the seven days of creation, Joachim sees the history of salvation as a sequence of seven ages, each lasting one millennium.[28] Using the forty-two generations (six ages times seven generations) leading up to Jesus (Matt 1:1–17), he divides the old covenant into seven parts: six ages each, with seven generations that precede Christ, and then Christ signifies the seventh epoch. In analogy to that, the new covenant is also divided into seven parts, there are six ages, each with seven generations. Each generation lasts thirty years, corresponding to Jesus's age at his death. These calculations show that the new covenant will last 1,260 years. After that comes the seventh epoch, which is the time of the Spirit. While the old covenant is the time of the Father, characterized by law and fear, the new covenant of the Son lasts until 1260 CE and is characterized by grace and faith. The third and final epoch was inaugurated already by Saint Benedict (ca. 480–ca. 515) and is characterized by love and the Spirit. These epochs, however, are not discreetly separated from one another but have their germinations in the prior epoch and are to some extent intertwined, since the persons of the Trinity are not separated either. Joachim writes:

> The first status of the world was begun from Adam, bore fruit from Abraham, and was consummated in Christ. The second was begun from Ozias, bore fruit from Zachary, the father of John the Baptist, and will have consummation in these times. The third had its beginning from Saint Benedict, began to bear fruit in the twenty-second generation from that saint, and will be consummated in the consummation of the world.[29]

---

27. Joachim of Fiore, *Exposition of the Apocalypse of John* f.34ra, in Bernard McGinn, *The Calabrian Abbot: Joachim of Fiore in the History of Western Thought* (New York: Macmillan, 1985), 179.
28. For the following see Medard Kehl, *Eschatologie* (Würzburg: Echter, 1986), 183–84.
29. Joachim of Fiore, *Concordie Novi ac Veteris Testamenti* 4.2.1, in McGinn, *Calabrian Abbot*, 187.

Joachim, who believed that he belonged to the second epoch, "did not draw any revolutionary conclusions from the implications of his historico-eschatological visions."[30] While he saw his own time as a century of radical decay, he projected a messianic leader to bring about spiritual renewal for the sake of the kingdom of Christ and to disclose to all people that which hitherto had been disguised in significant figures and in the sacraments. But his hope was not materialistic, antiecclesiastic, or anti-institutional, as with some of his successors. Even the thousand years of the new epoch he regarded to be only symbolic. Joachim opted more for a radical spiritualization of the world during the time of the Spirit than for an earthly renewal.

Later followers of Joachim were less patient than he had been and also more inclined to give his thoughts a material base. For instance, the Franciscan Spirituals in the thirteenth and fourteenth centuries attempted without compromise to achieve evangelical perfection in this third age.[31] It led them into open confrontation with the imperial messianism of Emperor Frederick II (1194–1250) and with the institutional Roman Catholic Church.

Joachim attacked Peter Lombard (1095/1100–1160), a scholastic theologian, bishop of Paris, and author of four books of Sentences, which became the standard textbook of theology and was still used by Martin Luther in his early years. Lombard had distinguished between the unity of God's essence and the Trinity of the three persons of the Godhead. Joachim made the accusation that Lombard did not teach "a Trinity but a quaternity of God, that is, three persons, and that common essence as a fourth."[32] The Fourth Lateran Council in 1215, however, refuted this accusation and in turn condemned Joachim's claim that the one essence or substance or nature of the Trinity is not a true and proper one but only a "collective" one. Since Joachim had handed over to the Holy See all his writings "to be approved or corrected," his monastery remained unharmed by this verdict.

But his idea of a total renewal and cleansing of this earth persisted.

---

30. So Karl Löwith, *Meaning in History* (Chicago: University of Chicago Press, 1949), 151, and Bernhard Töpfer, *Das kommende Reich des Friedens: Zur Entwicklung chiliastischer Zukunftshoffnungen im Hochmittelalter* (Berlin: Akademie-Verlag, 1964), 48–103, esp. 102–3, who shows that while Fiore's monastic idealism stayed within the boundaries of the church, it could be used as a revolutionary impetus to change the existing order of society.
31. For more extensive information see R. Kerstenberg-Gladstein, "The *Third Reich*: Fifteenth-Century Polemic against Joachism, and Its Background," in *Joachim of Fiore in Christian Thought: Essays on the Influence of the Calabrian Prophet*, ed. Delno C. West (New York: Burt Franklin, 1975), 2:559–609, esp. 562–64.
32. Fourth Lateran Council, chap. 2 (803), in Denzinger, *Compendium of Creeds*, 267.

Neo-Marxist philosopher Ernst Bloch (1885–1977) asserted that Joachim drew up "the most momentous social utopia of the Middle Ages," because it abolishes both church and state.[33] Its third age is an age of "universalized monastic and consumer communism, an 'age of free spirit.'"[34] Bloch sees the fundamental principle of Joachimism in the "unconcluded revelation."[35] He appreciates the active fight of Joachimism against the social principles of a Christianity that had associated itself with the class-conscious society since the time of Paul and consequently had to compromise its message. This third period of history, as prophesied by Joachim, seems to emerge in the Soviet Union and, quite naturally, find its archenemy in the clerical domination of the second period.[36] This clerical kingdom does not fully comprehend the third period, or if it does, it denounces it. These extrapolations show how much Bloch was interested in the anticlerical and political-revolutionary implications of Joachim's thought.[37] In Marxist fashion, Bloch also appreciates the "complete transfer of the kingdom of light *from the other world and the empty promises of the other world into history, even though into a final state of history.*"[38] According to Bloch, the relegation of our hopes to a better beyond must then cease. Moreover, the sectarian revolutionaries' attempt to date the projected kingdom of God made them employ their total energy, which for Bloch is a sign of the true sectarian. For centuries Joachim's writings were propagated, and pamphlets were written in his spirit and in his name.

Gotthold Ephraim Lessing (1729–81), for instance, one of the spiritual leaders of the Enlightenment in Germany, shows a familiarity with a tritheistic periodization of history and refers to the third age as an age of "a new eternal gospel."[39] It is of such farther-reaching consequence that even Friedrich Engels, coauthor of the *Communist Mani-*

---

33. Ernst Bloch, *The Principle of Hope*, trans. Neville Plaice, Stephen Plaice, and Paul Knight (Cambridge, MA: MIT Press, 1995), 2:509.
34. Ibid., 2:510.
35. Ibid., 2:514.
36. See ibid., 2:513.
37. Though Joachim's thought had an unmistakably revolutionary character (see Ernst Benz, *Evolution and Christian Hope: Man's Concept of the Future, from the Early Fathers to Teilhard de Chardin* [Garden City, NY: Doubleday, Anchor Books, 1966], 42), Gerhard Sauter rightly cautions us against Bloch's interpretation of Joachim. The anticlerical and political-revolutionary impulses of Joachim were less direct than Bloch assumes. See Sauter, *Zukunft und Verheissung: Das Problem der Zukunft in der gegenwärtigen theologischen und philosophischen Diskussion* (Stuttgart: Zwingli, 1965), 331.
38. Bloch, *Principle of Hope*, 2:510.
39. Gotthold Ephraim Lessing, *The Education of the Human Race*, trans. F. W. Robertson (London: Henry S. King, 1872), 70–71. Though not mentioning Joachim explicitly, he refers to some of the enthusiasts of the thirteenth and fourteenth centuries, who, according to Lessing, have perhaps caught a glimpse of this "new eternal gospel" and only erred in predicting its arrival as "so near to their own time."

festo, declared in 1842: "The self-confidence of humanity, the new Grail, around whose throne the nations jubilantly gather... this is our vocation: to become the Templers of this Grail, to gird our swords around our loins for its sake and cheerfully risk our lives in the last holy war, which will be followed by the millennium of freedom."[40] In the context of these secularized versions of millennialism, we must also mention the idea of the kingdom of God in America, a country that is not called the New World just because it was discovered relatively late. Even August Comte's idea of history as an ascent from the theological phase through the metaphysical up to the scientific phase is not unrelated to Joachim's notion of the three ages.[41]

Again, the Marxian dialectic of the three stages of primitive communism, class society, and the final communism as the realm of freedom, in which the state will have withered away, has its antecedents in Joachim's three ages. This is no less true of the phrase "the Third Reich" as a name for that "new order" that was to last a thousand years but fortunately only lasted from 1933-45. The messianic self-consciousness of Nazi ideology can be seen in the fact that Adolf Hitler was called *der Führer* ("leader") of this Reich ("empire" or "kingdom") and was greeted by millions with "*Heil!*" ("salvation").[42] As British historian Norman Cohn (1915-2007) perceptively writes:

> Communists no less than Nazis have been obsessed by the vision of a prodigious "final, decisive struggle" in which a "chosen people" will destroy a world tyranny and thereby inaugurate a new epoch in world history. As in the Nazi apocalypse the "Arian race" was to purify the earth by annihilating the "Jewish race," so in the Communist apocalypse the "bourgeoisie" is to be exterminated by the "proletariat." And here, too, we are faced with the secularized version of a phantasy that is many centuries old.[43]

While Joachim was still looking for a leader, both the communists and the Nazis thought well enough of themselves to provide this leader-

---

40. Friedrich Engels, *Schelling und die Offenbarung* (Leipzig: Robert Binder, 1842), in Karl Marx and Friedrich Engels, *Historisch-kritische Gesamtausgabe* (Frankfurt am Main: Marx-Engels-Archiv, 1927), 1/2:225-26; quoted in Eng. trans. in Bloch, *Principle of Hope*, 2:515.
41. So Norman Cohn, *The Pursuit of the Millennium: Revolutionary Messianism in Medieval and Reformation Europe and Its Bearing on Modern Totalitarian Movements*, 2nd ed. (New York: Harper Torchbooks, 1961), 101.
42. See Löwith, *Meaning in History*, 159. It seems strange that, in describing Joachim and his idea of the Third Reich, Bloch passes over Hitler and his utopian dreams with silence. Should this indicate that Hitler's program cannot be integrated into a "principle of hope"?
43. Cohn, *Pursuit of the Millennium*, 311.

ship. But as soon as finite humanity with its own finite spirit wants to inaugurate the conditions promised by the divine Spirit, of eternal peace and equality, only failure and terror can result. Having traced the impact of Joachim's Trinitarian speculations into modernity, let us now return to the late Middle Ages.

Honoring Tradition and the Bible

Through the liberation from ecclesial authority, the Reformation period made room for any kind of Trinitarian reflection, from the conservative affirmation of the tradition, as with Martin Luther (1483-1546) and John Calvin (1509-1564), to those who rejected the true Godhead of Christ and of the Holy Spirit, such as Spanish physician Michel Servetus (1511-53) and Italian theologian Fausto Sozzini (1539-1604), who spent most of his life in Poland and who had considerable influence on the anti-Trinitarians in Transylvania (present-day Romania). But for the Reformers the doctrine of the Trinity remained uncontested unless they thought they had to stand up against those who challenged its validity. Nevertheless, they had their own distinctive accents.

Martin Luther

During his time as monk Martin Luther (1483-1546) followed the scholastic distinctions of the doctrine of the Trinity.[44] As we notice in the Augsburg Confession of 1530, which was approved by Luther, he followed tradition:

> In the first place, it is with one accord taught and held, following the decree of the Council of Nicea that there is one divine essence which is named God and truly is God. But there are three persons in the same one essence, equally powerful, equally eternal: God the Father, God the Son, and God the Holy Spirit. All three are one divine essence, eternal, undivided, unending, of immeasurable power, wisdom, and goodness, the creator and preserver of all visible and invisible things.[45]

For Luther there was never any doubt that "Father, Son, and Holy Spirit are three different persons but one rightful and unified natural true

---

44. See Martin Luther, sermon of Dec. 24, 1514 (WA 1:20-24).
45. The Augsburg Confession, article 1, in *The Book of Concord*, ed. Robert Kolb and Timothy Wengert (Minneapolis: Fortress Press, 2000), 36.

THE TRINITY

God, creator of heaven and earth."[46] This he defended against all the usual deviations, such as the Arians and the Sabellians. And he continues: "These are three persons and one God who has given to us totally with everything that he is and has."[47] According to Luther, the Trinity is attested in Scripture, both in the Old and the New Testament: "It is most clearly testified that there are three persons and one God. Not only will I believe it because Augustine and the Fathers wrote it if not the Old and the New Testament would have most clearly shown us this article of the Trinity."[48] Unity and trinity are equally emphasized, since God is one and a threesome. But Luther does not like the term *threefoldness* (*Dreifaltigkeit*). He writes: "Threefoldness is really bad German. In the Godhead there is highest unity. Some call it threesome. But this sounds too facetious. Augustine also commiserates that he has no convenient word. . . . He calls it a third. I cannot give it a name." *Dreifaltigkeit*, a German term used for naming many Roman Catholic churches, or the Trinity, in general seems to have been shied away from by Lutherans because of Martin Luther's verdict. Luther did not know yet the term *triunity* (*Dreieinigkeit*) or *triune* (*dreieinig*), since it did not even exist in Latin. Only Johann Conrad Dannhauer (1603–1666), the teacher of famous representative of German pietism Philip Spener, used the Latin term *triunus* ("triune").[49]

There is one God in three persons, and each person is the whole Godhead, and nevertheless no person is for himself the Godhead without the other two. Luther finds this based on Scripture, and therefore he claims: "Here faith is necessary and not much astute speculation."[50] "Though natural reason does not grasp it, this is correct, faith alone shall grasp it, natural reason makes heresy and error, faith teaches and maintains the truth, because it stays by Scripture which does not betray nor deny."[51] Since reason is insufficient to understand this mystery and Scripture reveals it, faith is needed to grasp it. Yet it is not simple fideism according to the motto "don't think, just believe." Luther is cognizant of the scholastic discussions about the Trinity as he writes: "We should treat it most clearly and not like the school teach-

---

46. Martin Luther, *Vom Abendmahl Christi: Bekenntnis* (WA 26:500.27-29).
47. Ibid. (WA 26:505.38-39).
48. Martin Luther, *Promotionsdisputation Georg Major und Johannes Faber* (WA 39/2:305.9-12).
49. Johann Conrad Dannhauer, *Hodosophia Christiana seu theologia positive*, 4th ed. (Leipzig: Friedrich Groschuff, 1713 [1649]), 138, where he writes: "Ergo Deus triunus est verus Deus, ac reciproce verus Deus est triunus Deus" with reference to the God of Abraham, the God of Isaac, and the God of Jacob.
50. Martin Luther, *Kirchenpostille* (1522) (WA 10 I/1:157.15-16).
51. WA 10 I/1:191.13-16.

ers who have treated it with their invented subtlety which has hidden it from the common people and deterred them."[52]

Luther knows that

> the term *trinitas* is not expressed in Holy Scripture. But I must talk in this way that the weak understand it. And the truth of our faith requires that one talks this way: "hypostasis" means the person of the Father, of the Son, and the Holy Spirit; if you want to use a different term do it, but only preserve and express the proper item. "*Trinitas*" is a rather strange thought, but one must talk in this way because of the weak and of teaching.... The item we must maintain, we may talk in terms as we like it.[53]

For him the conviction "Scripture alone" is better than all human deliberations. This does not mean that he rejects tradition completely, as we notice with his reference to hypostasis. He can also say in conjunction with tradition that "Christ is unceasingly and eternally born from the Father" and that the external works of the Trinity cannot be divided and attributed to either Father, Son, or Holy Spirit alone.[54] As a good Augustinian, he affirms that the persons of the Trinity are distinguished from one another by nothing other than their mutual relations as Father, Son, and Holy Spirit. The terms are relatively unimportant for Luther, since there was not one term that was totally adequate. But the substance was what mattered to him, one in three and three in one.

While the external works of the Trinity are one, Luther can speak of the Holy Spirit as a gift that our faith receives, but then he corrects himself, saying, "he is not a gift but a vivifying God."[55] The Spirit illumines our hearts so that we become healthy and joyful to fulfill God's will. Though the Holy Spirit goes forth from the Father and is sent by the Son, the Spirit is "one God in both" but also a distinct person.[56] While the persons of the Trinity have their own peculiarity by their mutual relations, they act in a unified way. In a sermon of 1541 he explains this very nicely:

> This one Lord, king, and creator has portrayed and made himself known in such a way through his Son that in the Godhead it is thusly: the Word is spoken by the Father, the Holy Spirit (as one says) agrees; that there is a

---

52. WA 10 I/1:181.11-13.
53. Martin Luther, *Promotionsdisputation Georg Major und Johannes Faber* (WA 39/2:305, 15–23).
54. Luther, *Kirchenpostille* (1522) (WA 10 I/1:154.1).
55. Martin Luther, sermon of March 18, 1525 (WA 17/1:125.7).
56. Martin Luther, *Die drei Symbola oder Bekenntnis des Glaubens Christi* (1538) (WA 50:274.15).

third and nevertheless is in himself one, and if it is one, it is called creator of the world.

Augustine and other teachers of old have said: Opera *Trinitatis ab extra sunt indidivisa*. This means, the works of the Holy Trinity are externally undivided. Father, Son, and Holy Spirit are one unified creator, not three over against the created. This is how far the Turks, and Jews, and pagans get. But we should not perceive God only from the outside in his works but God also wants that we perceive him from inside. But how is he internally. Internally he is one being and three persons, Father, Son, and Holy Spirit, not three gods. We pray therefore only to one God. How is this? It is inexplicable. The angels cannot marvel enough out of joy. But us it is contained in word and preached.[57]

God as the Creator, Sustainer, and Redeemer is one God who can also be perceived by reason, as Luther often asserts. But this God is in himself three persons who show themselves to us as Father, Son, and Holy Spirit. Yet without Scripture and revelation contained in Scripture, we would not know that Jesus of Nazareth, the Son, and the enigmatic spirit, the Holy Spirit, are representing and indeed are the one Godhead. The economic Trinity of the salvific economic process is the expression of the immanent Trinity. The Trinitarian faith is therefore based on the experience of salvation through Christ.

John Calvin

When we come to John Calvin (1509-64), we notice at once that he too affirms the salvific aspect of the Trinity when he writes with reference to John 1:1 ("In the beginning was the Word"): with "these words, therefore, the Evangelist assures us that we do not withdraw from the only and eternal God, when we believe in Christ, and likewise that life is now restored to the dead through the kindness of him who was the source and cause of life, when the nature of man was still uncorrupted." Then Calvin continues to say that the eternal procession of the Son has been hidden for a long time and was only hazily hinted at to the Fathers under the law until it was shown us completely in the incarnation of Christ. Moreover, in their disputes with the heretics, the church fathers were forced to think of words that say nothing other than that which was handed on in Scripture: "They said that there are three Hypostases, or Subsistences, or Persons, in the one and simple essence of God."[58]

---

57. Martin Luther, sermon of Dec. 25, 1541 (WA 49:238.35-239.31).

Similar to Luther, for Calvin Scripture is the starting point for perception of the Trinity, while tradition informs him of the vocabulary to be used. Calvin devotes chapter 13 of the first book of his *Institutes* to the Trinity: since Scripture tells us of the immensity and the spirituality of God's essence, philosophy does not suffice to fathom God's essence. But there is a "special mark by which he designates himself, for the purpose of giving a more intimate knowledge of his nature. While he proclaims his unity, he distinctly sets it before us as existing in three persons." We must hold on to these three persons. Otherwise the name of the Deity becomes empty, unrelated to the true God. Then he explains that the word *person* means a kind of being (subsistence) by which one differs from the other, while the basic being (substance) is one and the same. The Western church used the term *person*, while the Eastern church, to show its unity with the West, taught that there are three *prosopa* ("aspects") in God. "All these, however, whether Greeks or Latins, though differing as to the word, are perfectly agreed in substance."[59] The church by strongest necessity was impelled to use the words person and Trinity to make plain and transparent the truth of Scripture. We encounter here almost the same kind of argument that Luther used. He did not feel comfortable with the traditional terminology but for the sake of Scripture he felt that he must use it.

In a second part of this chapter of the *Institutes* Calvin sets out "to prove" the Godhead of the Son and of the Holy Spirit, including the Godhead of Christ in the Old Testament. Once the Godhead of the three persons in the Trinity is "proven," Calvin affirms the unity and threeness of the Trinity (sections 16 and 17). With Paul he asserts that there is one faith, one Baptism, and one God (Eph 4:5), and on the other hand he acknowledges that "there is some distinction between the Father and the Word, the Word and the Spirit; but the magnitude of the mystery reminds us of the great reverence and soberness which ought to be employed in discussing it."[60] Not in God but between Father, Son, and Holy Spirit there is a real distinction but not a division. He does not think it is helpful to use analogies in human affairs in a metaphoric way to elucidate these distinctions, but he thinks that the distinctions mentioned in the Bible are at least worth noting. Examples of this include the Father as the beginning of all activity and therefore the wellspring

---

58. John Calvin, *Commentary of the Gospel according to John*, trans. William Pringle, vol. 1 (Grand Rapids: Christian Classics Ethereal Library), in his exegesis of John 1:1.
59. John Calvin, *Institutes of the Christian Religion*, ed. John T. McNeill, trans. Ford Lewis Battles (Louisville, KY: Westminster John Knox, 2006), 1.13.2 (pp. 110–11).
60. Ibid., 1.13.17 (p. 125).

and fountain; the Son as wisdom, council, and arrangement in action; and the Spirit as energy and efficacy of action. Nevertheless, each individual person is a hypostasis of the whole divine nature.

Then Calvin refutes all the wrong teachings concerning the Trinity and finally concludes:

> Whosoever will compare the writings of the ancient fathers with each other, will not find anything in Irenaeus different from what is taught by those who come after him. Justin is one of the most ancient, and he agrees with us out and out.... Moreover, the consent of the ancient fathers clearly appears from this, that in the Council of Nice, no attempt was made by Arius to cloak his heresy by the authority of any approved author; and no Greek or Latin writer apologises as dissenting from his predecessors.[61]

In sum: All the ancient authorities affirm the doctrine of the Trinity. Calvin did not answer the question as to the mystery of the Trinity, but he could answer the question of what God is: God is triune, one and three in one being. Just like Luther, Calvin was no innovator but affirmed the Trinity in line with the ancient tradition and that it is firmly founded on the biblical witness.

There were others who, similar to Calvin and Luther, were influenced by the Renaissance spirit and the new availability of the biblical sources in their original languages. Unlike the Reformers, though, they thought they could dispense with tradition altogether and stay with Scripture alone. Yet this kind of autonomous thinking was highly suspect to the Reformers, who abided by the christological and Trinitarian decisions of the church. These views were declared heretical by the Reformers and by the church at large, and those who supported them often had a violent and premature death.

An Ambiguous Return to Scripture

Scripture alone was the catchword of mainline reformation. But this did not imply a disdain for tradition as long as it was seen in congruence with Scripture. This, however, was different for others who also claimed Scripture on their side.

Michael Servetus

Michael Servetus (1509/11–1553), whom Calvin mentioned quite often

---

61. Ibid., 1.13.29 (p. 138).

in his *Institutes* (see 1.13.22, where he rejects the objections of Servetus to the Trinity), was a Spanish Renaissance polymath versed in many sciences and also in theology. He studied the Bible in its original languages and, outraged by the pomp and luxury displayed by the pope and his retinue, decided to follow the path of the Reformation. In October 1530 he visited Johannes Oecolampadius in Basel, and in May 1531 he met Martin Bucer and Wolfgang Fabricius Capito in Strasbourg. Two months later, in July 1531, Servetus published *De Trinitatis Erroribus* (*On the Errors of the Trinity*). The next year he published *Dialogorum de Trinitate* (*Dialogues on the Trinity*) and the supplementary work *De Iustitia Regni Christi* (*On the Justice of Christ's Reign*). Because of his nonorthodox views he was persecuted by the Inquisition. Servetus then studied medicine and became quite famous in his new profession. Through a friend who was also an acquaintance of John Calvin, Servetus and Calvin began to correspond. In 1553 Servetus published yet another work with further anti-Trinitarian views, titled *Christianismi Restitutio* (*The Restoration of Christianity*). There he sharply rejected the idea of predestination as the idea that God condemned souls to hell regardless of worth or merit. God, insisted Servetus, condemns no one who does not condemn himself through thought, word, or deed.

For Calvin, who had by then written his *Institutes*, Servetus's latest book was an attack on his personally held Christian belief that he put forth as an "established Christian doctrine." Calvin sent a copy of the *Institutes* as his reply. Servetus promptly returned it, thoroughly annotated with critical remarks. Calvin composed an extensive refutation of Servetus's position, at the conclusion writing to Servetus: "I neither hate you nor despise you; nor do I wish to persecute you; but I would be as hard as iron when I see you insulting sound doctrine with so great audacity."[62] In time their correspondence grew more heated, until Calvin ended it. Servetus sent Calvin several more letters, to which Calvin took offense. Calvin revealed the intentions of his offended pride when writing to his friend William Farel (1489–1565) on February 13, 1546: "Servetus has just sent me a long volume of his ravings. If I consent he will come here, but I will not give my word, for if he comes here, if my authority is worth anything, I will never permit him to depart alive."[63]

On April 4, 1553, Servetus was arrested by Roman Catholic authorities and imprisoned in Vienne, France. Servetus escaped from prison

---

62. John Calvin, *Fidelis Expositio Errorum Michaelis Serveti* (CO 8:495).
63. John Calvin, *Letter* 767 (CO 12:283).

three days later. He was then convicted of heresy and sentenced to be burned with his books. An effigy and his books were burned in his absence. Meaning to flee to Italy, Servetus stopped in Geneva, where Calvin and his followers had denounced him. On August 13 he attended a sermon by Calvin at Geneva. He was arrested after the service and imprisoned, and his property was confiscated. French Inquisitors asked Servetus to be extradited to them for execution. But Calvin wanted to show himself as a firm defender of Christian orthodoxy and wanted the trial to be held in Geneva. At the trial, Servetus was condemned on two counts, for spreading and preaching non-Trinitarianism, specifically, modalistic Monarchianism or Sabellianism, and anti-paedobaptism (anti-infant baptism). Calvin believed Servetus deserved death on account of what Calvin termed his "execrable blasphemies." Calvin expressed these sentiments in a letter to Farel, written about a week after Servetus's arrest, in which he also mentions an exchange with Servetus. Calvin writes: "I hope that sentence of death will at least be passed on him; but I desired that the severity of the punishment be mitigated."[64] The city council condemned Servetus to death for his denial of the Trinity and infant baptism. On October 27, 1553, Servetus was burned alive—atop a pyre of his own books.

But what did Servetus actually teach? In his first two books (*On the Errors of the Trinity*, and *Dialogues on the Trinity* plus the supplementary *On the Righteousness of Christ's Kingdom*) Servetus rejected the classical doctrine of the Trinity, claiming that it was not based on Scripture. He argued that it "was brought upon us by the Greeks, for they above all other men are most given to philosophy." The Trinity or three persons in the divine Being are "the new gods which have recently come, which our fathers did not worship." Servetus in turn advocated a return to the simple teachings of Paul and of the early church fathers "that Jesus Christ is the Son of God."[65] He is equal to God in power but not in nature or essence. We notice here an Arian tendency in order to preserve a strict monotheism. The same problem arises with the Holy Spirit. Servetus claims: "The philosophers have invented besides a third separate being, truly and really distinct from the other two, which they call the third Person, or the Holy Spirit; and thus they have contrived an imaginary Trinity, three beings in one Nature. But in reality three beings, three Gods, or one threefold God, are foisted upon us under the

---

64. John Calvin, *Letter* 1772 (CO 14:590).
65. Michael Servetus, *On the Errors of the Trinity* 1.60, in *The Two Treatises of Servetus on the Trinity*, trans. Earl Morse Wilbur (New York: Kraus Reprint, 1969 [1932]), 67.

pretense and with the names of a unity."⁶⁶ Servetus hoped that the dismissal of the Trinitarian dogma would make Christianity more appealing to Jews and Muslims, who had preserved the unity of God in their teachings. According to Servetus, Trinitarians had turned Christianity into a form of "tritheism," a belief in three gods. For him it was a Christian variation of the polytheism of antiquity.

Instead Servetus claimed that the Old Testament and the apostles teach a modalistic concept of God the Father. The Old Testament contains no prophecy of the coming of Christ but a sequence of a progressive manifestation of the same God. This same God then appears in the New Testament as Son and Spirit to reveal spiritual truth to humans and to effect the deification of humanity. Servetus affirmed that the divine Logos, the manifestation of God and not a separate divine person, was incarnated in a human being, Jesus, when God's spirit came into the womb of the Virgin Mary. Only from the moment of conception was the Son actually generated. Therefore, although the Logos from which he was formed was eternal, the Son himself was not eternal. According to Servetus, this would have led to two gods. But "to us, as to Paul, one God is enough, who is the Father, and one Lord Jesus Christ, who is the Son."[67] Even the incarnation is treated by Servetus in such a way that God really does not become human. He writes: "Again, John did not say, The Word became flesh, as they take it; but, The Word was flesh, the Word existed as flesh; and this is the most proper meaning of *ho logos sarx egeneto* [the word became flesh]."[68] In his *Treatise Concerning the Divine Trinity* Servetus teaches that the Logos was the reflection of Christ, and "that reflection of Christ was 'the Word with God'" that consisted of God himself, shining brightly in heaven, "and it was God Himself," and that "the Word was the very essence of God or the manifestation of God's essence, and there was in God no other substance or hypostasis than His Word, in a bright cloud where God then seemed to subsist. And in that very spot the face and personality of Christ shone bright."[69]

Servetus states his view clearly in the preamble to *The Restoration of Christianity* (1553): "There is nothing greater, reader, than to recognize that God has been manifested as substance, and that His divine nature has been truly communicated to mankind. It is in Christ alone that we

---

66. Ibid., 1.30, in *Two Treatises of Servetus on the Trinity*, 33–34.
67. Ibid., 1.21, in *Two Treatises of Servetus on the Trinity*, 26.
68. Ibid., 7.5, in *Two Treatises of Servetus on the Trinity*, 174.
69. Michael Servetus, *The Restoration of Christianity—An English Translation of Christianismi restitutio, 1553*, trans. Christopher A. Hoffman and Marian Hillar (Lewiston, NY: Mellen, 2007), 75.

shall fully apprehend the manifestation of God Himself through the Word and His communication to mankind through the spirit."[70] Yet in this book he also advocates a dualistic worldview, culminating in the appearance of the millennial age commencing in 1585, when God will overcome Satan and the kingdom of the saints will arrive. Even gnostic ideas come to the fore in the views of Servetus. His theology, though original in some respects, has often been compared to adoptionism, Arianism, and Sabellianism. Nevertheless, Servetus rejected these ideas: adoptionism, because it denied the divinity of Jesus; Arianism, because it multiplied the hypostases and established a rank; and Sabellianism, because it seemingly confused the Father with the Son.

But Servetus also rejected the Trinitarian understanding of one God in three persons. For him the incomprehensible God is known through Christ, by faith, rather than by philosophical speculations. Christ manifests God to us, being the expression of his very being, and through him alone, God can be known. The Scriptures reveal him to those who have faith; and thus we come to know the Holy Spirit as the divine impulse within us. Under severe pressure from Catholics and Protestants alike, Servetus clarified this explanation in his second book, *Dialogues*, to show that the Logos was coterminous with Christ. He asserts that "this body [i.e., Christ] now has the same Substance that the Word once had. But Christ was there typified and prefigured."[71] He was nevertheless accused of heresy because of his insistence on denying the dogma of the Trinity and the distinctions between the three divine persons in one God. The one God stays in heaven, whence his Word and his Spirit are/were sent. While almost every aspect of his teachings has been severely criticized, he "is one of the most original thinkers of the 16th century."[72]

Unitarian theologian Earl Morse Wilbur (1866–1956), who translated *The Two Treatises of Servetus on the Trinity*, states concerning Servetus: "Whatever the Bible may say he accepts as authority not to be questioned. In his interpretation of it he is the biblical literalist." Yet the doctrine of the Trinity, "which had once been esteemed the very heart of Christian faith, upon the acceptance of which one's eternal salvation depended, had degenerated, Servetus felt, into something wholly artificial, abstract, speculative, sterile, and fatal to the vital piety."[73] Wilbur

---

70. Ibid., 1.
71. Michael Servetus, *Dialogues on the Trinity* 1.2, in *Two Treatises of Servetus on the Trinity*, 190.
72. So rightly Jerome Friedman, "Servet, Michael (1509/1511-1553)," in *TRE* 31:173.
73. Earl Morse Wilbur, introduction to *Two Treatises of Servetus on the Trinity*, x, xi.

concludes that Servetus did not reject the Trinity altogether but its unbiblical interpretation. He also thinks that the Reformers initially gave not much attention to the terms in which that doctrine was traditionally stated, but then on account of the attack of Servetus treated the doctrine of the Trinity much more extensively. He may very well be correct in this assessment.

Fausto Sozzini

One person who protested against the execution of Servetus and who publicly confessed his agreement with him was Italian theologian and humanist Lelio Sozzini (1525–62).[74] Through his extensive travels in Europe, he had contact with many reform-minded groups, Calvinists, Lutherans, Anabaptists, and free thinkers, and even exerted influence on Polish anti-Trinitarians. His nephew Fausto Paolo Sozzini (1539–1604) underwent no regular schooling but was self-taught and traveled extensively and thereby acquired a good general knowledge in the humanities. As was quite common among Italian intellectuals, he was convinced that religion must correspond to reason and thus be explainable by reason. In 1578 he was invited by the anti-Trinitarians in Transylvania (present-day Romania) to help them in their controversies with a radical member of the group. He had lived in Poland since 1579 and became the authority and leader of the anti-Trinitarian movement there, which called itself Sozzinianism after its spiritual mentor.

Sozzini's anti-Trinitarianism is founded on a literal interpretation of Scripture and on reason. He rejected the Godhead of Christ and of the Holy Spirit. Christ was basically a human being who surpassed other humans by his supernatural conception, his perfect holiness, and his role as a mediator between us and God. Though one should not pray to him as to God, he can be venerated. Sozzini collapsed the Trinity into a unitarian view of God. Since reason ruled supreme, he was tolerant of other views, which distinguished him from virtually all representatives of orthodox Christianity.

The movement in Poland was initially characterized by free thinking, ranging with regard to the Trinity from tritheism, advocating three Gods; to ditheism, advancing two Gods; and unitarianism, having just one Supreme Being. The so-called Rakau Catechism was started by Fausto Sozzini but finally completed and published in Polish by oth-

---

74. For the following see Waclaw Urban, "Sozzini/Sozinianer," in *TRE* 31:598–604.

ers in 1605 after his death.[75] This catechism claims to derive its theological positions from Scripture only but is also open to reasonable investigation. It is anti-speculative and Bible centered. It opens with the trustworthiness, sufficiency, and clarity of Scripture before it deals with the doctrine of God. Jesus is seen as a human being who was conceived by the Holy Spirit and born by the Virgin Mary, but not pre-existent. Though he is the Son of God the Father, "everything which is divine in Christ, is a gift of his Father." He is not of divine nature, but "the man Jesus Christ is a mediator between God and humans."[76] Then human free will is advanced, and original sin is rejected as non-biblical. Scripture does not show that after the fall humans no longer have a free will. Water Baptism is an "external ceremony," and infant Baptism is not commanded by Scripture.[77] But those who perform this erroneous ceremony may do it. Naturally, this catechism was immediately rejected by the Anglican, Lutheran, and Reformed churches, and by decision of the English Parliament was committed to the flames in 1614. Yet the Sozzinian movement spread to other countries, such as Germany, Ukraine, and Slovakia. When the Polish Brethren, as they called themselves in Poland, were exiled in the mid-seventeenth century, many of them settled in Transylvania, where in Cluj, Romania, there is still today a Unitarian theological faculty, albeit in conjunction with the Reformed church.

Thomas Müntzer

While the so-called left wing of the Reformation, the Spiritualists, Anabaptists, and Enthusiasts, had little interest in Trinitarian reflections and often were negligently or openly anti-Trinitarian, one person deserves special mention, Thomas Müntzer (ca. 1490–1525). Similar to Luther, he was born in the foothills of the Harz Mountains in the small town of Stolberg to a middle-class family. He studied at the universities of Leipzig and Frankfurt/Oder, was consecrated to be a priest, and moved in 1517 to Wittenberg to deepen his theological studies. He supplied at several charges but never stayed long in one and finally received in April 1523 a pastorate in Allstedt, a small agricultural town in electoral Saxony. He married a former nun and reformed the service

---

75. Martin Schmeisser, ed., *Sozinianische Bekenntnisschriften—Der Rakóẃer Katechismus des Valentin Schmalz (1608) und der sogenannte Soner-Katechismus* (Berlin: Akademie-Verlag, 2012). It contains the German translation of 1608 by Valentin Schmalz (107–212).
76. Ibid., 126–27.
77. Ibid., 173.

according to his own ideas. He also warned the people in Stolberg to flee the pleasures of this world to prepare for the coming judgment.

Martin Luther became more critical of Müntzer and his increasingly radical thoughts.[78] In two publications, *Protest or Offering* and *On Contrived Faith*, Müntzer laid down his ideas. His relations with electoral Saxony too were severely disrupted when he arranged that Allstedt not pay its dues to a nunnery and even plundered and burned down a chapel. As the situation escalated, Müntzer moved to the free imperial city of Mühlhausen. There too he caused problems and was exiled. Soon he played a leading role in the peasants' insurrection in Thuringia, announcing in a sermon to the peasants on May 15, 1525, that God would intervene in their favor in this last battle to purify the world. Yet the army of the princes won on that day a decisive victory in which thousands of peasants were killed. He claimed that this happened because the peasants did not seek God's honor and his kingdom but their own advantage, which always leads to destruction. Müntzer was put to death on May 27, 1525, at Frankenhausen.

As an apocalyptic utopian and the "new Daniel," Müntzer wanted to rigorously enforce God's will in this eschatological end time and refers to Joachim of Fiore.[79] In a letter attached to his discourse *On Contrived Faith* (1524), he mentions that his enemies call Joachim's teaching "with great mockery" the "Eternal Gospel." Müntzer holds Joachim in high esteem, though he claims that he does not derive his revolutionary ideas from Joachim, "but rather from the living speech of God."[80] Martin Luther and his followers, however, rejected categorically any utopian ideas in the Augsburg Confession of 1530, where they state: "Rejected are some Jewish teachings, which have also appeared in the present, that before the resurrection of the dead saints and righteous people alone will possess a secular kingdom and will annihilate all the ungodly."[81] Yet these dreams of a Third Reich, the age of the Spirit implying a tritheistic progression instead of a triune advancement of world history, coupled with apocalyptic scenarios of the end of the

---

78. See Erich Gritsch, *Reformer without a Church: Thomas Muentzer 1488[?]-1525* (Philadelphia: Fortress, 1967); and Michael J. Baylor, trans. and ed., *Revelation and Revolution: The Basic Writings of Thomas Müntzer* (Bethlehem, PA: Lehigh University Press, 1993).
79. See the extensive biography by Walter Elliger, *Thomas Müntzer: Leben und Werk*, 3rd ed. (Göttingen: Vandenhoeck & Ruprecht, 1976), 444–45.
80. As reprinted in Baylor, *Revelation and Revolution*, 84. See also Bloch, *Principle of Hope*, 2:512. When Müntzer mentions here that he has read Joachim's *Commentary on Jeremiah*, this is based on a misunderstanding. The *Commentary on Jeremiah* was a pseudo-Joachimite document, printed in Venice in 1516 (see Baylor, *Revelation and Revolution*, 213n20). This shows us what popularity Joachim enjoyed in the sixteenth century.
81. Augsburg Confession XVII, in *Book of Concord*, 50.

world, have resurfaced even in our own time in the twenty-first century. Humans seem to long for a spiritual guide who will lead them to a golden age.

6

Post-Reformation Developments

Following the intra-Lutheran controversies that resulted in the Formula of Concord and the Book of Concord in 1580, a period of confessional orthodoxy and scholastic Lutheranism flourished. The same move can also be traced in the Reformed tradition and even in the Roman Catholic Church. In Lutheranism a singular emphasis on pure teaching and proper formulations replaced the fuller Lutheran emphasis on the gospel's power and purpose for the whole person as a justified sinner in this world. And yet, a thoroughly biblical and soundly confessional theology was never totally exclusive of a deeply felt personal spirituality. Martin Luther's own piety exhibited an interplay of objective doctrines with existential application.

Affirmation of the Trinitarian Faith (Orthodoxy and Enlightenment)

While for the representatives of the Reformation theology was an existential matter, even at its extremes, orthodoxy picked up the insights of the Reformers and wedded them with the concerns of the scholastics. Their premise was that the Christian faith, which orthodoxy steadfastly affirmed, must be intelligible. To this effect voluminous tomes expounding the Christian truth were composed.

Johann Gerhard

One example of this approach is seen with Johann Gerhard (1582–1637), one of the most prominent exponents of Lutheran orthodoxy and who, beginning in 1616, became a professor at Jena. He published his *Loci Theologici* in nine volumes (1610–22). Having treated Holy Scripture (chap. 1) and the nature and attributes of God (chap. 2), he arrives in chapter 3 at "The Most Holy Mystery of the Trinity." In thesis 1 he asserts that "it is necessary to know and believe the mystery of the Trinity for all who want to be saved."[1] Not only those who deny the Trinity are excluded from salvation but also those who are ignorant of it. Yet he comforts his readers by saying that equal knowledge of the Trinity is not required of everyone. According to Gerhard, the mystery of the Trinity can be confirmed from both the New Testament and the Old Testament.[2] Similar to Thomas Aquinas he says that "the mystery of the Trinity cannot and ought not be proved a priori by natural reason."[3] But then Gerhard turns the argument around and says that natural reason cannot disprove the mystery of the Trinity either. The reason for this is that things that are believed cannot be judged by things that are within the sphere of understanding. Moreover, human reason is corrupt and cannot clearly perceive things that are matters of faith.

In the next chapter Gerhard deals with Trinitarian terminology and states in his first thesis that in explicating the mystery of the Trinity one may use terms that are not used in Scripture.[4] Having gone through the various terms such as *ousia*, *essentia*, *persona*, *substantia*, and *trinity*, including their etymology, he sums up: "But God is not called three in respect to his essence, which is one, not with respect to his essential peculiarities, which are simply the same as the essence itself, not in respect to genus and species, since in God there is neither genus nor species, but with respect to his three basic ways of being which are the uncreated in the Father, the created in the Son, the coming forth in the Holy Spirit."[5] He also mentions there with reference to Martin Chemnitz (1522–86), another prominent representative of Lutheran orthodoxy, that the Latin *trinitas* ("Trinity") is in

---

1. Johann Gerhard, *Loci Theologici* (Berlin: Gustav Schlawitz, 1863), 1:371.
2. Ibid., 1:377.
3. Ibid., 1:377–78.
4. Ibid., 1:386.
5. Ibid., 1:398.

German called *Dreifaltigkeit*, which is actually "threefoldness," (*triplicitas*); *Dreieinigkeit* ("triunity") is more appropriate.

The next brief chapter is devoted to the general arguments from Scripture concerning the Trinity. The argument from the New Testament is continued in the next chapter, starting with Jesus's baptism as a manifestation of the Trinity. As Gerhard reminds us: "The pious of old said: '*If you do not believe in the Trinity, follow John to the Jordan and you will see.*'"[6] The argument is carried into the next chapter, with Matt. 28:19, "the institution of our baptism," as the second scriptural witness to the Trinity. As Robert D. Preus (1924–95) states in his lucid exposition of Lutheran orthodoxy: "The Lutheran teachers remark that only God has the authority to institute such a rite. For such a rite is a means of salvation, and salvation is the work of God alone. The mention of all Three Persons indicates that all Three are the author of the sacraments and that all Three are divine."[7] The third witness to the Trinity is adduced from John 14:16. The paraclete suffices to affirm the personhood of the Holy Spirit. Finally, the so-called *Comma Johanneum* (1 John 5:7–8), is, as mentioned earlier, a later insertion into the text and is briefly mentioned as a New Testament testimony to the Trinity. After giving these four main attestations to the Trinity in the New Testament, Gerhard moves to the Old Testament.

The first attestation of the Trinity given is deduced from creation. Though we read that only the one God is the Creator, the Hebrew term *'elōhîm* is plural, indicating not just the essential unity but also the plurality of the persons.[8] The second argument comes from the liberation from Egypt. The angel who led the Israelites through the desert is identified with Christ, an argument that Gerhard gleans from such church fathers as Justin Martyr and Eusebius of Caesarea. Since in Isaiah 63:7–11 the Holy Spirit is also mentioned next to the angel, Gerhard claims it is evident that there are three distinct persons involved in the liberation from Egypt. Three persons are in the divine essence, as we can gather from this passage. The third main argument is then derived from the promise of the Messiah in passages from Moses, the Psalms, and the Prophets. In this regard Gerhard cites Genesis 1:15 as well as Psalm 110:1; Isaiah 9:5–6; and many other passages. As a fourth main argument, Gerhard briefly cites the Aaronic or priestly blessing

---

6. Ibid., 1:406.
7. Robert D. Preus, *The Theology of Post-Reformation Lutheranism*, vol. 2, *God and His Creation* (St. Louis: Concordia, 1972), 129.
8. See Gerhard, *Loci Theologici*, 1:418.

in Numbers 6:24–26. The unity of the divine essence as well as the three persons of the Trinity are indicated here. In conclusion, Gerhard divides the biblical references according to the plurality or the trinity of the persons, using both direct or indirect references. Throughout his deliberations he devotes ample space to the Sozzinians, refuting their Arian leanings and also their assertion of the inferiority of the Son. According to Gerhard, they rejected any argument for the Trinity from the Old Testament and denied that the Holy Spirit is either God or a divine person.[9]

As Preus concedes, Gerhard and other orthodox theologians exhibit "an exegesis which rigidly adheres to a set of dogmatic conclusions before it even approaches a given text and tends to ignore the historical setting of the text."[10] When one reads their argumentation, one also quickly notices that they were heavily indebted to the church fathers, not just with regard to Trinitarian terminology but also in their use of biblical references. Since the orthodox theologians maintained that the New Testament always interpreted the Old Testament correctly, they could see the Old Testament passages in light of the New. Their thinking included the premise that Scripture interprets itself and that one clear passage interprets and opens up the implications of another clear passage. The problem was that others, such as the Sozzinians, claimed too that they did not depart from the literal sense of Scripture, but they arrived at very different results. With extensive scholastic rhetoric orthodox theologians introduced no new dogmatic developments but held onto the common Western tradition.

Johann Arndt

Soon orthodoxy was seen as too distant from the real life of Christians, and pietism arose, with its emphasis on the Bible and theology for the Christian life. The most renowned forerunner of pietism, Johann Arndt (1555–1621), held to doctrinal purity with a high degree of spiritual sensitivity. Arndt's devotional work *True Christianity* emphasized the Christian's life, which was not merely a product of orthodox doctrines but involved an inner relationship based on the justified believer's union with God. *True Christianity*, which has been translated into most European languages, has served as the foundation of many books of devotion, both Roman Catholic and Protestant, and by 1740 it had been

---

9. See ibid., 1:431, 433.
10. Preus, *Theology of Post-Reformation Lutheranism*, 136.

published in 123 editions. Johann Gerhard also followed Arndt's example and wrote in his youth in 1610 *Sacred Meditations*, an almost mystical expression of personal devotion. Lutheran scholasticism, as the Aristotelian and highly dogmatic approach has frequently been called, became more and more polemical and insensitive as it grew in influence and dominance in the seventeenth century. The aridity of such orthodoxy in the latter half of the century, coupled with the despair produced by the Thirty Years' War a generation earlier, resulted in conditions that were ripe for pietism. Dry, dogmatic theology had suppressed the full expression of the Christian faith, and pietism arose as a corrective.

Nicolaus Ludwig von Zinzendorf

Karl Barth claimed that Count Nicolaus Ludwig von Zinzendorf (1700–1760) "was perhaps the only genuine Christocentric of the modern age."[11] As Zinzendorf asserts: "The Holy Trinity is concentrated in the person of Jesus Christ.... The Father, the Holy Spirit and the Word live in the person of Christ, all three. He is the reflection."[12] For Zinzendorf Christ is the creator. Though Father and the Holy Spirit are co-creators, "we know positively that he [Christ] is the God for whose sake are all things as he has made them." It is again "the Father's own teaching that the Son has created the world."[13] The Father rules over the world until all the enemies of Christ are laid at his footstool by his Father. In this second period from Christ's incarnation until judgment day, Christ remains the secret center of activity, while God the Father and God the Holy Spirit act for the Son. Christ, the creator of the world, the God of the Old and New Testament, who in an interactive manner participates in the rule of the world during his time on earth until the final judgment, will then assume his position and rise from his rest to become again the focal person of the Trinity.

While for the Reformers God the Father occupied the central place, for Zinzendorf it is the Son. He therefore rejects the idea of an eternal

---

11. Karl Barth, *Church Dogmatics*, vol. 4, *The Doctrine of Reconciliation*, part 1, ed. and trans. G. W. Bromiley (Edinburgh: T&T Clark, 1956), 683.
12. August Gottlieb Spangenberg, *Apologetische Schluß-Schrift*, in Nikolaus Ludwig von Zinzendorf, *Ergänzungsbände zu den Hauptschriften*, ed. Erich Beyreuther and Gerhard Meyer (Hildesheim: Georg Olms, 1964), 3:571. For more details on Zinzendorf's view of the Trinity see Erich Beyreuther, "Christozentrismus und Trinitätsauffassung," in Erich Beyreuther, *Studien zur Theologie Zinzendorfs*, 2nd ed. (New York: Georg Olms, 2000), 9–34.
13. Nikolaus Ludwig von Zinzendorf, *Hauptschriften*, vol. 5, *Londoner Predigten*, ed. Erich Beyreuther and Gerhard Meyer (Hildesheim: Georg Olms, 1963), 287–88 (the second London sermon of Dec. 26, 1754).

procession of the Son from the Father and the coming forth of the Holy Spirit if it is understood as an ontological statement, since this would imply some kind of subordination. If one wants to talk about persons in the Godhead, Zinzendorf asserts, one should not look in the Godhead—as orthodoxy has done—but in God's self-disclosure, in revelation. Zinzendorf rejected speculation about the inner Trinity. He differed from scholastic theologians and wanted to establish the doctrine of the Trinity on the basis of Scripture alone. While he rejected speculation, for him the knowledge of the Trinity depends not only on the correct exegesis of Scripture but primarily on the experience of redemption. But this latter emphasis also got him into trouble when he talked about the Holy Spirit as mother.

Zinzendorf illustrates that the Holy Spirit is our protector by saying that the Spirit leads us through this world as if with his motherly hands. From this concept of motherly care he develops the idea of the Holy Family, God as Father, the Holy Spirit as Mother, and Christ as the Son. According to this primal effigy of the inner Trinity, Zinzendorf develops the image of his community, the Bohemian or Moravian Brethren, and of the family in general. As Samuel Powell relates: "The potentially most controversial innovation lay in calling the Holy Spirit our Mother, lacking as it does specific Biblical grounding. Apart from the lack of express Biblical warrant, it seems to establish a marital relation between the Father and the Spirit. This image particularly appalled Johann Albrecht Bengel, the Biblical scholar, who attacked Zinzendorf for this and other doctrinal novelties."[14] Gary Steven Kinkel explains that Zinzendorf, by referring to the Spirit as "Mother" and to God as "Father," did not want to speculate about the inner life of the Trinity. "The language of the Holy Spirit as Mother referred instead to God revealed in personal, saving relation to human beings."[15] With the term *mother* he sought to express God's gracious salvific activity as it came to the fore in Jesus's suffering, death, and resurrection. It was the nurturing and caring aspect of the Spirit that came to expression in the term *mother*. But soon the pendulum swung in the opposite direction, when the Age of Reason dawned. The focus was no longer on the experience of the Christian community but on the human intellect.

---

14. Samuel M. Powell, *The Trinity in German Thought* (Cambridge: Cambridge University Press, 2001), 40. See also Johann Albrecht Bengel, *Abriß der so genannten Brüdergemeine* (New York: Georg Olms, 1972), esp. 71–73, where he attacks the notion that the Holy Spirit is "feminine" and "mother."
15. Gary Steven Kinkel, *Our Dear Mother the Spirit. An Investigation of Count Zinzendorf's Theology and Praxis* (Lanham, MD: University Press of America, 1990), 9.

The Christian Faith Is Not Mysterious (Enlightenment)

During the period of the Enlightenment in the seventeenth and eighteenth century, there was more interest in the deconstruction of the Trinity than in its construction.

Ralph Cudworth

Cambridge Platonist Ralph Cudworth (1617–88) still wanted to stem this tide on the subject. In his *True Intellectual System of the Universe* (1678) he attempts to reject all atheism that might be derived from the new scientific worldview. He also tries to establish the doctrine of the Trinity in the larger context of philosophical and religious traditions. Traversing the religious history of antiquity, he asserts that a great deal of the polytheism of antiquity was really nothing other than the worshiping of one and the same supreme god, under many different names and notions. Furthermore, he poses the question whether, among those several names for God, some might not signify distinct divine hypostases; and particularly, whether there are not some "footsteps of such a trinity" to be found in the different theologies of antiquity.[16] Cudworth then estimates that this "theology of the divine tradition or revelation" first emerged among the Hebrews and from there spread to other nations. Yet these are only footprints, not a fully understood and developed doctrine of the Trinity. Therefore he clarifies concerning the Christian Trinity:

> First, that it is not a trinity of mere names or words, nor a trinity of partial notions and inadequate conceptions, of one and the same thing.... We conclude it to be a trinity of hypostases, or substances, or persons. The second thing that we observe concerning the Christian Trinity is this, that though the second hypostasis or person thereof, was begotten from the first, and the third proceedeths both from the first and second; yet are neither this second nor third creatures.[17]

This means that the three persons are equal in every respect. "In the last place, we add, that these three hypostases, or persons, are truly and really one God."[18] Here the unity of the Godhead is maintained.

---

16. Ralph Cudworth, *The True Intellectual System of the Universe* (1.4), (Bristol: Thoemmes Press, 1995 [1678]), 2:313.
17. Ibid., 2:340–42.
18. Ibid., 2:342.

John Locke

Yet philosopher John Locke (1632–1704), one of the main representatives of empiricism, was much more restrained. First of all, the notion of God was for him not an innate idea. He also made no mention of the Trinity in his *Essay Concerning Human Understanding* (1690), since he questioned whether the doctrine of the Trinity was a "clear and distinct" notion.[19] Doctrines received by others may not satisfy some if they do not know how these others have received them. One cannot "own" a notion if there is no prior understanding of this notion. Reason has priority over any other means of knowledge.

Gotthold Ephraim Lessing

The Education of the Human Race (1777), by German philosopher and literary critic Gotthold Ephraim Lessing (1729–81), is widely regarded as the manifesto of his theological/philosophical thoughts. In this treatise written toward the end of his career, he juxtaposes the simple truth of revelation and the searching truth of reason using the doctrine of the Trinity as an example. The truth of revelation states "a Son begotten [by God] from Eternity."[20] Reason must postulate a transcendental unity in God that does not exclude some kind of plurality. This divine plurality leads to the consequence that "God can either have no perfect conception of himself at all, or this perfect conception is just as necessarily, *i.e.*, actually existent, as He Himself." While revelation provides a rather simple answer, reason wanders endlessly back and forth without a satisfying answer. Yet revelation sets reason on the right track to understand even such a matter as the Trinity.

In the fragment *Christianity of Reason* (1751/53) Lessing states more explicitly his understanding of the Trinity. Next to God himself there is the Son of God. "This being is God himself and is not to be distinguished from God, because one thinks it as soon as one thinks of God, and because one cannot think it without God" (§7).[21] Lessing then ponders that the more two things have in common, the greater is their har-

---

19. John Locke, "Mr. Locke's Letter to the Bishop of Worcester," in *The Works of John Locke in Ten Volumes* (Aalen: Scientia Verlag 1963 [1823]), 4:68; see also 4:198.
20. Gotthold Ephraim Lessing, *The Education of the Human Race*, trans. F. W. Robertson, 3rd ed. (London: Henry S. King, 1872), 59–60, for this and the following quote.
21. The § numbers in parenthesis refer to Gotthold Ephraim Lessing, *The Christianity of Reason*, in *Lessing's Theological Writings*, selected and trans. Henry Chadwick (Stanford, CA: Stanford University Press, 2006 [1956]).

mony. The greatest harmony, then, exists if the two have everything in common and together they are only one. "Two such things are God and the Son-God, or the identical image of God; and the harmony which exists between them is called by Scripture *the Spirit who proceeds from the Father and the Son*" (§10). Lessing continues: "This harmony is God in such a way that it would not be God if the Father were not God and the Son were not God, and that both could not be God unless this harmony existed; that is, *all three are one*" (§12). It is interesting that Lessing calls this harmony the Spirit. Once he has established the Trinity, Lessing proceeds to talk about creation, through which God attributes something of his perfection to all the created beings. While the Spirit is the bond between Father and Son, he does not seem to have any other function. This is not really surprising, since the created order perceptible in the world can be traced to God the Father, and the historical events are associated with Jesus of Nazareth, God the Son. Since Lessing does not reflect on the church, the Spirit remains the bond between Father and Son but is not in any way connected with Jesus Christ and his ongoing presence in the world.

In his brief statement *The Religion of Christ* (1780), he elaborates: "How these two religions, the religion of Christ and the Christian religion, can exist in Christ in one and the same person, is inconceivable."[22] With such doubts in his mind it is not surprising that he published *The Fragments by an Anonymous Writer* (1774–78), knowing full well that these were parts of *An Apology for, or Some Words in Defense of, Reasoning Worshipers of God*, composed by Hamburg philosopher Hermann Samuel Reimarus (1694–1768).

Hermann Samuel Reimarus

While Reimarus rejected both materialistic atheism and pantheism, he was influenced by British deism and agreed with John Toland's 1696 publication *Christianity Not Mysterious* that the revelation of the Bible contains no true mysteries; rather, all the dogmas of the faith can be understood and demonstrated by properly trained reason from natural principles. Yet he also knew that Toland had been prosecuted in London, and therefore Lessing kept the manuscript in his desk during his lifetime.

While the whole manuscript of Reimarus had never been published,

---

22. Gotthold Ephraim Lessing, *The Christian Religion*, in *Lessing's Theological Writings*, 106.

the section "Concerning the Intention of Jesus and His Teaching" made quite an impact when it was published by Lessing. Reimarus asserts:

> Since nowadays the doctrine of the trinity of persons in God and the doctrine of the work of salvation through Jesus as the Son of God and God-man constitute the main articles and mysteries of the Christian faith, I shall specifically demonstrate that they are not to be found in Jesus's discourses. To this end I shall explain in what sense he is called Son of God, what the Holy Spirit signifies, and finally, what it means when Father, Son, and Holy Spirit are joined together in baptism.[23]

Perusing sources of the Old and the New Testament, Reimarus concludes that "by a son of God the Jews understood nothing other than a pious or just man whom God loved particularly and whose part he would take in some miraculous manner."[24]

When it comes to the Holy Spirit, Reimarus informs us: "In general, the Hebrews play with the word 'spirit.' For them it means (1) the soul itself, (2) the talents and aptitudes of the personality, and (3) the condition and stirrings of the same." "In the New Testament there is frequent mention of the Holy Spirit, but in the same threefold sense. (1) It means God himself.... (2) Among such references both ordinary and extraordinary gifts are most frequently to be understood.... There is no concept of a special person in God hidden in them."[25]

Concerning the three persons of the Godhead, "there are only two such places in the evangelists, one in the baptism of Jesus and the other in the baptismal formula that Jesus is said to have prescribed to his disciples." At Jesus's Baptism only John sees and hears things that the others are not aware of. This means, according to Reimarus, that it is a vision, just like Stephen's at his death. And "John and the apostles use the phrase 'to be baptized with the Holy Spirit' when they want to say that men are endowed with special spiritual gifts."[26] Reimarus concludes that the things reported about Jesus's Baptism are no more than a vision of John the Baptist. Reimarus asks rhetorically: "If Jesus himself had wished to expound this strange doctrine of three different persons in one divine nature, utterly unknown to the Jews, or if he had regarded explaining it one of a teacher's duties, would he have kept silent about it until after his resurrection?" When Jesus says "I

---

23. Hermann Samuel Reimarus, *The Intention of Jesus and His Disciples*, in *Reimarus: Fragments*, ed. Charles H. Talbert (Philadelphia: Fortress Press, 1970), 76.
24. Ibid., 81.
25. Ibid., 88, 90–91.
26. Ibid., 91–92.

and the Father are one," he does not intend to say that by nature he is equal to God or of one substance with the Father, but "simply intends to express in a striking manner his love for the Father and the Father's love for him." But it was not Jesus's intention "to present a triune God or to make himself God's equal."[27] Reimarus makes it clear: on biblical grounds the doctrine of the Trinity and Christ's Godhead are unfounded. There is no Trinity, and Jesus is not equal to God.

Reimarus was not alone in his skepticism. Immanuel Kant (1724–1804) too has nothing positive to say about the Trinity when he asserts:

> The doctrine of the Trinity, taken literally, has *no practical relevance at all*, even if we think we understand it; and it is even more clearly irrelevant if we realize that it transcends all our concepts. Whether we are to worship three or ten persons in the Divinity makes no difference: the pupil will implicitly accept one as readily as the other because he has no concept at all of a number of persons in one God (hypostases), and still more so because this distinction can make no difference in his rules of conduct.[28]

And Thomas Jefferson (1743–1826), one of the founding fathers of the United States and its third president, talks in a similar tone about the Trinity as a three-headed monster when he claims:

> The hocus-pocus phantasm of a God like another Cerberus, with one body and three heads, had its birth and growth in the blood of thousands and thousands of martyrs. And a strong proof of the solidity of the primitive faith, is its restoration, as soon as a nation arises which vindicates to itself the freedom of religious opinion, and its external divorce from the civil authority.
>
> In fact, the Athanasian paradox that one is three, and three but one, is so incomprehensible to the human mind, that no candid man can say he has any idea of it, and how can he believe what presents no idea? He who thinks he does, only deceives himself. He proves, also, that man, once surrendering his reason, has no remaining guard against absurdities the most monstrous, and like a ship without a rudder, is the sport of every wind. With such persons, gullibility which they call faith, takes the helm from the hand of reason, and the mind becomes a wreck.[29]

---

27. Ibid., 95–96, 98.
28. Immanuel Kant, *The Conflict of the Faculties: Der Streit der Fakultäten*, trans. and introduced by Mary J. Gregor (New York: Abaris, 1979), 65–67.
29. *Jefferson's letter to Rev. James Smith, December 8, 1822*, https://founders.archives.gov/documents/Jefferson/98-01-02-3202 (accessed April 25, 2017).

But this doctrine, declared silenced and dead, enjoyed a remarkable rejuvenation. This occurred first with Hegel in the nineteenth century and then with Karl Barth and those who followed his steps ever since the beginning of the twentieth century. But the rise of Trinitarian theology should not obliterate the fact that this doctrine is little understood and held but in low esteem by most laypersons, as many proponents of this doctrine readily admit.

The Return of the Trinity (From the Nineteenth Century to the Present)

While most Enlightenment thinkers had largely abandoned Trinitarian thinking and rendered the Trinity obsolete, it was up to a philosopher, Georg Wilhelm Friedrich Hegel (1770–1831), to recoup Trinitarian thinking and make it his central theme.

Georg Wilhelm Friedrich Hegel

Hegel's thoughts were so influential that in the twentieth century both Jürgen Moltmann and Wolfhart Pannenberg, among others, drew on them. But, similar to the representatives of the Enlightenment, he starts his reflections on the Trinity as a true philosopher, with thinking and not with the biblical documents. He is convinced that the thoughts of humanity, insofar as they are true and touch on being itself, coincide with the thoughts of the world spirit who creates things by thinking of them so that thinking, truth, and being coincide. Because of this correlation between the human thinking and that of the world spirit, Hegel can then make statements regarding "God and the world" that also involve statements about the Trinity.

The revealed religion, namely Christianity, was for Hegel the Absolute Religion. The decisive point for him is the incarnation. "Here the Divine Being is known as Spirit; this religion is the Divine Being's consciousness concerning itself that it is Spirit. For spirit is knowledge of self in a state of alienation of self: spirit is the Being which is the process of retaining identity with itself in its otherness."[30] This means that the divine being makes itself known as spirit by alienating itself from itself, yet at the same time retaining its identity with itself in that otherness. He follows the thoughts of Martin Luther's famous Christ-

---

30. Georg Wilhelm Friedrich Hegel, *Phenomenology of Mind*, trans. J. B. Baillie (New York: Harper Torchbooks, 1967), §759.

mas hymn when he states: "The infinite being, filling the immeasurability of space, exists at the same time in a definite space, as it is said, for instance, in the verse:

> 'He whom all heavens' heaven ne'er contained
> Lies now in Mary's womb.'[31]

There is a dialectic of the finite and the infinite, and a coincidence of opposites. Incarnation made possible God's self-disclosure and still does to this today.

God is "triune" from eternity, as "the God who differentiates himself but remains identical with himself in the process," and thus "in the Christian religion this is what is called the *Trinity*."[32] But Hegel also concedes, "The Trinity is called the *mystery* of God; its content is mystical, i.e., speculative." The eternal Trinity is the Father, then the Son, as the divinity objectified in itself, and the Spirit, the abolition of this differentiation, since "*the Holy Spirit is eternal love*." The universal spirit posits itself in its three determinations. This is for Hegel the dialectic history of the Spirit. The "Spirit is the divine history, the process of self-differentiation, of diremption and return into itself." This self-renunciation of God and his self-interpretation in the historical specificity is the realm of the Son. As Hegel explains: "God, considered in terms of his eternal idea, *has* to generate the Son, has to distinguish himself from himself, in such a way that what is distinguished is wholly he himself; and their union is love and the Spirit." "God appears as the concrete God." He has no other choice "than that of the sensible mode of the spirit that is spirit itself in itself—the shape of the *singular human being*." The self-manifestation of the Spirit, his necessity to appear as himself, is an expression of the creative being of God and occurs in the human being of Jesus of Nazareth.[33]

Hegel modifies the Christian doctrine of the Trinity to fit into his philosophy, since "the relationship of Father, Son, and Spirit ... is a childlike relationship, a childlike form." It is not to be taken literally but is "a merely figurative relationship." We must be aware "that all three are spirit." The Father is the universal, the Son is infinite particularity, and the Spirit is singularity. But when we say that God is

---

31. G. W. F. Hegel, *Fragment of a System*, trans. Richard Kroner, in Hegel, *Early Theological Writings* (New York: Harper Torchbooks, 1961), 315. See Martin Luther's hymn "Gelobet seist du, Jesus Christ," stanza 3. The English rendition "All Praise to You, Eternal Lord" is quite different.
32. Georg Wilhelm Friedrich Hegel, *Lectures on the Philosophy of Religion*, vol. 3, *The Consummate Religion*, ed. Peter C. Hodgson (Berkeley: University of California Press, 1998), 192.
33. Ibid., 276, 186, 215, 214.

the Spirit, then the third is also the first. This differentiation in which the divine life struggles with particularity is the process of self-maintenance, in which the Spirit is its own presupposition. "The process gives rise to nothing new; what is brought forth is already [there] from the beginning." Yet Hegel does not view this process, which is also carried on in the life process of nature, as something eternal. There is no eternal recurrence of the same. Hegel follows the incarnational process in which the subject, that is, humanity, "has to bring itself conclusively together with its original spiritual nature." There is the explication of the life of love, "of the same process which *is* God and which is *represented* in Christ." "The subject receives the assurance of its unity with God, of its reconciliation."[34] The unity with the divine and therewith the unity with the universal spirit is attained.

In his *Lectures on the Philosophy of Religion* of 1831 Hegel attempted to elaborate the Trinitarian structure of the Christian religion as clearly as possible, as Peter Hodgson, the translator and editor of these lectures, assures us. But one nevertheless wonders whether Hegel really follows the doctrine of the Trinity. Here Hegel talks about three spheres, the kingdom of the Father, the kingdom of the Son, and the kingdom of the Spirit. "God is immediately present to himself through his differentiation, which, however, is not yet externalized." God as Father is the first universality, that which is indeterminate and unknowable but also that which differentiates itself. Yet at this initial stage the idea does not develop into any further determinations, and God is only comprehended as a subject with many properties. This would mean that revelation is not yet actualized. The second stage or the second sphere "consists of the determination of the Son." The Son is not associated with creation and with the world. As Hegel explains: "Spirit relates itself to the other; this means that it is no longer absolute but finite spirit that is posited; and inasmuch as what is differentiated is itself something internally differentiated into nature and finite spirit, we have the creation of the world, the form in which the Son actually becomes the other." God no longer appears in natural immediacy but in spiritual immediacy, in human shape, in form of the unity of divine and human nature in a single human being. When we come to the kingdom of the Spirit, then, as noted above, we encounter and return to the original spiritual nature in the self-consciousness of the community. As Hegel explains the whole process: "The abstract-

---

34. Ibid., 194-95, 371, 373, 372.

ness of the Father is given up in the Son.... But the negation of this negation is the unity of Father and Son—love, or the Spirit."[35] The Spirit that has started the whole process is also the Spirit that encounters us at the end. If we ask whether the philosopher Hegel rendered the doctrine of the Trinity in theologically adequate ways, we are confronted with a modalistic framework in which one form of the Spirit is transformed into another.[36] Though he uses the term *person* for the three entities of the Trinity, he makes little use of their personhood except in case of the Son. Yet Hegel is cognizant of his limits as the philosopher claiming that philosophy does not "place itself above religion but only above the form of faith as representation."[37] Therefore he can work with the form but not with the content of faith. Whether the two can be that clearly distinguished is debatable, since the two always influence each other.

As Samuel Powell claims, however, Hegel is not too modest in his assumptions, since he was convinced "that he had captured the overall thrust of the Scriptures and creeds and in fact had done so in a way superior to that of theologians."[38] Powell agrees that Scripture and creeds contributed considerably to Hegel's exposition of the Trinity. But Hegel went a decisive step further by assuming that with the aid of dialectical thought he had discovered the ultimate truth in these texts. For Hegel this truth was the historical process. "The economic Trinity was for him a moving image of an eternal reality, for this eternal reality possesses a movement that is structurally identical to the historical movement, even if it occurs outside time."[39] What was prefigured in Trinitarian terms in heaven was to be executed in dialectical fashion on earth through human consciousness, in which the absolute spirit actualizes itself.

Through his thoroughgoing dialectic thinking from the Absolute to the finite (world) and back again, and by designating the Absolute as Spirit and the Son also as world, Hegel can rejuvenate Trinitarian thought in a highly speculative way. Theologians who followed him

---

35. Ibid., 51, 362, 365, 370.
36. Cyril O'Regan, "The Trinity in Kant, Hegel, and Schelling," in *Oxford Handbook of the Trinity*, ed. Gilles Emery and Matthew Levering (Oxford: Oxford University Press, 2011), 261, also points to "Hegel's modalism," though emphasizing that in contrast to ancient modalism Hegel's modalism is "dynamic and developmental."
37. Hegel, *Consummate Religion*, 374.
38. Powell, *Trinity in German Thought*, 139, in his extensive treatment of nineteenth-century Trinitarian thinking in Germany.
39. Ibid., 140.

could pick up this mood. Yet the ecclesiastical tradition served him largely as a springboard to enter new intellectual heights.

Friedrich Schleiermacher

Friedrich Schleiermacher (1768–1834) was much more restrained than Hegel. He remembered too well the Enlightenment verdict against the doctrine of the Trinity. Therefore he treats the doctrine of the Trinity only as a conclusion, cautioning that it *"is not an immediate utterance concerning the Christian self-consciousness, but only a combination of several such utterances."*[40] Indeed, the Trinity is not immediately connected with the Christian self-consciousness. As Schleiermacher explains, initially the aim of this doctrine was to assure the unity of the divine essence with the human nature—Christ being fully human and fully divine. Schleiermacher leaves it open whether there is an eternal distinction in the Supreme Being. Moreover, since in John's Gospel the Spirit is often mentioned, John could easily have accorded the Spirit the same place as the Word that was in the beginning as was God. The doctrine of the Trinity is therefore not "the true and the only natural completion of the Johannine statements." Only the need to guard against a semblance of polytheism necessitated the doctrine of the Trinity. When Schleiermacher claims that "the main pivots of the ecclesiastical doctrine—the being of God in Christ and in the Christian Church—are independent of the doctrine of the Trinity," this shows of how little existential significance this doctrine is.[41]

In the next paragraph Schleiermacher shows that *"the ecclesiastical doctrine of the Trinity demands that we think of each of the three Persons as equal to the Divine Essence, and vice versa, and each of the three Persons as equal to the others."*[42] Yet he claims that we can do neither the one nor the other. If, for instance, there is the eternal generation of the Son from the Father, there must be at least a relationship of dependence. The same holds true for the Spirit, whether he proceeds from the Father only or from the Father and the Son. Considering the attributes of the deity, one usually thinks of the Father. If there is a unity of the divine essence, then Son and Spirit cannot be treated differently.

Schleiermacher then refers to the time when the doctrine of the Trinity was conceived and admits that pagan descriptions of plurality

---

40. Friedrich Schleiermacher, *The Christian Faith*, ed. H. R. Mackintosh and J. S. Stewart (New York: Harper & Row, 1963), 2:738.
41. Ibid., 2:740, 741.
42. Ibid., 2:742.

may have entered the description that later on were no longer suitable. Yet, he claims, one should go back to the original tendency of the doctrine, that it is an "expression of our consciousness of Christ and of the common Spirit of the Church to assert that God is in both." God in God's self and God in relation to the world are at stake here. The problem, however, is that "we have no formula for the being of God in Himself as distinct from the being of God in the world" and therefore have to engage in speculation. How can we then distinguish properly "the peculiar being of God in Christ as an individual, and in the Christian Church as an historical whole, from the omnipotent presence of God in the world in general, of which these are parts"? he asks.[43] Since this task has not been solved properly, Schleiermacher contends that we should not be surprised that every now and then anti-Trinitarian opinions emerge. He appeals for patience with persons who hold such opinions and also questions whether the doctrine in its older form must still be maintained, since the acceptance of the doctrine of the Trinity is not the necessary precondition of faith in redemption.

Schleiermacher goes one step further, claiming that the "first unsolved difficulty lies in the relation of the unity of the Essence to the Trinity of the Persons; and here everything depends on the original and eternal existence of distinctions within the Divine Essence."[44] Then he questions whether this relation is so clearly expressed in the New Testament and whether the Sabellian view would not merit serious consideration of Father, Son, and Holy Spirit being different modes or aspects of the one God. If answered in the negative, Schleiermacher concludes that we must continue to express this doctrine without doing harm to the biblical witness. If answered in the affirmative, the exegetical undergirding of the ecclesiastical doctrine would be missing, and the Athanasian position could be seen as being on par with the Sabellian view. Even the immutability ascribed to the Supreme Being could be maintained if we distinguish between the divine decree in eternity and the fulfillment of salvation in time. In sum, Schleiermacher shows that the position of Athanasius is not cast in stone. It could be perceived as just one option. But Schleiermacher does not want to jettison the doctrine of the Trinity. He wants to be true to the biblical heritage and the ecclesiastical tradition without succumbing to the stifling effects of this tradition in view of its inner tensions.

---

43. Ibid., 2:747–48.
44. Ibid., 2:750.

Albrecht Ritschl

When we come to Albrecht Ritschl (1822-89), who was in Germany the major theological figure in the second part of the nineteenth century and far beyond, we notice in the indexes of his massive three-volume work, *The Christian Doctrine of Justification and Reconciliation*, not one entry for the Trinity.[45] He also tells us that through the imperial edict *De summa Trinitate et fide Catholica* of 380 the Nicene doctrine of the Trinity became public law. "The Reformers did not divest themselves of this.... They never disputed the doctrine of the Trinity."[46] We might assume that Ritschl follows the Reformers at this point, since the Trinity does not occupy an important position in his system of thought. But with regard to the Holy Spirit, Ritschl already observes: "The neglect of the subject has had this unfortunate practical consequence, that theologians either abstain from using the idea altogether, or understand by it a kind of resistless natural force which runs athwart the regular course of knowledge and the normal exercise of the will." Yet Ritschl understands the Holy Spirit as "the power of God which enables the community to appropriate His self-revelation as Father through His Son." For Ritschl the Holy Spirit is the Spirit of God who is "the ground of that knowledge of God and that specific moral and religious life which exist in the Christian community."[47] This means that the Holy Spirit, whom Ritschl usually calls "the Spirit of God," mediates to us the knowledge of God and enables us to exist as a Christian community. The Spirit has primarily an ecclesial function. Yet God's self-revelation as Father comes through his Son. Ritschl can talk about "the congruity between the Son of God and God as His Father" and "the eternal Godhead of the Son." We can gather from this that the preexistent Son is indeed attributed full divinity, while the Spirit is subordinated to God the Father. Ritschl calls Christ "the Bearer of the perfect revelation of God, through His solidarity with the Father, in the right exercise of His love and patience over the world, demonstrated His Godhead as man for the salvation of those whom, as His community, He at the same time represented before the Father by His obedience, and still represents."[48] Important for Ritschl is the practical aspect of God and Christ, mean-

---

45. Albrecht Ritschl, *The Christian Doctrine of Justification and Reconciliation*, vol. 3, *The Positive Development of the Doctrine*, trans. H. R. Mackintosh and A. B. Macaulay (Edinburgh: T&T Clark, 1900).
46. Albrecht Ritschl, *A Critical History of the Christian Doctrine of Justification and Reconciliation*, trans. John S. Black (Edinburgh: Edmonston and Douglas, 1872), 127.
47. Ibid., 533, 273, 471.
48. Ibid., 470-71, 591-92.

ing their salvific work for the benefit of humanity. While his emphasis on Christ's solidarity with God the Father can be attributed to the influence of Schleiermacher, the ethical bent betrays his indebtedness to Kant.

In his *Lectures on Dogmatics* (1881/82) Ritschl devotes a whole chapter to the doctrine of the Trinity. Similar to Schleiermacher, he declares: "This doctrine comes at the end of the system because one cannot understand the combination of the three persons without having understood the individual members. And this doctrine comes at the end of the system because it is an expression of our knowledge of God which is founded through the Holy Spirit in the [Christian] community as an expression of the complete and exhaustive knowledge of God."[49] Being derived from Scripture, this doctrine should come at the end, Ritschl concludes, and looking at its origin in the fourth century Ritschl rightly perceives it as a corollary to the doctrine of the Godhead of Christ. Ritschl then rejects the psychological interpretation of the Trinity given by Augustine as pure speculation. Since in the baptismal formulas the term *name* is used for Father, Son, and Holy Spirit, Ritschl concludes "that God becomes totally revealed in the mutual relationship of the three mentioned entities in such a way in which we as Christians are convinced that the revelation in Christ is the exhaustive, concluding, and final revelation."[50] Therefore Ritschl rejects the distinction between the immanent and the economic Trinity because we cannot know God's essence apart from God's self-disclosure.

Since God discloses himself as the Father through the Son and through the Holy Spirit in the Christian community, Ritschl concludes that "the content of the three persons is identical." As a result, he then can call the three persons *homoousios*, since they are the bearers of the eternal love of God. Moreover, they are hypostatically distinct from one another because God discloses himself as Father, the Son is the direct organ of this disclosure, and the Holy Spirit is the bearer of the continued self-disclosure in the Christian community. This does not mean, however, that we are confronted with three gods but that they represent the one God, who has fully self-disclosed himself. He is the one God "who cannot be called the Father if his self-disclosure through the identical being of the Son is not recognized as inseparable from him and in the same wise also the continuation through the Holy Spirit in

---

49. Rolf Schäfer, *Grundlinien eines fast verschollenen dogmatischen Systems* (Tübingen: Mohr, 1968), 203, who reprinted a few pages from the 679-page manuscript of Ritschl's *Lectures on Dogmatics*.
50. Ibid., 204.

the Christian community through the self-disclosure concentrated in the Son."[51] This means the Son has been the historical carrier of God's self-disclosure, and the Holy Spirit continues this now in the Christian community. With this proposition Ritschl led back to a Scripture-oriented understanding of the Trinity without much of the speculation that clouded the doctrine of the Triune God once it entered the Hellenistic environment. With his reduction of the doctrine of the Trinity to its biblical basis, he avoided the post-Nicene problematic that had been created by the preoccupation with "intradivine" distinctions while still affirming that one divine essence subsists in three persons, as the decisions of Nicea and Constantinople declared.[52]

Karl Barth

In contrast to Schleiermacher, who concluded his *Christian Faith* with the doctrine of the Trinity, Karl Barth (1886–1968) starts his *Church Dogmatics* with that doctrine. Since *God* reveals himself, he reveals himself *through himself* to reveal *himself*, and therefore the doctrine of revelation must begin with the doctrine of the Triune God. Barth writes: "Thus, to the same God who in unimpaired unity is Revealer, Revelation, and Revealedness, is also ascribed in unimpaired variety in Himself precisely this threefold mode of being. Only now, by consideration of the unity and variety of God in His revelation attested in Scripture—and also really by that—we are confronted with the problem of the doctrine of the Trinity."[53]

Barth realizes that it is quite unusual to place the doctrine of the Trinity, at the beginning of dogmatics, and yet he refers to Peter Lombard and Bonaventure, who had followed the same pattern. While most theologians, including Melanchthon and Calvin, started with Holy Scripture and the doctrine of God, Barth thinks very little of this procedure. He contends that it is difficult to see how we can talk about Holy Scripture and about God unless we first consider the Triune God whose revelation makes Scripture holy and who speaks to us as God. By starting with the doctrine of God, pondering whether God exists, what he is, and finally who God is, we directly contradict the highly important explanations we receive from the doctrine of the Trinity. With the whole weight of tradition, from Calvin to Schlatter, Barth emphasizes

---

51. Ibid., 205.
52. See ibid., 151.
53. Karl Barth, *Church Dogmatics*, vol. 1, *The Doctrine of the Word of God*, part 1, trans. G. T. Thomson (Edinburgh: T&T Clark, 1960 [1936]), 344.

that if we do not know God in the way in which God reveals himself as the one triune God, we miss the Christian God. The Trinitarian name of God expresses the specifically Christian consciousness of God, and this consciousness is the basis and the content of our faith. Barth assures us that it is not important which place is given to the Trinity, but placing at the beginning shows that the content of the Trinity "may be made decisive and dominant for the whole of dogmatics."[54] Here we receive the answer of who the self-revealing God is and also what he does and effects.

Since, according to Barth, God's revelation is God's own immediate speaking, God's word is identical with God himself. This identity is albeit an indirect one, since the word of God is mediated through human persons, who received and handed it on. Though in the Bible and in the church the proclamation of the word of God is God himself, this is so because these things bear witness to this word in revelation. By this event the one word of God is indistinguishable from God's own speaking, and therefore it marks revelation as distinct from Holy Scripture and from the church's proclamation. God's revelation is grounded in itself, and therefore "its reality and likewise its truth do not rest upon a superior reality and truth." While Scripture and proclamation must become the word of God, revelation must not first become it, since it "reposes and lives in the fullness of the original being of the Word of God, existent in itself."[55] Revelation is therefore identical with God's own speaking.

That God reveals himself as the Lord is an analytical judgment, since we cannot distinguish here between form and content. "To be Lord means to be what God in his revelation is towards man."[56] Without revelation, Barth assures us, we are unaware that there is a Lord and that God is this Lord. Lordship means freedom, and in the decisions made in this freedom of God the divinely good becomes an event. Here the truthfulness, righteousness, holiness, and mercy of God enter in. The revelation of the Lordship is not an abstract matter but a concrete one, since God "in this freedom speaks as *I* and addresses by *thou*." The statement "God reveals Himself as the Lord" is, according to Barth, the root of the doctrine of the Trinity.

---

54. Ibid., 1/1:348.
55. Ibid., 1/1:350-51.
56. Ibid., 1/1:352.

> The God who has revealed Himself according to the witness of Scripture, is the same in unimpaired unity, yet also the same in unimpaired variety thrice in a different way. Or, in the phraseology of the dogma of the Trinity in the Church, the Father, the Son and the Holy Spirit in the Bible's witness to revelation are the one God in the unity of their essence, and the one God in the Bible's witness to revelation is in the variety of His Persons the Father, the Son, and the Holy Spirit.[57]

This statement actually summarizes Barth's understanding of the Trinity, one God in three persons, as presented by the witness of Scripture. Yet Barth realizes that the doctrine of the Trinity is not simply given by revelation but also "is a work of the Church."[58] While this doctrine refers to texts of the Bible, the church translates and expounds them. Barth counters the charge that this doctrine is not contained in the Bible with the remark that, similar to every aspect of proclamation, it is an explanation over and above the reading of the Bible. Explanation means repeating in different words what has been said already.

Barth's claim that "revelation is the root of the doctrine of the Trinity" is now modified, suggesting that propositions given only indirectly about the Trinity are identical with the proposition about revelation. Barth calls the dogma of the Trinity "a just interpretation of the Bible." He sees a genuine and truly established connection between the biblical witness to God in his revelation and the doctrine of the Trinity. And he calls it a "fact, that the doctrine of the Trinity is the basic presupposition of the doctrine of God as such."[59] From the doctrine of the Trinity Barth arrives at the doctrine of God, and not vice versa. From the doctrine of the Trinity we can comprehend who the God who reveals himself actually is.

Barth states, "Revelation in the Bible means the self-unveiling, imparted to men, of the God who according to His nature cannot be unveiled to man." God reveals himself as the Father of the Son, in whom he assumes form for our benefit. This is where history enters in, because the revelation attested in the Bible claims to be an historical event. Especially with the doctrine of the Trinity we are referred to history, since this doctrine "is nothing else than the unfolding of the knowledge that Jesus is the Christ or the Lord."[60]

Before extensively dealing with the Trinity, Barth considers the ves-

---

57. Ibid., 1/1:353.
58. Ibid., 1/1:354.
59. Ibid., 1/1:356, 358.
60. Ibid., 1/1:368, 384.

tiges of the Trinity in nature, history, and religion, and also in the human soul, such as the existence and mutual relationship of spring, stream, and lake (nature); the idea of three kingdoms (history); and the subjective religious consciousness of cognition, meditation, and contemplation (religion). Barth considers these as supplementary illustrations of the doctrine. Barth cautions, however, that we should not let ourselves "be actually supported, strengthened, and confirmed by an entity different from revelation."[61] In the proclamation of the word of God, Barth contents that God himself creates a vestige of himself and so of his three-in-oneness.

After having stated these initial considerations, Barth unfolds the church's doctrine of the Trinity, showing how it developed. From the outset he insists that the unity of the essence of God "is not only not removed by the threeness of the 'Persons,' but it is rather in the threeness of the 'Persons' that its unity consists."[62] In the threefold repetition of Father, Son, and Holy Spirit God is the one God. If the equality of the nature of Son and Holy Spirit with God the Father is not maintained, the unity of God is called into question. They cannot be regarded as subordinate hypostases without calling into question revelation as the presence of God.

To express more clearly the unity of God, Barth uses the term "the three 'modes of being' in God" instead of the three "Persons." The reason for this is, among other concerns, that *person* is usually associated with individuality and personality, which would move in the direction of tritheism. This does not mean that Barth would abandon the concept of person for God. He says: "The statement 'God is one in three modes of being, Father, Son, and Holy Spirit' thus means that the one God, i.e. the one Lord, the one personal God is what He is not in one mode only, but . . . in the mode of the Father, in the mode of the Son, in the mode of the Holy Spirit."[63] These modes of God's existence should not be confused or mixed up with one another. They are also not three divine attributes, since one is God the Creator, the other God the Reconciler, and the third God the Redeemer. None of the three can be taken by itself, since "the divine modes of existence condition and permeate one another mutually with such perfection, that one is as invariably in the other two as the other two are in the one." This perichoresis or mutual penetration should guard against any Sabellian monarchi-

---

61. Ibid., 1/1:397.
62. Ibid., 1/1:402.
63. Ibid., 1/1:407, 413.

THE TRINITY

anism. Yet talking about "threeness in oneness" and the "oneness in threeness," terms that Barth uses, is, as he concedes, "both one-sided and unsatisfactory." This agrees with his admission of "the inconceivability of God, the inadequacy of all knowledge of the revealed God."[64] Underlying these problems is perhaps also Barth's endeavor to establish a doctrine of the Trinity totally from within the biblical self-disclosure of God.

Yet Barth is adamant: God's revelation, attested to in Scripture, forces us to distinguish the three modes of existence of the one God. "It shows us God in His operation as Revealer, Revelation, and Revealedness, or as Creator, Reconciler, and Redeemer, or as Holiness, Mercy, and Loving-Kindness."[65] While we cannot talk about any of the three modes of being separately, we must nevertheless attribute each individual word or work of God to one of the three modes of being. At the same time, we should never forget or deny the presence of the one God in all these three modes of existence.

Barth admits that the doctrine of the Trinity is not to be found in the Old and the New Testaments. But he claims it arose from these texts in a later historical situation. Therefore it belongs to the church and is a dogma of the church. Yet why would the church formulate this doctrine, he asks? His response is that the church answered with this doctrine the question "Who it is that reveals Himself."[66]

> The doctrine of the Trinity declares ... that and how far He who reveals Himself to man according to the witness of Scripture can be our God, that and how far He can be our God. He can be our God, because He is equal to Himself in all His modes of existence, is one and the same Lord. ... And this Lord can be our God, He can meet us and unite us to Himself, because He is God in these three modes of existence as Father, Son, and Spirit, because creation, reconciliation, redemption, the entire being, language, and action in which He wills to be our God is grounded and typified in His own essence, in His Godness itself.[67]

The doctrine of the Trinity answers the question left open in Scripture of who that God is who has disclosed his own self to us. God is the Triune God who is Creator, Reconciler, and Redeemer. Once this is clear, Barth proceeds to expound each mode of being for itself. Concerning God the Father he states: *"The one God reveals Himself according to Scrip-*

---

64. Ibid., 1/1:425, 423, 426.
65. Ibid., 1/1:427.
66. Ibid., 1/1:436.
67. Ibid., 1/1:439-40.

ture as the Creator, that is, as the Lord of our existence. As such He is God our Father, because as the Father of God the Son He is so antecedently in Himself." With regard to God the Son he writes: "*The one God reveals Himself according to Scripture as the Reconciler, i.e. as the Lord, amidst our enmity towards Him. As such He is the Son come to us, or the Word spoken to us, because He is so antecedently in Himself, as the Son for the Word of God the Father.*" God is the eternal Father of the eternal Son "as the Revealer with the power of the Creator," through whom everything was created.

Finally we come to the Spirit. Barth writes: "*The one God who reveals Himself according to Scripture as the Redeemer, i.e. as the Lord who sets us free. As such He is the Holy Spirit, by receiving whom we become the children of God, because, as the Spirit of the love of God the Father and God the Son, He is so previously in Himself.*"[68] For Barth redemption and reconciliation are not identical, since reconciliation refers to what has been and is accomplished, while redemption concerns itself with the still-outstanding fulfillment. Though distinct from the Father and the Son, the Holy Spirit is no less than Father and Son. Similar to the Son, through whom all things were made, we hear in the Nicene Creed of the life-creating Spirit, attesting to his divinity. The affirmation of the Holy Spirit proceeding from the Father and the Son also shows that he is not a creature but "an emanation of the divine essence."[69]

Barth very strongly defends the *filioque* that the Spirit proceeds from the Father and the Son with the argument that in revelation the Spirit is a gift of the Father and the Son. With this the Eastern Church agrees. But, according to Barth, "it reaches out beyond revelation, in order to arrive at a quite different picture of God," claiming that in the eternal inter-Trinitarian being of God the Holy Spirit proceeds immediately from God the Father (through the Son). In contrast, Barth contends that "the *Filioque* is the expression of the knowledge of the communion between Father and Son, knowledge that the Holy Spirit is the love, which is the essence of the relation between these two modes of existence of God. And the knowledge of this communion is nothing else than the knowledge of the ground and confirmation of the communion between God and man, as a divine, eternal truth, as created in revelation by the Holy Spirit."[70] For Barth the *filioque* expresses and assures the communion between God and humanity and also the love that exists between Father and Son. Since Barth starts his reflections

68. Ibid., 1/1:441, 457, 511, 513.
69. Ibid., 1/1:541.
70. Ibid., 1/1:549–50.

on God with the Trinity, he has little room to appreciatively consider the Orthodox position.

For Barth the Orthodox position is an "error," since "in this conception the Spirit loses His mediating position between Father and Son, and Father and Son lose that mutual connection in the Spirit. . . . But above all it is the unity of the Trinity which throughout we must hold to be endangered by the denial of the *Filioque*."[71] Barth is certainly correct in his assessment that something basic is at stake here in the difference between the Eastern and the Western positions, given his starting point for of the doctrine of God. Yet if we start with the traditional approach, assuming a general knowledge of God, and then move to the specific Christian knowledge of God, the issue looks very different. It is no longer the Trinity that is at stake here but the function of the Holy Spirit. Is the Spirit God's Spirit, or is he a mode of being of the Triune God? In the latter case, which Barth pursues, the Spirit seems to lose his function as God's agent in the world. Yet Barth continues the agenda of Hegel by placing the Trinity at the center of his reflections. But whereas for Hegel the Trinity was, so to speak, the clockwork of the world and its history, for Barth it seems much more removed from the affairs of the world.

Karl Rahner

Exactly at this point Karl Rahner (1904–84), the premier theologian of the Roman Catholic Church in the twentieth century, expresses his uneasiness with the Trinity. He states that much has been done in the research of the history of the Trinity, but very few impulses propelled this doctrine toward the future. Orthodox confession to the Trinity notwithstanding, most Christians are monotheists in their day-to-day Christian practice. He even goes so far as to say that if the doctrine of the Trinity were eliminated as wrong, most Christian literature would remain unchanged. Even in the doctrine of the incarnation the Trinity comes hardly into focus, since one usually speaks about that fact that God became human. This means for many Christians that their understanding "of the incarnation will not have to be changed if there were no Trinity."[72] Rahner contends "that the assertions about the Trinity in their catechetical formulations are almost unintelligible to people

---

71. Ibid., 1/1:552.
72. Karl Rahner, "Der dreifaltige Gott als transzendenter Urgrund der Heilsgeschichte," in Karl Rahner, *Sämtliche Werke* (Freiburg: Herder, 2013), 22/1b:519.

today, and that they almost inevitably occasion misunderstandings."[73] The reason for this is that when a human being today hears of "one God in three persons" without any further explanations, he or she associates with the word *person* content that is associated with this word elsewhere. Moreover, when we hear of the terms *hypostasis*, *essence*, and *nature* in connection with the Trinity, these concepts are far from being clear and unambiguous. Especially when talking about a person today, we think of someone who has his or her own free center of consciousness and free activity, which is contrary to what is meant with *person* in regard to the Trinity. There the unity of the three persons is of utmost significance. In the Trinity there is a unicity of essence, which implies and includes the unicity of one single consciousness and one single freedom. The traditional vocabulary concerning the Trinity is more confusing than explanatory. This kind of assessment is typical today, even for most theologians who advocate a Trinitarian theology.

Rahner sees the same problems with the so-called psychological theory of the Trinity. The imposing speculations with which Christian theology has tried to conceive of the inner life of God since the time of Augustine do not explain anymore what they are supposed to explain, namely, why the Father expresses himself in Word, and with the Logos breathes a Spirit that is different from him. "The psychological theory of the Trinity neglects the experience of the Trinity in the economy of salvation in favor of a seemingly almost gnostic speculation about what goes on in the inner life of God."[74] One forgets here that in the Trinity the countenance of God is turned toward us in God's self-communication. Rahner therefore insists that in the history of salvation and revelation the Trinity is the immanent Trinity, because through grace and incarnation God really gives himself and appears as he is in himself in the economy of salvation, as attested in the Old and New Testaments. As the following quotation shows, for Rahner the economy of salvation is the immanent Trinity.

> Insofar as he has come as the salvation which divinizes us in the innermost center of the existence of the individual person, we call him really and truly "Holy Spirit" or "Holy Ghost." Insofar as in the concrete historicity of our existence one and the same God strictly as himself is present for us in Jesus Christ, and in himself, not in a representation, we call him "Logos" or the Son in an absolute sense. Insofar as this very God, who

---

73. Karl Rahner, *Foundations of Christian Faith: An Introduction to the Idea of Christianity*, trans. William V. Dych (New York: Seabury, 1978), 134.
74. Ibid., 135.

> comes to us as Spirit and as Logos, is and always remains the ineffable and holy mystery, the incomprehensible ground and origin of his coming in the Son and in the Spirit, we call him the one God, the Father.[75]

The assertion that one and the same God is present for us as Father, as Son or Logos, and as Holy Spirit, that the Father gives himself to us through the Son in the Holy Spirit—these are in the strict sense assertions about God as he is in himself. This also shows "that of the doctrine of the Trinity is not at subtle theological and speculative game, but rather is an assertion which cannot be avoided."[76] God as the incomprehensible ground of our being is not only the God of infinite distance but also the God of absolute closeness in true self-communication. The Trinity is not just a reality as a doctrine; it discloses to us the experience of grace. We know of the Trinity because the Word of the Father has entered our history and has imparted to us his Spirit. This fact of the history of revelation cannot be the tacit presupposition of the doctrine of the Trinity but must be its starting point.

Rahner sees two ways of starting: one, as the older confessions and Eastern theology did, to begin with the one God, who is the Father of Jesus Christ and the one who sends the Holy Spirit through Christ. The other possibility is to start with the Trinity, the one God, whose essence subsists in three persons. Unlike Barth, Rahner prefers the first option. As we have seen, Rahner holds the descriptor "three persons" to be problematic for the Trinity. In turn he introduces the descriptor "three distinct ways of subsistence" (*drei distinkte Subsistenzweisen*) in explaining the term "three persons." Yet he does not go as far as Barth, who simply replaced "three persons" with "three modes of being."[77] Rahner's continuous reference to the salvation history of God and the biblical witness as the starting point for Trinitarian reflections make his approach appear less dogmatic and less speculative. The joining together of the immanent Trinity (God in God's self in all eternity) with the economic Trinity (God in his salvific activity) has become known as Rahner's Rule and has had great influence in shaping Trinitarian theological conversations henceforth.[78]

---

75. Ibid., 136.
76. Ibid., 137.
77. See Rahner, "Der dreifaltige Gott," 22/1b:565, 619.
78. So rightly Stanley J. Grenz, *Rediscovering the Triune God: The Trinity in Contemporary Theology* (Minneapolis: Fortress Press, 2004), 217.

Paul Tillich

Paul Tillich (1886–1965), another giant of twentieth-century theology, devotes very little space to the Trinity in his three-volume *Systematic Theology*. He states: "The doctrine of the Trinity has independent roots in the encounter with God in all his manifestations."[79] When Schleiermacher put this doctrine at the conclusion of his theological system, a significant step was taken in the direction of an existential understanding of theological concepts, through his emphasis on the "Christian consciousness." For that reason, Tillich has little sympathy for Karl Barth, who began his "prolegomena" with something that actually was "post-legomena," namely the doctrine of the Trinity. "One could say that in his system this doctrine falls down from heaven, the heaven of an unrelated biblical and ecclesial authority."[80] For Tillich, similar to Rahner, the experiential dimension of the Trinity is important.

According to Tillich, the Christian doctrine of the Trinity adds to Trinitarian thought a decisive element, namely the relation of Christ to the Logos. The decision of Nicea in 325, so says Tillich, rescued Christianity from lapsing back into the veneration of demigods. The enlargement of the creed at the Council of Constantinople in 381 affirmed the divinity of the Holy Spirit. This, according to Tillich, was a christological necessity. If the being of Jesus as the Christ is the new being, then it cannot be the human spiritual life of Jesus that makes him the Christ. It must be the divine Spirit, who, equal to the Logos, cannot be less than God.

Trinitarian symbols become empty if they are cut off from their experiential roots, namely the experience of the living God and the experience of the new being in Christ. The Trinitarian dogma became a supporting part of the christological dogma. God himself and not a demigod was present in the human being of Jesus of Nazareth. This move, however, always carried with it the danger that Jesus the Christ would lose his fully human nature. The faithful wanted a God who walked on this earth and who was not involved in the problematic nature of this world. Yet the decision of the Council of Chalcedon that Jesus was fully human and fully divine mitigated against this temptation.

According to Tillich, the Trinitarian symbolism must be understood as an answer to the questions that are implied in the human situation.

---

79. Paul Tillich, *Systematic Theology* (Chicago: University of Chicago Press, 1957), 2:143.
80. Paul Tillich, *Systematic Theology* (London: SCM, 1978), 3:327.

They are threefold: finitude with regard to the essential being of humans as creatures, estrangement in regard to the existential being of humans in time and space, and ambiguity with regard to the participation of humans in universal life. The doctrine of God answers the questions of finitude; the doctrine of Christ the questions of the laws of estrangement; and the doctrine of the Spirit those of ambiguity. Each of these answers is an expression of our relation to the unconditional, and each of these answers follows from a special experience of revelation. This means that Trinitarian reflection results from experiences of revelation or from the working of the divine Spirit. This divine Spirit is present as the Spirit of God and through him in the church and in each individual Christian.

Yet there is still one basic problem: "How can ultimate concern be expressed in more than one divine *hypostasis*?"[81] We encounter this problem in religious devotion: is the prayer that is directed toward one of the three persons directed to the one in distinction from the other two, to whom another prayer may be directed? If there is no difference, why does one not simply address the prayer to God? Yet if there is a difference, do we not encounter then a kind of tritheism? Here the classical terms of *ousia, hypostasis, substantia,* and *persona* are of no help. Even the psychological analogies introduced by Augustine to show the difference between the hypostases provide no solution. Through the criticism of the doctrine of the Trinity during the Enlightenment, Tillich claims there developed in most Protestant churches some kind of christocentric unitarianism in which Christ absorbs in himself God and the Holy Spirit. Tillich concludes: "The doctrine of the Trinity is not closed. It can be neither discarded nor accepted in its traditional form. It must be kept open in order to fulfill its original function—to express in embracing symbols the self-manifestation of the Divine Life to man."[82]

---

81. Ibid., 3:289.
82. Ibid., 3:294.

7

Perspectives of the Present Scene

Through the dominance of Karl Barth in twentieth-century Protestant theology, Trinitarian reflection received an immense boost. This is true for the Reformed side, as we will notice with Jürgen Moltmann and his followers, as well as for the Lutheran wing, as we gather from Wolfhart Pannenberg. Both Moltmann and Pannenberg were students of Karl Barth and were influenced by his Trinitarian theology. Yet, as we will detect, Trinitarian perspectives have been mined far beyond confessional considerations, from liberation theology to feminist concerns and even to orthodox considerations.

The Long Shadow of Karl Barth

Both Moltmann and Pannenberg were not just students of Karl Barth; they became theologians in their own right. Moreover, they were also influenced by Hegel in their appreciation of the doctrine of the Trinity. Yet they did not follow their mentors blindly.

Jürgen Moltmann

Jürgen Moltmann (1926–) readily admits: "Many people view the theological doctrine of the Trinity as a speculation for theological specialists, which has nothing to do with real life."[1] Similar to Rahner, Moltmann observes that most Christians in the West are actually monotheists. That God is one and triune makes little difference to their doctrine of faith and to ethics. Most theological approaches do not begin with the Trinity. This means that this doctrine is of little importance. Since Moltmann senses that today it is important that we talk about the Triune God out of personal experience, he refers to Schleiermacher's statement that God is indirectly experienced in our feeling of absolute dependence. Schleiermacher put the doctrine of the Trinity at the end of his Christian faith, since it was not a direct statement about the Christian self-consciousness. The feeling of absolute dependence refers us to God as one, and the doctrine of the three divine persons is then considered secondary. Moltmann concludes with regard to Schleiermacher: "The doctrine of the Trinity is superfluous."[2]

Moltmann questions whether the experience of God can be adequately expressed in the concept of one God. The feeling of absolute dependence grasps only one side of the relationship with whom we call God. The other side remains unknown because the living relationship, which faith ought to be, considers only my dependence but not God's relationship with me. If it is the relationship of covenant and love, as the biblical witness tells us, it cannot be one-sided; it must be reciprocal. "The expression 'experience of God' therefore does not only mean our experience of God; it also means God's experience with us."[3] The Bible witnesses to God's history with us and also to God's experiences with us. Here believers feel the infinite passion of God's love; God suffers with us, God suffers from us, and God suffers for us. Moltmann concludes that today the discussion about the access to the doctrine of the Trinity is carried out in the context of the question about God's capacity or incapacity to suffer.

Another objection to the doctrine of the Trinity comes from the present-day issue of practical application. There seems to be nothing in the doctrine of the Trinity that is useful. Yet Moltmann contends that this one-sided, pragmatic thinking must be overcome and refers here to the Greek philosophers and fathers of the church, who realized that knowing does not involve just practical application but also wonder. One does not just appropriate what one knows, but one is also transformed through what one perceives. Trinitarian thinking, Moltmann

---

1. Jürgen Moltmann, *The Trinity and the Kingdom of God: The Doctrine of God*, trans. Margaret Kohl (Minneapolis: Fortress Press, 1981), 1.
2. Ibid., 3.
3. Ibid., 4.

claims, "should prepare the way for a liberating and healing concern for the reality that has been destroyed." The question, however, is how we should approach the doctrine of the Trinity. Neither the old idea of one substance and three persons nor the more modern version of one subject and three modes of being seems to suffice. Moltmann therefore attempts "to start with the special Christian tradition of the history of Jesus the Son, and from that to develop a historical doctrine of the Trinity."[4]

Moltmann writes:

> In distinction to the trinity of substance and to the trinity of subject we shall be attempting to develop a social doctrine of the Trinity. We understand the scriptures as the testimony to the history of the Trinity's relations of fellowship, which are open to men and women, and open to the world. This trinitarian hermeneutics leads us to think in terms of relationships and communities; it supersedes the subjective thinking which cannot work without the separation and isolation of its objects.[5]

Against a totally apathetic understanding of God, a God who cannot and does not suffer, Moltmann points to the suffering of Christ as the suffering of the passionate God. "If we start from the pathos of God, then we do not consider God in his absolute nature, but understand him in his passion and in his interest in history."[6] Concerning the Old Testament, Moltmann now refers to the concept of *Shekinah*, a term that is not used in the Old Testament but that denotes the divine presence of God and his glory. Moltmann sees this Shekinah as the present indwelling of God in Israel, the condescension of the eternal one, and the anticipations of the glory of the one who is to come. This history of God's Shekinah allows one to comprehend the Jewish people's history of suffering. While English theology in the nineteenth and twentieth century carried on a discussion about God's possibility, whether God could suffer, Continental theology remained silent on this topic. It was instead picked up by Spanish philosopher Miguel de Unamuno (1864–1936) and Russian philosopher Nikolai Berdyaev (1874–1948), who perceived the tragedy of human freedom as the history of the sufferings of divine love. This leads Moltmann to consider the issue of theodicy.

Though there is an undeniable connection between sin and suffer-

---

4. Ibid., 9, 19.
5. Ibid., 19.
6. Ibid., 26.

ing, innocent suffering, the suffering of the righteous, of the poor, and of children, it is an actual attack on theodicy. The experience of suffering, however, goes beyond the question of guilt and innocence. Yet Moltmann does not provide a real answer. Instead he points out that "suffering reaches as far as love itself, and love grows through the suffering it experiences—that is the signpost that points to true life." This is then connected with the crucified Christ on Golgotha. This leaves the interpretation of Christ's death far from settled. Moltmann considers in the context of theodicy God's freedom and states that this freedom does not just mean Lordship, power, and possession, but rather God's freedom primarily lies in the friendship that he offers us and by which he makes us his friends. But this kind of freedom is vulnerable, since God suffers with human beings who love and becomes their advocate, "thereby throwing open their future to them."[7]

The divine compassion, founded on the biblical witness that God is love, Moltmann summarizes in six propositions: (1) Love is the self-communication of the good. (2) Every self-communication presupposes the capacity for self-differentiation. (3) By deciding to communicate himself, God discloses his own being; otherwise his position would not be as self-communication of the good that he is. (4) That God is love means, in Trinitarian terms, that in eternity and out of the very necessity of his being the Father loves the only begotten Son. (5) With the creation of the world, which is not God but which nonetheless corresponds to him, God's self-humiliation begins—of the self-limitation of the one who is omnipresent, and the suffering of the eternal love. (6) This means that the creation of the world and human beings for freedom and fellowship is always bound up with the process of God's deliverance from the sufferings of his love.[8]

After these preliminary considerations and propositions, Moltmann finally deals with the New Testament witness, centering on "the history of the Son." Moltmann rightly claims that "according to the witness of the New Testament Jesus is manifested as 'the Son.'" But he continues in the next sentence: "His history springs from the co-efficacy of the Father, the Son and the Spirit." Then follows the presupposition: "*The New Testament talks about God by proclaiming in narrative the relationships of the Father, the Son and the Spirit, which are relationships of fellowship and are open to the world.*" This presupposition is expounded in his deliberations about the doctrine of the Trinity. The history of Jesus

---

7. Ibid., 52, 56.
8. Ibid., 57–60.

begins with the statement that "he is the revealer of the Trinity." We read here mainly about Jesus as the Son and the mutual loving of the Father and the Son as a love of like for like that is exclusive. In unique authority Jesus knows and proclaims the Lord of the coming kingdom as his Father. In the synoptic story of Jesus's baptism and call, as well as in Jesus's own manifestation of the Father, Moltmann finds a clearly perceptible Trinitarian form. It is contained in the self-differentiation of God "inherent in the Jewish idea of the divine Wisdom, which is in eternity God's beloved child and seeks a home on earth."[9]

In the giving up of the Son by the Father, Moltmann discerns the revelation of the Trinity. The same is true for the resurrection, since the Father raises the Son through the Spirit. In the encounter with the sending of the creative Spirit through the Son, and in the eschatological consummation and glorification, we again notice a Trinitarian order. In the New Testament we find, according to Moltmann, at Trinitarian coworking of Father, Son, and Spirit, but with changing patterns, namely Father—Spirit—Son, Father—Son—Spirit, and finally Spirit—Son—Father. If the three divine subjects are coactive in the history of God and of his kingdom, then the unity of the Trinity cannot be a monadic unity but must be a union and fellowship of Father, Son, and Spirit. From the high-priestly prayer "that they all may be one. As you, Father, in me and I am in you, may they also be in us" (John 17:21), Moltmann concludes that the fellowship of the disciples with one another is to resemble the union of the Son with the Father. "But not only does it have to resemble that trinitarian union; in addition it has to be a union within this union. It is a *fellowship with* God and, beyond that, a *fellowship in* God. But that presupposes that the triunity is open in such a way that the whole creation can be united with it and can be one within it."[10] This means that the Trinity is an open Trinity for uniting and including the whole of creation.

Once Moltmann has established this open Trinity, he perceives the figure of the Son against the comprehensive horizon of the history of the Triune God with the world. Christology too is now perceived as an open Christology, considering the creation of the world through the Father of Jesus Christ and the perception of the transfiguration of the world through the Holy Spirit, who proceeds from the Father of Jesus, the Son. We now hear again about creation, incarnation, and resurrection and glorification. Moltmann concludes:

9. Ibid., 64–65, 74.
10. Ibid., 95–96.

> The trinitarian movement of the sending of the Spirit from the Father through the Son may still be viewed as a "work outwards" although it too is preceded by inner changes in the divine Trinity—changes from which this movement arises. But the trinitarian movement of the gathering of the Spirit through the Son to the Father is at work "inwards," a movement of the Trinity; by virtue of the opening of the Trinity in the sending of the Spirit, however, it is a movement into which the whole creation is gathered.[11]

Since all things are assembled under Christ as the head, and all tongues confess him as Lord, all people and things partake of the inner-Trinitarian life of God. The Triune God is at home in the world, and history exists out of his inexhaustible glory. In the end, this is Moltmann's conviction, that there will be a universal homecoming of all that exists. With this foundational Trinitarian presupposition, Moltmann is now ready to criticize Christian monotheists of every kind, from Arius to Karl Rahner.

Moltmann asserts that since the dogma of the Trinity evolved out of Christology, this doctrine cannot be termed "a speculation." Rather, "On the contrary, it is the theological premise for christology and soteriology."[12] One might ask here how it can be the premise for Christology if it evolved out of Christology. Trinitarian and christological controversies seem to be so much intertwined that at least in the first four centuries the debates on the Trinity and on Christ cannot be easily separated. Moltmann asserts that a strict monotheism has to be theocratically conceived and implemented, as shown by Islam. Therefore the conquest of the fundamental monotheistic monarchic idea through the doctrine of the Trinity was one of the great theological achievements of the early church. For Christians, at stake was the capacity for Christ to be redeemer and reconciler if he were not fully equal with God. Even Karl Barth is not appreciated by Moltmann, since he puts the divine Lordship before the Trinity and therefore establishes a Christian monotheism under the guise of the doctrine of the Trinity. Karl Rahner too developed his doctrine of the Trinity talking about a single divine subject in three "distinct modes of subsistence."[13]

---

11. Ibid., 127.
12. Ibid., 129.
13. Ibid., 144.

Moltmann perceptively notes that "trinitarian theology grew up through the theological remoulding of philosophical terms."[14] He rightly claims that it seems to make more sense theologically to start from the biblical history rather than from philosophical postulates. Since in the biblical witness we encounter Father, Son, and Holy Spirit and at the same time one God, there seems to be a personal self-differentiation of God, and not merely a modal differentiation, for only persons, not modes of being or modes of subjectivity, can be one with one another. The concept of God's unity must be perceived in the perichoresis of the divine persons, in their mutual fellowship and interpenetration. It is no surprise that for Moltmann the distinction between the economic Trinity, meaning the revealed Trinity in the process of salvation, and the immanent Trinity, meaning how God is in himself, is no speculative matter but one of utmost significance. "The distinction between an immanent Trinity and economic Trinity secures God's liberty and his grace. It is the logically necessary presupposition for the correct understanding of God's saving revelation."[15] While the immanent Trinity cannot undo what the economic Trinity does, and vice versa, the two form a continuity and merge into each other. But they have different purposes. The immanent Trinity is the object of doxology, while the economic Trinity is the object of kerygmatic and practical theology. How God is in himself leads to praise and adoration, and how he is for us leads to salvific consequences.

Salvation for Moltmann is an event neither of the past nor of the hoped-for future. The history of salvation is the history of the Triune God, who draws us into and includes us in his eternal triune life, with all the fullness of its relationships. This means that we become part of this triune interpenetration. Moltmann explains: "The perichoretic at-oneness of the triune God corresponds to the experience of the community of Christ, the community which the spirit unites through respect, and affection and love. The more open-mindedly people live with one another, for one another and in one another in the fellowship of the Spirit, the more they will become one with the Son and the Father, and one in the Son and the Father (John 17:21)."[16] The Christian community, then, becomes a semblance of the Trinity, at least in its interpersonal relationships. When we look at the Scripture passage to which Moltmann refers, we notice that such consequences for the

---

14. Ibid., 148.
15. Ibid., 151.
16. Ibid., 157–58.

Christian community are not phrased in the indicative mode but in the form of a petition for the future. Here Moltmann is much more optimistic.

The same holds true for his perception of the immanent Trinity. He claims that with unveiled face already here and now we recognize in the obscurity of history the glory of the Triune God. While we can only in a fragmentary way express the mystery of the Trinity, Moltmann is adamant that the concepts and terms must correspond to and be suited to the thing that has to be conceived and comprehended. Keeping this in mind, he approaches the "constitution of the Trinity." In explaining the significance of Father, Son, and Holy Spirit, Moltmann points out that the Christian understanding of God the Father is defined by the relationship to the Son and the relationship of the Son Jesus Christ to God the Father. The Son is the eternal Son of the Father and has everything in common with him, "except his 'Personal' characteristics." While the personal concepts associated with Father and Son are fairly clear, "the 'third Person' of the Trinity has a certain anonymity. It is not always clear from the New Testament that the Holy Spirit is not merely a divine energy, but a divine subject too." Moltmann also concedes: "The concept of the Holy Spirit really has no organic connection with the doctrine of God the Father and the Son."[17] Nevertheless, he asserts that the Holy Spirit is of the same essence or substance as the Father.

The issue of the *filioque*, that the Holy Spirit proceeds from both the Father and the Son, is clearly seen by Moltmann as divisive. Yet, as he declares, this need not be so, since Orthodox theologians admit that the Son is not removed from the procession of the Spirit from the Father, nor uninvolved in it. Moltmann therefore suggests that the Western church should admit that the *filioque* is a later addition to the creedal text and was in no way intended as an attack on the Eastern church. It was simply an attempt to interpret and define that Trinitarian statement of the Nicene Creed more clearly. Moltmann suggests that the *filioque* should be withdrawn, and at the same time a common discussion about the doctrine of the Trinity should commence. One must remember that Moltmann contends that the aim of the affirmation of the procession of the Holy Spirit from the Father alone was to emphasize the Spirit's full divinity. Since the Cappadocian theologians talked about the Son's relationship to the Holy Spirit, calling him "the Spirit

---

17. Ibid., 162, 166, 168–69.

of the Son" and the "Spirit of Christ," we might then be allowed to promulgate a statement that also includes the Son in the procession of the Holy Spirit. Moltmann suggests that we should talk about *"the Holy Spirit who proceeds from the Father of the Son."*[18] This would mean an indirect participation of the Son in the procession of the Spirit from the Father, in the sense that this participation is mediated by the Father's Fatherhood.

Important for Moltmann's understanding of the Trinity is the concept of perichoresis, first introduced by John of Damascus.[19] By virtue of their love, the Father, Son, and Spirit live in one another to such an extent and are developed in one another to the extent that they are one. This is a process of most perfect and intense empathy. Yet through their personal characteristics they are distinguished from one another as Father, Son, and Holy Spirit. It is this oneness and still distinction that makes the Trinity so valuable. Moltmann explains: "Monotheism was and is the religion of patriarchy, just as pantheism is probably the religion of earlier matriarchy. It is only the doctrine of the Trinity ... which makes the first approach towards overcoming sexist language in the concept of God. It leads to a fellowship of men and women without privilege and subjection."[20]

When Moltmann talks about the kingdom of freedom, we notice how important the doctrine of the Trinity is for his concept of the kingdom of God. From the idea of divine Lordship comes the idea of a theocracy, either of a political or a clerical version, while the doctrine of the Trinity constitutes the church as a community free of dominion. Moltmann asks us here to return to Joachim of Fiore and "to rediscover the truth of his Trinitarian view of history."[21] According to Moltmann, Joachim attempted in a modalistic way to divide the history of the kingdom chronologically in three successive eras. Yet for Moltmann the kingdom of the Son presupposes and absorbs the kingdom of the Father, so that the kingdom of the Spirit presupposes the kingdom of the Son and absorbs it. There are three continually present strata and transitions in this kingdom history. Joachim already viewed the Trinitarian history of the kingdom as the history of humanity's progressive and growing liberty. Father, Son, and Holy Spirit as the three determining factors

---

18. Ibid., 185.
19. See John of Damascus, *Exposition of the Orthodox Faith* (NPNF[2] 9:91), where John uses the term *perichoresis*, albeit speaking of the permeation of "divinity and flesh" in Christ, whereas concerning the Trinity he does not use this term. There he speaks about "union."
20. Moltmann, *Trinity and the Kingdom of God*, 165.
21. Ibid., 203.

of the history of God's kingdom point to the eschatological kingdom of glory, in which people will finally, wholly, and completely be gathered into the eternal life of the Triune God and be deified. Then the history of the kingdom of God will correspond to the freedom of servants, children, and God's friends. These strata in the experience of freedom will involve a process of maturing through experiences that are continually new. Since "freedom itself is indivisible and all-comprehensive ... every partial freedom presses forward to total freedom and to the freedom of the whole creation."[22] For Moltmann the Trinity foreshadows the eschatological perfection, when the whole creation will be lifted up into union with God.

Roughly ten years after the publication of his book *The Trinity and the Kingdom of God*, Moltmann published *History and the Triune God: Contributions to Trinitarian Theology*, basically a collection of essays. In the introduction he states that within the past ten years the doctrine of the Trinity has become important in formulating the distinguishing Christian characteristic. Especially four moments have become important: (1) the concept of the Trinitarian fellowship, (2) the issue of masculine and feminine metaphors, (3) the further development of the Trinitarian theology of the cross, and finally (4) perspectives of a Trinitarian view of history.

The first point evolved directly from Moltmann's social concept of the Trinity. The Triune God is perceived as a community; it invites into its community and becomes the prototype for a just and livable community in the world of nature and the world of humans. According to this understanding, the community of the Holy Spirit, which undergirds the unity of the church, is not a monarchic centralism but the unified people of God, unified by the unity of Father, Son, and Holy Spirit.[23]

In the Trinitarian theology of the cross, Moltmann asks what the suffering and dying of Christ means for God. As the Father of Jesus Christ, God becomes the cosufferer, which leads to the divine passion and to

---

22. Ibid., 222.
23. When feminist theology posed the question of male and female metaphors for the Godhead and especially for the persons of the Trinity, it was especially the male domination and the patriarchy that were questioned. Here it was again that Trinitarian concept of community that proved attractive. The Trinitarian concept of the reciprocal perichoresis of the three divine persons expressed a communication that disallowed domination. "The divine persons are there for one another: the Father for the Son, the Son for the Father, the Spirit for the Father and the Son. They achieve this perfect representation for one another.... They interpenetrate each other mutually to such a degree that they exist in one another and indwell one another mutually" (Jürgen Moltmann, *History and the Triune God: Contributions to Trinitarian Theology*, trans. John Bowden [Minneapolis: Fortress Press, 1991], xv).

the pain of the Father. "In this way it becomes possible to see the cross of Golgotha in the heart of the triune God, so as to perceive the revelation of God in the crucified Jesus."[24] With regard to the Trinitarian concept of history, the ideas of Joachim of Fiore loom in the background. If the historical recognition of the Triune God discloses the reality as history with an eschatological goal, then it makes sense to perceive a movement from the initial creation via the historical reconciliation to the eschatological completion. Past, present, and future are directed toward the future in which time is completed and finished. The realms of nature, grace, and glory are then three stages on the way to completion. This shows for Moltmann what fertile ground for theology the doctrine of the Trinity has become. When he remarks about the concepts of an author, "I certainly cannot follow all the author's speculative trains of thought," then this may also hold true with Moltmann's own Trinitarian proposals.[25] While the systematic constructs are impressive, the biblical undergirding is quite often very selective. This also leads to undue speculation, especially about the inner Trinity. At that point one might want to ask: How does Moltmann know this?

Thomas F. Torrance

Thomas F. Torrance (1913-2007), the premier Scottish systematic theologian and former doctoral student of Karl Barth, devoted three books to the doctrine of the Trinity. In his 1988 publication, *The Trinitarian Faith: The Evangelical Theology of the Ancient Catholic Church*, he identifies the immanent Trinity as the economic Trinity, saying: "In the Gospel God has revealed himself to us as Father, Son and Holy Spirit, but in such a way that we know that he is in himself what he is toward us in his saving acts in history, eternally Father, Son and Holy Spirit in his one divine being, and that what he is eternally in himself as Father, Son and Holy Spirit, he is in his activity toward us through the Son and in the Spirit."[26] The movement of the divine activity toward us is from the Father, through the Son, and in the Holy Spirit, while the movement from us to God is in reverse order. While Torrance follows in this book the line of thought of the Nicene Creed, in contrast to Barth, he covers the Trinity in the last chapter.

---

24. Ibid., xvi.
25. Ibid., xvii; he says this with reference to Norbert Hoffmann and his book *Kreuz und Trinität: Zur Theologie der Sühne* (Einsiedeln: Johannes-Verlag, 1982).
26. Thomas F. Torrance, *The Trinitarian Faith: The Evangelical Theology of the Ancient Catholic Church* (Edinburgh: T&T Clark, 1988), 5.

In this last chapter, called "The Triunity of God," Torrance masterfully traces the development of the doctrine of the Trinity, even conceding with regard to the Council of Constantinople concerning the Holy Spirit it said that "'he proceeds from the *being* of the Father' which it had not said of the Son." It also did not speak of the Holy Spirit as *homoousios* with the Father. But then Torrance adds that the confession of "the Holy Spirit as 'Lord and Giver of Life, who proceeds from the Father, who with the Father and the Son together is worshiped and glorified', was meant to rank the Holy Spirit fully with the Father in the lordship and glory of the Godhead."[27] The creedal pronouncements in the Nicene-Constantinopolitan Creed about the Holy Spirit had the effect of establishing the doctrine of the Holy Spirit as perfectly coequal with the Father and the Son in the Trinity.

But Torrance also notes: "Though grounding the unity of the Godhead in the Father as the unique and exclusive Principle of Deity and thus as the one Cause of the being and existence of the Son and the Spirit, the Cappadocian way of steering between unipersonalism and tritheism . . . led to a serious difference between East and West." Western theologians went for the *filioque*, while those in the East maintained that the Holy Spirit proceeded from the Father only, in order to preserve the unity of the divine monarchy. It was then up to Cyril of Alexandria, who in Torrance's eyes might have provided a mediating point with his doctrine of coinherence in the one identical being of God. According to Cyril, Father, Son, and Holy Spirit mutually indwell and contain one another while remaining what they are. The result was, as Torrance sees it, a "succinct theological expression in the identification of the *Monarchia* with the *Triunity* of God."[28] There was one being of the Godhead in the Trinity and at the same time a consubstantial Trinity in unity.

Evidently this largely historical treatment of the doctrine of the Trinity did not suffice, because in his 1996 publication, *The Christian Doctrine of God: One Being Three Persons*, Torrance begins with the telling statement: "This monograph is devoted to clarifying understanding of the most profound article of the Christian Faith, the doctrine of the Holy Trinity." He also concedes at the outset: "The Holy Scriptures do not give us dogmatic propositions about the Trinity, but they do present us with definite witness to the oneness and differentiation between the Father, the Son and the Holy Spirit."[29] Especially impor-

---

27. Ibid., 334–35.
28. Ibid., 336–37, 340.

tant for Torrance is the formulation of the *homoousion* at the Council of Nicea, because it provided a deeper understanding of the gospel and the all-important relation between the incarnate Son and God the Father. Yet he also claims that this term is not sacrosanct beyond reconsideration, since all theological terms and concepts fall short of the realities they intend and are open to further modification.

Torrance starts with the Christian notion of God, which is to be understood from within the unique, definitive, and final self-disclosure of God in Jesus Christ in accordance with the proclamation of the gospel and its actualization through the Holy Spirit. Torrance asserts: "In sharp contrast with every other religion, Christianity stands for the fact that in Jesus Christ God has communicated to us his *Word* and has imparted to us his *Spirit*, so that we may really know him as he is in himself although not apart from his saving activity in history."[30] In distinction from Thomas Aquinas, there is no separate doctrine of the one God without the doctrine of the Triune God. Especially that separation, Torrance maintains, has intended to treat the doctrine of the Trinity as irrelevant, only of peripheral significance for the Christian faith and for Christian living. Yet Barth, per Torrance, has rescued the doctrine of the Trinity and put it back again at center stage. Contrary to Rahner, Torrance does not want to collapse the economic Trinity and the ontological Trinity into one, but of course he knows very well that only through the economic Trinity do we understand who God really is in his very being, namely Father, Son, and Holy Spirit. The Christian conceptions of God for us and God in himself must be inseparably held together.

According to Torrance, the Trinity is essential for God's self-disclosure and for our understanding of this self-disclosure. He writes: "Only in Christ, God become man for us, does he communicate his self-revelation to us by the power of his Spirit in such redeeming and enlightening way that we may apprehend it and, human beings though we are, really know God in himself, both in his oneness as the Lord God and in his differentiation of Father, Son and Holy Spirit, one Being, three Persons."[31]

There is only one way of knowing about God and knowing God properly, and that is through his triune self-disclosure. "God reveals himself

---

29. Thomas F. Torrance, *The Christian Doctrine of God: One Being Three Persons* (Edinburgh: T&T Clark, 1996), ix.
30. Ibid., 3.
31. Ibid., 15.

through himself, and what God communicates to us is not something of himself but his very Self, through God from true God." The triune self-disclosure is therefore not partial or incomplete but the full and comprehensive self-disclosure of God. Nevertheless, "the incarnation must not be understood as involving any surrender of God's transcendence, or any compromising of his eternal freedom." While Torrance talks about the full self-disclosure of God, he maintains the distinction between the ontological and the economic Trinity. This allows for the full self-disclosure, maintaining at the same time the ontological being of God. In talking about the economic Trinity "as the freely predetermined manifestation in the history of salvation of the eternal Trinity which God himself was before the foundation of the world, and eternally is," we notice the influence of Calvin.[32] Everything is prearranged, and the world is the stage on which God reveals his glory. But Torrance is cognizant of the limits of theological reflections when he writes:

> The God whom we have come to know through his infinite condescension in Jesus Christ, we know to be infinitely greater than what we can ever conceive, so that it would be sheer presumption and theological sin on our part to identify the Trinitarian structures in *our* thinking and speaking of God with the *real* constitutive relations in the triune Being-in-Communion of the Godhead. All true theological concepts and statements inevitably fall short of the God to whom they refer.[33]

Especially by comparing scientific reasoning with theological reflection, Torrance is mindful of the provisional character of all our theological statements. He therefore rightly concludes his investigation by pointing to the liturgy of the church, which has been intrinsically Trinitarian.

Torrance picks up the doctrine of the Trinity again in a collection of essays, *Trinitarian Perspectives: Toward Doctrinal Agreement*. There he calls the doctrine of the Trinity "the innermost heart of the Christian faith, the central dogma of classical theology, the fundamental grammar of our knowledge of God."[34] The reason for his highly appreciative words is that the doctrine of the Trinity manifests that God has opened himself to us in such a way that we may know him in the inner relations of his divine Being and have communion with him in his divine

---

32. Ibid., 21, 108–9.
33. Ibid., 110.
34. Thomas F. Torrance, *Trinitarian Perspectives: Toward Doctrinal Agreement* (Edinburgh: T&T Clark, 1999 [1994]), 1.

life as Father, Son, and Holy Spirit. This self-communication of God sets Christianity apart from every other religion. In other religions God remains ultimately lawful, namely as incomprehensible, whom we cannot know in himself and in his inner life. "Christianity stands for something very different: the fact that in Jesus Christ God has communicated to us his *Word* and has imparted to us his *Spirit*, so that we may really know him as he is in himself."[35]

Especially important are Torrance's remarks about the Agreed Statement on the Holy Trinity of 1991 between the Orthodox Church and the World Alliance of Reformed Churches. Torrance lists several important features of this doctrinal consensus:[36]

1. Concerning the historic formula of one being in three persons, it was often held that Father, Son and Holy Spirit are personal; the one Being of God, common to the three persons, however, is not. But now it was asserted that God is a personal being made known to us in his self-disclosure as Father, Son, and Holy Spirit. God therefore is intrinsically personal.

2. Concerning the ultimate principle of the Godhead, in which all three persons share equally, "the whole indivisible Being of God belongs to each of them as it belongs to all of them."[37] There is no subordination in the Trinity, and there are no degrees of deity among the divine persons. All three share equally in the "monarchy" of God.

3. Since the doctrine of the one monarchy of God is not restricted to one divine person, and since there is the complete interpenetration of the three divine persons in one another within the one indivisible being of the Trinity, the procession of the Spirit from the Father can be considered in a different way. Torrance contends that the one Being of God the Father belongs as fully to the Son and the Spirit as to the Father, which then means "that the Holy Spirit proceeds ultimately from the Triune Being of the Godhead." Since God is Spirit, "'Spirit' cannot be restricted to the Person of the Holy Spirit but applies to the whole Being of God to which the Father and the Son with the Holy Spirit belong in their eternal Communion with one another."[38] There are not two ultimate principles in God from which the Spirit would proceed, as the *filioque* was interpreted by the East. The procession of the Spirit must be thought of in a holistic way as a procession from

---

35. Ibid., 2.
36. Ibid., 111–14.
37. Ibid., 112.
38. Ibid., 112–13.

the completely mutual relations within the one indivisible being of the Lord God, who is Trinity in unity and unity in Trinity. This way the divisive issue of the *filioque* is overcome.

4. Finally, the agreement overcomes the division between Western theology, which moves from the one being of God to the three persons, and Eastern theology, which in reverse moves from the three persons to the one being of God. Torrance concludes that "It is preeminently a statement on that dynamic Triunity of God as Trinity in Unity and Unity in Trinity."[39]

While it is highly desirable that the ancient controversies be overcome by moving the conversations to another level, one wonders how these results hold up against the biblical testimony. As Torrance himself realized, the biblical documents do not give us a dogmatic statement on the Trinity. At most they give us some indications about the one God, who works in and through different manifestations. Anything further is highly speculative, including what has been agreed on between the Orthodox and the Reformed concerning the inner-Trinitarian relations. We simply do not know anything beyond the economic Trinity. The rest is shaky inference.

Robert W. Jenson

Especially in the late twentieth century, many theologians followed the lead of Barth and Moltmann to emphasize the need for Trinitarian language and reflection. American Lutheran theologian Robert W. Jenson (1930–) in 1982 wrote *God according to the Gospel: The Triune Identity*. His goal was to make the Trinitarian tradition lucid and "to develop proposals for its reform and further development."[40] He thinks that especially in an age of pluralism it is vitally important to answer the question as to what God we are talking about. In the Christian church Father, Son, and Holy Spirit occupy the place occupied by Yahweh in Israel. This Trinitarian naming of God goes all the way back to the New Testament. This Trinitarian phrase immediately summarizes the primal Christian interpretation of God, since it embodies the church's primal experience of God. "The gospel identifies its God thus: God is the one who raised Israel's Jesus from the dead. The whole task of theology

---

39. Ibid., 113–14.
40. Robert W. Jenson, *God according to the Gospel: The Triune Identity* (Philadelphia: Fortress Press, 1982), xii.

can be described as the unpacking of this sentence in various ways. One of these produces the church's trinitarian language and thought."[41]

Jenson asserts that in order to identify the God of the gospel we must identify Jesus, since that God "is" Jesus. The Trinitarian discourse becomes evident especially in prayer, when Christians speak to the Father, with the Son, and in the Spirit while addressing their prayer to God. Jenson asserts that when we pray "to" God, and it is not determined also "with" and "in," then it is not the true God whom we identify in our address but rather some distant and timelessly uninvolved divinity. Therefore it is decisive that our address to God is always Trinitarian. That God is not some god but has a proper name "means among other things that not all addresses to deity are equally true." One can simply err at the very base of religious life. Jenson assures us "that we may in God's own Spirit approach him as Father, because we do so with the man Jesus."[42] This Trinitarian approach to God encapsulates the specifically Christian proclamation and the Christian faith.

It comes as no surprise that Jenson devotes the first volume of his *Systematic Theology* to the Triune God. Starting from the biblical narrative, he finds the crucifixion especially problematic for Trinitarian discourse, since the one called "Father" here hands the one called "Son" over to oppositional and deadly creatures. Here the identity of God "must be constituted precisely in the integration of this abandonment."[43] Yet there is the Lord's resolve to meet and overcome death in the resurrection. With regard to the Trinity, Jenson points to the Johannine Jesus, who "speaks in his own person as one of the Trinity and straight-forwardly of the Spirit as another such. He thus speaks from within God himself. So speaking, he speaks of 'the Father' by whom he and the Spirit are sent and with whom they are one, who is his own role with them." Therefore he finds the Gospel of John as "a chief New Testament inspiration of developed trinitarian doctrine."[44]

For Jenson the triune name and the Trinitarian logic and iconology determine the language of the Christian faith. Otherwise other explicit Christian teachings will become arbitrary puzzles. Jenson then postulates: "Christians can live only in a dramatic and linguistic space determined by the coordinates of the triune name: to the Father, with the Son, in the Spirit." Father, Son, and Holy Spirit are the three persons of

---

41. Ibid., 21.
42. Ibid., 186–87.
43. Robert W. Jenson, *Systematic Theology*, vol. 1, *The Triune God* (New York: Oxford University Press, 1997), 65.
44. Ibid., 89, 93.

the story that is at once God's story and ours. They are the three agents of what the one God does with the creatures. They are the one united agency of the Triune God. Jenson is concerned that the Triune God may be split into a tritheism or even into four identities, Father, Son, Spirit, and the Trinity. He therefore suggests that the three be treated "not as persons but as inner functions of the exclusively personal Trinity."[45]

Concerning the *filioque*, Jenson asserts that it cannot be abandoned, because, according to the biblical narrative, "the Spirit indeed comes to us not only from the Father but also from the Son." According to John 20:22, the disciples received the Holy Spirit from Jesus Christ. The *filioque* then reads this giving of the Holy Spirit into God himself. That the Son is begotten by the Father, and that the Spirit proceeds ineffably otherwise from the Father, are irreducible starting points for Christian thinking. Overcoming the impasse of the *filioque*, Jenson suggests: "the Father begets the Son and freely breathes his Spirit; the Spirit liberates the Father for the Son and the Son from and for the Father; the Son is begotten and liberated, and so reconciles the Father with the future his Spirit is." Whether this suggestion is intelligible and solves the issue at stake of how the Spirit is related to the Father remains to be seen. Nevertheless, Jenson is optimistic, since he is convinced that "the very function of trinitarian propositions [is] to say that the relations that appear in the biblical narrative between Father, Son, and Spirit are the truth about God himself.[46]" And that truth to discover is the task of theology. While we may agree to this charge for theology, we must also remember that according to the Lutheran principle of "Scripture alone," we cannot know more than Scripture discloses to us. The rest is speculation. It is exactly this limitation that seems to have been transgressed by Jenson.

Colin Gunton

Colin Gunton (1941–2003), British systematic theologian and former doctoral student of Robert Jenson, writes in the preface of the first edition of his book *The Promise of Trinitarian Theology* that "the loss of the trinitarian dimension has gravely impoverished the Christian tradition over recent decades, and one of the hopeful signs of recent years has been a renewal of interest." Barely six years later he writes in the preface to the second edition: "Suddenly we are all trinitarians, or so it

---

45. Ibid., 93–94, 123.
46. Ibid., 150, 161.

would seem. As the result of the number of influences, both churchly and secular, the doctrine of the Trinity is now discussed in places where even a short time ago it would have been regarded as an irrelevance." Since the doctrine of the Trinity is now used for many different purposes, Gunton warns against two dangers, "of limiting expression to the economic Trinity and of using an ontological trinitarianism as an immanent principle of reality."[47] One should not collapse the immanent Trinity into the economic Trinity, because the former serves also as a foundation for the relative independence and integrity of worldly reality and thus for human freedom. On the other hand, if the immanent or ontological Trinity is used as a kind of principle saying that because God is like this then the world is or ought to be like that, the danger of idealizing and projecting looms large. The Trinity is in this case used as a model for personal relations in human social order. Gunton sees the chief defect in turning Christ into a world principle at the expense of Jesus of Nazareth, and then treating the cross as a focus for the suffering of God rather than as the center of history, in which God overcomes sin and evil.

In order to avoid these twin dangers, Gunton follows Irenaeus, who provides an essentially biblically based starting point. Irenaeus discerns that the economy of creation, recapitulation, and redemption is constituted by the achievement of the Father's work by the Son and the Spirit. They mediate the will and work of the Father, "perfecting through redemption of what was created perfect in the beginning." His careful self-limitation to Scripture avoids speculations about the being of the immanent Trinity and holds together the immanent and the economic Trinity. According to Irenaeus, "the Son and the Spirit are the ways by which God himself is *personally* involved in the created order." They are in some ways the two hands of God. As Gunton explains: "Here, as in Scripture, the Father calls the tune, so to speak, and is played in different modes by his two hands."[48] It does not follow from this, however, that because of the distinctive forms of action of the three persons of the Triune God they can be conceived to be or to act separately. There is no way of severing the Spirit from Jesus Christ or from God the Father. The works of the Triune God are undivided. To speak with the metaphor of Irenaeus, the left hand knows and approves of what the right hand does, and vice versa. Gunton cau-

---

47. Colin E. Gunton, *The Promise of Trinitarian Theology*, 2nd ed. (London: T&T Clark, 1997 [1991]), xi, xv, xxi.
48. Ibid., xxii, xxv, xxvii.

tions again: "There must be limits on speculation, certainly about to the inner being of the deity, if the doctrine of the ontological Trinity is not to fly free from its basis in revelation." He contends that "the value of the theology of the Trinity lies more in enabling a rethinking of the topics of theology and culture than in offering a privileged view of the being of God."[49] It is important for him to establish a concrete rather than a theoretical trinitarianism and to think about the world and the church in a Trinitarian way through Christ and the Holy Spirit.

Gunton then exemplifies this concrete trinitarianism by looking at church and society. The church is the human institution that is called in Christ and the Spirit to echo the communion that God is eternally. It is therefore called to be a being of persons-in-relation that receives its character as communion by virtue of its relation to God, and so is enabled to reflect something of that being in the world. Similarly, taking Father, Son, and Spirit by virtue of their otherness-in-relation, so that each particular is unique and absolutely necessary to the being of the whole, is a model in its own way for our being in society. We are relational beings and as such necessary for the whole societal web to function. That indispensable interrelatedness extends beyond the human level to all of creation. Gunton observes: "As the creation of the love of God the world is not an impersonal process, a machine or a self-developing organism . . . but that which itself has a destiny along with the human."[50]

The doctrine of the Trinity enables us to understand the world as truly created by God real and good, but also in continued dependence on his conserving action. Creation through the Son and the Spirit affirms the relatedness of the world to its maker and also its dynamic teleology, directed to eschatological perfection. As much as he can, Gunton shies away from speculation, keeping in mind the unknowability of God, which is to preserve the freedom and, so to speak, personal privacy of God's being. "To be personal is to exist in relation, indeed, but also to be defined by one's otherness to all other beings. There are therefore strict limits to what we may claim to know of any other person, let alone of God." There are the limits of our personal and conceptual possibilities and also limits of God's revelation. Keeping those in mind, God is not totally unknowable. There are concepts for our knowledge of God, such as the understanding of God as the personal Creator and Redeemer of the world. But in what sense, asks Gunton, is God per-

---

49. Ibid., xxix.
50. Ibid., 14.

sonal? His answer is that God "is personal as being three persons in relation, of having his being in what Father, Son and Holy Spirit give to and receive from each other in the freedom of their unknowable eternity."[51] To be personal, according to Gunton, means to be one whose being consists in relations of mutual constitution with other persons. Being, therefore, is being in relation. Communion is then a function of the relations of all three, Father, Son, and Spirit. Gunton concludes:

> Thus the Father is what he is not only because he begets the Son, but also because the Son responds in the way made known in his obedience as incarnate, and so can be understood to be the one who shares in the constitution of the being of God by means of his eternal response of obedience and love. Similarly, the movement of the Spirit can be argued also to be constitutive of the being of God the Father, in that it is the Spirit who ensures that the love of Father and Son is not simply mutual love, but moves outward, so that creation and redemption are indeed free acts of God, but acts grounded in his being as love.[52]

The question must be raised again, as Gunton himself does, whether this is "a matter of pointless speculation." He denies that it is and shows that it is not pointless. Nevertheless, it is highly speculative.

Gunton also upholds the *homoousion*, since it is able to express that oneness of the being as an act of God in the Trinity. And he affirms that the Son and the Spirit are "as truly and fully God as is the Father, in and through their economically subordinate functions of doing the will of the Father in the world." While *homoousios* and perichoresis are seen as vital devices to ensure the Trinitarian language, "it is equally important to maintain a way of speaking of the distinct modes of divine action that are made known in biblical revelation." While one appreciates the reference to the scriptural basis, one still wonders whether that basis is really foundational. But Gunton assures us that he undertakes the struggle for an adequate Trinitarian conceptuality to express coherently and as well as possible "what it is that we are granted to know of the God to whom we are related by the Spirit through Jesus Christ."[53] It is not speculation that moves Gunton in his deliberations but the concern to express and know as well as possible the God whom we encounter in the biblical documents. That endeavor must certainly be lauded.

---

51. Ibid., 193, 195.
52. Ibid., 196.
53. Ibid., 198, 200.

Ted Peters

Ted Peters (1941–), an American Lutheran theologian, rejects the idea that the Trinitarian doctrine is a mystery. As a doctrine it is a construction for "bringing faith to understanding, for the purpose of explaining the significance of what happened in the Christ event."[54] He follows the lead of Jenson to incorporate the dynamics of temporal movement into the proper life of God and to perceive the deity of Christ as the final outcome of the divine intercourse with creation. "Eternity, then, would incorporate the consummation of time into the eschaton, which is the reality of God. Between now and then the future is genuinely open, and God's freedom to act is maintained."[55] Important for Peters is the temporal moment, which he introduces into the concept of the Trinity.

Instructive for our later discussion is his admission that "in the construction of the doctrine of the Trinity there is no intrinsic interest in the number three. . . . We need not assume that the three persons of the Trinity are of the same kind or order." Through the introduction of a temporal dynamic work in the divine eternity there is a clear preference for "becoming" over "being." The Trinitarian being of God is still open, and "God has a future in history as well as an eschatological future." Having traced a host of issues and problems and having attempted to solve them even-handedly, Peters concludes with five theses, the first of which reads: *"To understand God as Trinity in the economy of salvation requires that God be both temporal and eternal."*[56] While the symbol of the Father communicates the sense of the beyond, the symbol of the Son communicates a sense of the intimate, and the Holy Spirit as love binds the two, assuring us that we are speaking here of one divine reality. We notice here that the Holy Spirit is much more a functional entity than a personal one. Important for Peters is that by being triune God is perceived as both transcendent and immanent, eternal and temporal, independent and dependable in the eschatological fulfillment of creation and history. He also cautions that *"the image of the immanent Trinity is not be used as a model for human society; rather, we should seek to transform human society on the basis of our vision of the coming kingdom of God in which God alone is the absolute."*[57]

---

54. Ted Peters, *God as Trinity: Relationality and Temporality in Divine Life* (Louisville, KY: Westminster John Knox, 1993), 17.
55. Ibid., 23.
56. Ibid., 24, 25, 173.
57. Ibid., 184.

Wolfhart Pannenberg

Stanley Grenz (1950–2005), a former doctoral student of Wolfhart Pannenberg (1928–2014) and a leading evangelical theologian, speaks for many Christians when he writes: "For as long as I can remember I have been a trinitarian. Like most Christians who have been raised in the church, at an early age I came to accept as self-evident that God is three persons yet one divine being."[58] In his *Systematic Theology* Pannenberg attempts to show in a historical analysis that the doctrine of the Trinity is indeed self-evident. The doctrine of the Trinity, according to Pannenberg, grew out of Christology. In the light of Easter, the Son had to appear as the Son of the Father whom Jesus had proclaimed. According to Romans 1:3, Jesus was accorded the Sonship of God through his resurrection from the dead. The concept of Christ's preexistence does not mitigate against this, because, according to apocalyptic thinking, that which is anticipated as the eschatological completion, namely the resurrection of Jesus, is already present in heaven.[59] The full Sonship we find in Jesus Christ, who is called the *kyrios*. The confession of Jesus Christ as the only *kyrios* does not diminish the confession to the one God, because everything comes from the one God, the Father, but at the same time is mediated through the one *kyrios* (1 Cor 8:6).

This correlation between Father and Son is complemented by a third member, the Holy Spirit. The Spirit is the medium of the communion of Jesus with the Father. Evidently, the communion of Jesus as the Son with God as the Father can only be expressed if one also talks about a third, namely the Holy Spirit. But "so long as the Spirit was not differentiated from the Son as a separate hypostatic entity, he could be viewed as the power of the Father filling the Son, while the Son for his part could be seen as the Word of the Father in which the Spirit of the Father expresses itself. On the other hand, one might see in the hypostatic differentiation of the Spirit as a third alongside the Father and the Son a consequence of the hypostatizing of the Son."[60] While Pannenberg discerns in Paul an occasional identification of *kyrios* and *pneuma* ("Spirit"), he does not concede a full identity of both, because the *pneuma* is the Spirit of the Lord (2 Cor 3:17). Pannenberg also admits that "although the concept of the Holy Spirit of God is a familiar one

---

58. Stanley J. Grenz, *Rediscovering the Triune God: The Trinity in Contemporary Theology* (Minneapolis: Fortress Press, 2004), ix.
59. Wolfhart Pannenberg, *Systematic Theology*, trans. Geoffrey W. Bromiley (Grand Rapids: Eerdmans, 1991), 1:265.
60. Ibid., 1:267, 269.

from the OT, only in connection with the relation of Father and Son is the Spirit seen to be an independent third principle of the divine reality."[61]

When the councils of Nicea and Constantinople affirmed the full Godhead of the Son and the Spirit, these decisions implied that the forms of God's presence and self-disclosure in the world are one of the transcendent God, which means that he is both present and transcendent with regard to our world.[62] But Pannenberg also cautions that once these decisions were made, the doctrine of the Trinity is by no means sufficiently clarified. There was still work to do for future theologians. Nevertheless, theology since the Reformation emphasized that the Christian understanding of God was attained only through the doctrine of the Trinity, without which it would remain incomplete. But how can the three persons of the Trinity be correlated to one another without falling into some kind of modalism or subordinationism, meaning that the three persons are just different modes of the Godhead or that the persons are in different ways subordinated to the "supreme" God? Here Pannenberg maintains that the starting point must be how Father, Son, and Spirit appear in the revelatory events and how they relate to one another in these events. One can properly speak about God's being and attributes only in the context of the Trinitarian self-disclosure of God as Father, Son, and Holy Spirit.[63]

Starting with the relationship between Jesus and the Father and between Jesus and the Spirit of the Father has consequences for the terms that are used to describe these relationships. The prime purpose of Jesus's mission is to establish among people the rule of the Father, and in carrying out this mission he proves to be the Son who serves the goal of the Father. The title "Son" therefore reflects Jesus's message of the Father. "The Son is not only the representative of the rule of God; but executes it." This also implies Jesus's suffering and death, so that one can only say of the Son of God that he was crucified, died, and was buried. Since the Father acts through the Spirit and the Son is resurrected through the power of the Spirit, Pannenberg even asserts that Father and Son are dependent on the working of the Spirit.[64]

While Pannenberg agrees with Augustine that the Spirit is the bond of communion between Father and Son, he disagrees that the Spirit

---

61. Ibid., 1:272.
62. See ibid., 1:277.
63. Ibid., 1:299.
64. Ibid., 312, 315. The German original even reads: "Insofern darf gesagt werden, dass Vater und Sohn hier auf das Wirken des Geistes angewiesen sind" (*Systematische Theologie*, 1:342).

proceeds from the Father and the Son. He claims that the concept of *filioque* is wrong, if for no other reason than that the Son receives the Spirit from no one other than the Father.[65] Therefore we must say that the Spirit proceeds from the Father and is received by the Son, a fact that does not preclude that the Son then hands on the Spirit to his followers.

Since for Pannenberg the inter-Trinitarian relationships between Father, Son, and Spirit have the form of mutual self-distinction, they cannot be only different modes of being of a singular divine subject but must be perceived as living actors of independent centers of activity. The divine consciousness therefore subsists in the threefold way in which each of the three persons relates to the other two and therefore distinguishes itself from them. Since the Triune God is no other than the God proclaimed by Jesus, Pannenberg suggests that "even the Lord's Prayer is seen as an invocation of the whole Trinity and not just of the Father of Jesus Christ."[66] While Pannenberg agrees with the distinction between the immanent and the economic Trinity, he asserts that the unity of the Trinitarian God cannot properly be maintained without the revelation and the therein-contained salvation-economic activity of God in creation. But this does not seem to pertain to the Lord's Prayer in the same way as we have seen with regard to Jesus's suffering and death. As the Lord's Prayer indicates, it is addressed to the Father alone, the same way that suffering and death is undergone by the Son alone. Otherwise Jesus's prayer in Gethsemane would make little sense.

For Pannenberg the increasing independence of the immanent Trinity over against the economic Trinity lost more and more of its function in terms of the salvific economy. This also led to a loss of the biblical basis for the Trinity. He also rightly observes that the threefoldness has not been a problem since Nicea and Constantinople, but the unity of the Trinitarian God has been.[67] Without abandoning the three entities, Father, Son, and Spirit, and their basic unity, one must ask whether the Trinitarian reflections have proceeded in the proper direction. To this fundamental question we will return later.

---

65. Pannenberg, *Systematic Theology*, 1:317.
66. Ibid., 1:319, 326.
67. Ibid., 1:342.

Roman Catholic and Orthodox Voices

When we come to the Roman Catholic side, it is not without significance that here we encounter less speculation than with Moltmann and some of his followers, and also a decided emphasis on the economic Trinity over against the immanent Trinity. This holds true even for the Orthodox view, as we can see from John Zizioulas below. For the Roman Catholic view this is not surprising, given the influence of Karl Rahner. But it may also be due to connectedness with tradition, which is more formative for both Roman Catholic and Orthodox theologians.

Catherine Mowry LaCugna

When Catherine Mowry LaCugna (1952–97), a Roman Catholic theologian and, until her premature death from cancer, a faculty member at Notre Dame, wrote *God for Us: The Trinity and Christian Life* (1991), she stated: "Today, a trinitarian theology of God is something of an anomaly. Even though at one time the question of the Trinity was at the center of a vital debate, Christianity and Christian theology seem to have functioned quite well, for several centuries, with a doctrine of the Trinity relegated to the margins."[68] Once her book had been published this statement soon became anachronistic.

LaCugna wanted to show in this book "that the doctrine of the Trinity, properly understood, is the affirmation of God's intimate communion with us through Jesus Christ in the Holy Spirit."[69] In order to do this, of course, she first has to delve into the historic development of the doctrine of the Trinity.

LaCugna notes that in their confrontation with Arians and other heresies, the Cappadocians—Gregory of Nyssa, Gregory of Nazianzus, and Basil the Great—strongly distinguished between the hypostasis and *ousia* to defend the coequality of the divine persons. This led to a gap between the mystery of God (*ousia*) and the mystery of redemption (hypostases). Therefore, the economy of salvation, including the creaturely Jesus of Nazareth, was more difficult to perceive and was "replaced by the eternal divine Son." Augustine's dictum that the external works of the Trinity are one, although valid in itself, furthered the idea that the Trinity has only one relationship to creation. "Then

---

68. Catherine Mowray LaCugna, *God for Us: The Trinity and Christian Life* (San Francisco: HarperSanFrancisco, 1991), ix.
69. Ibid.

there is no further need to refer to what is distinctive about the divine persons in the economy of salvation." Without intending to do so, Augustine's "legacy to Western theology was an approach to the Trinity largely cut off from the economy of salvation." When we come to Thomas Aquinas, this tendency continues. The treatise about the one God became a philosophical issue concerning the divine nature and attributes that reason alone, apart from revelation, could determine. "The treatise on the Trinity then assumed not just second place but became of quite diminished importance except as a formal treatment of processions, persons, relations."[70]

LaCugna then sums up her argument:

> Thomas' method not only conceals the economy of redemption even while presupposing it; it is also at odds with the typical patterns of Christian prayer and worship in which prayer is addressed to God the Father through Jesus Christ by the power of the Holy Spirit.
>
> A nontrinitarian account of creation will always make it seem as if God is not *essentially* involved with the creature. This belies religious faith. A trinitarian doctrine of creation, on the other hand, thinks together divine relationality and created relationality. Divine relationality becomes the paradigm for every type of relationality in creation. And, every type of created relation reality insinuates divine relationality.[71]

Once LaCugna has traced the history of the doctrine of the Trinity, its emergence and defeat, she ponders "whether there is a different way to establish and retain an essential correlation between *oikonomia* and *theologia* short of postulating an 'intradivine' realm of persons and relations, or essence and energies, that lie on the other side of the ontological divide." The eternal essence of God (*theologia*) must be brought together with the economy of redemption (*oikonomia*), which was so decisive in early Christian reflection. Otherwise God becomes unintelligible for present-day humanity. LaCugna therefore wants to reconceive "the doctrine of the Trinity as the mystery of God who saves through Christ by the power of the Holy Spirit."[72] She wants to follow here Karl Rahner, who emphasized the essential unity of the immanent and the economic Trinity premised on the idea that God is by nature self-communicating. Since God is by nature self-expressive and seeks to communicate God's self, theology is then "the contemplation of the

---

70. Ibid., 73, 102, 167.
71. Ibid., 168.
72. Ibid., 198, 210.

one self-communication of God (Father) in the Incarnation of Christ and in the divinizing presence of the Spirit (grace)."[73]

In the economy of redemption God relates to us and we to God, and finally we relate to each other. LaCugna states: "The doctrine of the Trinity affirms that the 'essence' of God is relational, other-ward, that God exists as diverse persons united in a communion of freedom, love, and knowledge." Since she insists on the correspondence between *theologia* and *oikonomia*, the focus of the doctrine of the Trinity is on the communion between God and ourselves. She continues: "When we affirm that the 'economic' Trinity is the 'immanent' Trinity and vice versa, or that God's energies express the divine essence, we are saying that God's way of being in relationship *with us*—which is God's personhood—is a perfect expression of God's being as God."[74] Thereby the term *person* whether in the singular or the plural is not a description of the essence of God as God is in God's self but points to the ineffability of God. Surprisingly, it does not matter for LaCugna whether we say (with Karl Barth) that God is one person in three modalities, or (with the classical orthodox expression) one nature in three persons; decisive for her is that God is personal and therefore can relate to us.

LaCugna sees the purpose of the doctrine of the Trinity as "to speak as truthfully as possible about the mystery of God who saves us through Christ in the Holy Spirit."[75] It is an attempt to say something about the encounter between God and humanity and with everything that exists. The doctrine of the Trinity therefore permeates the whole theological undertaking. Eventually it will lead to doxology, praising God for what God is doing, has done, and will do on our behalf and for the whole of creation. According to La Cugna, Trinitarian theology is inherently doxological. "Its goal is to understand something of what it means both to confess and to live out faith in the God of Jesus Christ. Its central theme is the mystery of persons in communion. Theology itself is the fruit of communion with God and can also be a means of union with God."[76] With these considerations LaCugna has gone a step beyond Karl Rahner's proposal of equating the immanent Trinity with the eco-

---

73. While it makes no sense to talk about God's essence as it is in itself, the distinction between the immanent and the economic Trinity cannot be totally eradicated, since there still is the mystery of God. Though God really, utterly, and completely discloses God's own self, humans as creatures are "incapable of fully receiving or understanding the One who is imparted" (ibid., 231).
74. Ibid., 243, 304–5.
75. Ibid., 320.
76. Ibid., 368.

nomic Trinity, since she links this up with the Orthodox emphasis on communion by John Zizioulas.

John Zizioulas

John D. Zizioulas (1931–), a student of Georges Florovsky at Harvard, was professor of dogmatics in Thessaloniki (1986-96), and before that held professorships in Athens (1964-70), Edinburgh (1970-73) and Glasgow (1973-86). He is titular metropolitan of Pergamon (present-day Turkey) and one of the most influential Orthodox theologians today. According to Zizioulas, being means life, and life means communion, which especially holds true for God, since the being of God is the relation of being: "Without the concept of communion it would not be possible to speak of the being of God. . . . It would be unthinkable to speak of the 'one God' before speaking of the God who is 'communion,' that is to say, of the Holy Trinity. The Holy Trinity is a *primordial* ontological concept and not a notion which is added to the divine substance or rather which follows it."[77] The abyss between the primordial ontology and the economy of salvation, or between God and the world, is bridged by the concept of communion. Zizioulas claims that nothing exists without communion, "not even God."[78]

Patristic theology insisted from its very beginnings that we can approach God only through the Son and in the Holy Spirit. Through the economy of the Trinity, which means the work of Christ and the Spirit in history, in the church humans are the image of God. Zizioulas explains: "The Church is built by the historical work of the divine economy but leads finally to the vision of God 'as He is,' to the vision of the Triune God in his eternal existence."[79] In the divine economy the Triune God, Father, Son, and Holy Spirit, built the church, where humans are constituted in the image of God and where they can approach God the Father through the Son in the Holy Spirit. Especially in the eucharistic worship, the metahistorical, eschatological, and iconological dimension of the church comes into focus as we contemplate the being of God.

For Zizioulas the Eucharist is not one sacrament among others and not a means of grace; it is the manifestation and the realization of the church. Here the church contemplates its eschatological nature

---

77. John D. Zizioulas, *Being as Communion: Studies in Personhood and the Church* (London: Darton, Longman, and Todd, 1985), 17.
78. Ibid.
79. Ibid., 19.

and realizes humanity's true being as the image of God's own being. The Eucharist constitutes the church's being. "The Eucharist manifests the *historical* form of the divine economy" through the life, death, and resurrection of Jesus Christ.[80] It links each church to the first apostolic communities and to the historical Christ. This is the historical and institutional anchor. Through the epiclesis and the presence of the Holy Spirit the eschatological anchor is provided. This gives the church

> the taste of eternal life as love and communion, as the image of the being of God. The Eucharist, as distinct from other expressions of ecclesial life, is unthinkable without the gathering of the whole Church in one place, that is, without an event of *communion*; consequently, it manifests the Church not simply as something instituted, that is historically *given*, but also as something *con-stituted*, that is *constantly* realized as an event of free communion, prefiguring the divine life and the Kingdom to come.[81]

The church is central in Zizioulas's Trinitarian reflections, and the Eucharist becomes the focal point in the church.[82] The experience of communion in the Eucharist reveals that the being of God really communes with that which is not God, meaning the individual believer. That this communion is realized in Christ by the power of the Holy Spirit discloses that God's being is a communion of Father, Son, and Holy Spirit. In the Eucharist, so to speak, the whole doctrine of the Trinity is brought together.

Especially important for Zizioulas is the identification of being with life, for which particularly Ignatius and Irenaeus are mentioned.[83] Again, it was the Eucharist that led to the identification of existence with life. The concepts of immortality and incorruptibility, with their ontological connotations, are used to establish the relationship between creation and the Eucharist. The conferral of new life through communion with God is actualized within the members of the eucharistic community. Zizioulas affirms that from the beginning Christians understood the Eucharist as an event of communion with the body of Christ in the Holy Spirit, which led to the affirmation of the full divinity of Christ and the Holy Spirit—in short to the doctrine of the Trinity.

---

80. Ibid., 21.
81. Ibid., 22.
82. He cautions that "the Church," according to the one, holy, catholic, and apostolic church, has a local and a universal dimension and should not be identified with a congregation or a denomination.
83. See ibid., 80–81.

The other major accomplishment of the Greek fathers was that for them the unity of God, the one God, so to speak the ontological principle of the being and life of God, did not consist in one substance but in the hypostasis, meaning the person of the Father. "The one God is not the one substance but the Father, who is the 'cause' both of the generation of the Son and of the procession of the Spirit." The ontological principle of God is therefore traced back to the person. From this then come God's personal freedom and his free will to exist, to beget the Son, and to bring forth the Spirit. This way Zizioulas can claim: "The being of God is identified with the person."[84]

As a Greek Orthodox theologian, Zizioulas opens our understanding of the central significance of the eucharistic mystery, both for Christian life and also for understanding the doctrine of the Trinity. He mines the insights of the Greek fathers in the freeing of the static ontological principle of God's being by emphasizing the fatherhood of God, which then necessarily leads to Trinitarian thinking. Yet by grounding the being of God in the freedom of the Father, one wonders whether the Son and the Spirit have the same freedom as the Father and are therefore persons in the same way as the Father.[85]

Mining Trinitarian Insights for Feminist and Liberationist Concerns

Given Jürgen Moltmann's emphasis on the Trinitarian perichoresis as a model for liberation and nonoppression, we need not be surprised that feminist theologians as well as liberation theologians showed that Trinitarian reflections have a decided impact on their theological work. Indeed, since the Trinity involves talk about God, it should not leave feminist theologians unconcerned about how one talks about God. Moreover, they also remind us that in early Christian reflections Sophia ("wisdom") could serve as a substitute for the Spirit or be mentioned alongside the Spirit. With liberation theologians, however, it is not so much the talk about God but the relationship between Father, Son, and Holy Spirit, and their "role model" for human relationships, that comes to the fore.

---

84. Ibid., 40–41.
85. This caution has been rightly raised by Aristotle Papanikolaou, "Contemporary Orthodox Currents on the Trinity," in *The Oxford Handbook of the Trinity*, ed. Gilles Emery and Matthew Levering (Oxford: Oxford University Press, 2011), 337.

Elizabeth A. Johnson

Elizabeth A. Johnson (1941–), Distinguished Professor of Theology at Fordham University in New York and a member of the Sisters of St. Joseph, addresses the Trinity from a feminist perspective. Neither Christology nor the doctrine of the Trinity was a problem for the early biblical communities, according to Johnson, since they had concentrated on what God had done for them in Jesus and who Jesus is in a functional way. Yet moving into the wider Hellenistic world, Christians began making use of philosophical categories and wondered about Jesus in an ontological way. They asked who he was in himself that enabled him to function as our Savior. Understanding that he is from God, the question arose whether he was equal to God, and therefore the issue of two Gods arose. We are confronted here with the christological controversies, and later on those dealing with Trinitarian issues. But the result of asserting one God in three persons did not really solve the problem. "Most people today hear that word 'person' in a contemporary sense, a psychological sense, as a center of consciousness and freedom related to other persons. This leads to the problem that in talking about the three persons in God, many Catholic people are really tritheists and think of three 'people' in God: Father, a Son, and an amorphous Holy Spirit (we never quite get the Spirit personalized)."[86]

Johnson is convinced that we cannot grasp God in a single concept. Therefore the doctrine of the Trinity safeguards the understanding of divine nature as a mystery of self-communicating love. In following Moltmann's interpretation of the crucifixion, Johnson states that, while Jesus suffers on the cross, both Father and Son are suffering, though in different ways. The Father is suffering the grief of the loss of his Son, and the Son is suffering the loss of his own life and his abandonment by his Father. Yet in their suffering they are deeply united in one love to save the world regardless of the cost. This is revealed in the Holy Spirit, who is the love of the Father and the Son. "At Jesus's death his Spirit, God's love, is let loose on the world. The love between Father and Son is released into creation and begins to bring about redemption."[87] While her feminist concern does not come to the fore in this publication, it is eloquently expressed in *She Who Is: The Mystery of God in Feminist Theological Discourse*.

---

86. Elizabeth A. Johnson, *Consider Jesus: Waves of Renewal in Christology* (New York: Crossroad, 1990), 26–27.
87. Ibid., 121.

The main concern in *She Who Is* is to speak appropriately about God. To talk about God in feminine metaphors not only challenges the traditional structures of patriarchy but also introduces a different concept of community, characterized by mutual acceptance, love, and justice. Yet to accord God feminine characteristics still leaves God as predominantly male, whereby the female attributes are subordinated to the male God. To remedy the situation, one could refer to the Holy Spirit, who in Hebrew is grammatically accorded the feminine form. That too, however, has its problems, because the Son has appeared in human form, and we can also produce a mental image of the Father. Yet the Spirit is without image. Theologically speaking the Spirit remains "the most mysterious of the three divine persons." Moreover, the male principle is still predominant and sovereign, even as God the Spirit remains the "third" person. The point is that simply adding a male or female dimension does not do justice to the whole God. "If women are created in the image of God, then God can be spoken of in female metaphors in as full and as limited a way, as God is imagined in male ones, without talk of feminine dimensions reducing the impact of this imagery."[88]

Johnson asserts that naming characteristics or dimensions does not lead to appropriate speech about God, but only using metaphors of both male and female who are of equal rank. She starts her investigation of speaking about God with the Spirit, with the liveliness of God that in a subtle and yet powerful way permeates the world. This results in a theology of the Triune God that starts with the experience of the Spirit. The activities of the Spirit-Sophia embrace the width, the depth, and the duration of the whole world. Johnson is apprehensive about the procession of the Spirit, whether from the Father or from the Son or from both, since that implies some subordination. Instead she prefers to talk about the Spirit as a freely self-giving gift. Since the Spirit of the living God is present everywhere in the world and in human history, talking about the Spirit is actually talking about the mystery of God. Johnson concludes: "The activities of vivifying, renewing, empowering, and gracing, with their consequent names and images bring us in an initial way to three key insights important for feminist theology of God, namely, the transcendent God's immanence, divine passion for liberation, and the constitutive nature of relation."[89]

---

88. Elizabeth A. Johnson, *She Who Is: The Mystery of God in Feminist Theological Discourse* (New York: Herder & Herder, 2007 [1992]), 50, 54.
89. Ibid., 146–47.

When she comes to Jesus Christ, Johnson asserts that Jesus the Christ is the Messiah, the anointed one, who was anointed by the Spirit. "Through his human history the Spirit who pervades the universe becomes concretely present in a small bit of it; Sophia pitches her tent in the midst of the world; the Shekinah dwells among the suffering people in a new way." She discerns that the feminine figure of the personified wisdom has great influence in biblical Christology (see 1 Cor 1:24), and this opens a large field to interpret the salvific significance of Jesus. "A relation to the whole cosmos is already built into the biblical wisdom tradition, and this orients Christology beyond the human world to the ecology of the earth, and indeed, to the universe, a vital move in this era of planetary crisis." The language of wisdom also points faith to a global ecumenical perspective that respects the righteous ways. Finally, by becoming one with humanity in the incarnation and in suffering, Sophia shows ways of justice and peace. In conclusion Johnson points out: "Jesus the Christ is the Wisdom of God in a concrete, historical gestalt."[90]

When Johnson comes to God the Father or, as she calls God, the Mother Sophia, she realizes that God is "even in being manifest, always and forever absolute mystery." "The story of Jesus reprised in history through the power of the Spirit manifests the character of God's absolute mystery as one of graciousness and compassion, bent especially upon the hurt, captive, and lost." The motherly Creator is not just the uncreated source of all existence and the one who keeps alive and comforts, but is also the one who strives to overcome everything that threatens to destroy the beloved creation. As Johnson maintains: "Christian-eschatological hope can be expressed in images of birth and new life redolent of the experience of mothering."[91]

Once Johnson has outlined the vivifying ways of the Spirit, that caring and liberating history of Jesus-Sophia and the generating mystery of the Creator-Mother, she addresses the issue of how to relate the three. Both a monolithic concept of God and a tritheistic understanding mitigate against the liberating aspect of the Trinity. She reminds us "that this symbol of holy mystery arises from the historical experience of salvation, and that it speaks about divine reality not literally but by way of analogy." It is a symbol that developed historically from the religious experience of the gracious God who was encountered by the Jewish people, and later by non-Jewish people through Jesus

---

90. Ibid., 150, 165–66, 167.
91. Ibid., 170, 181.

of Nazareth in the power of the Spirit. "It is a theological construct which codifies the liberating God encountered in history."[92] Yet Johnson reminds us that in the course of history it was occasionally forgotten that there is the greatest possible dissimilarity between the analogies we use and the holy mystery of the Triune God. Moreover, the attribution of the metaphors has been in flux, as Scripture and tradition show. For instance, "spirit," "wisdom," and "mother" have been applied to each of the three Trinitarian persons. Therefore Johnson maintains: "It is not essential for the truth of God's triune mystery to speak always in the metaphors of father, son and spirit."[93] The Trinity is Holy Wisdom, which does not exist in lifeless self-identity but corresponds to itself in threefold repetition, through which it can freely embrace the world. Unoriginated origin, incomprehensible mother of all; once and for all she leaves the hiddenness as its clear self-enunciating word. This eternal divine movement of self-differentiation directed toward the outside is the foundation of creation, and it becomes personally concrete in the incarnation and takes shape in continual yet fragmentary anticipations of redemption. At the same time, Holy Wisdom unfolds itself always as the unique self-giving Spirit. Here Johnson weds together the three persons of the Trinity in their involvement from creation to its fulfillment. Decisive for the symbol of the Trinity is a living community of mutual personal relationships of equal rank. Since, according to Johnson, "ideas of God are cultural creatures related to the time and place in which they were conceived," she is free to color these concepts with feminist Christian speech: "the Spirit's universal quickening and liberating presence, the living memory of Wisdom's particular path in the history of Jesus, and the inconceivable Holy Wisdom herself who brings forth and orients the universe."[94] This project draws on biblical heritage and Christian tradition, showing that the doctrine of the Trinity can also be opened up to feminist interpretation without destroying this doctrine.

Leonardo Boff

Finally we come to Leonardo Boff (1938–), a Brazilian Roman Catholic theologian and member of the Franciscan Order who devoted two books to the doctrine of the Trinity, a 1986 publication, *Trinity and Soci-*

---

92. Ibid., 197–98.
93. Ibid., 212.
94. Ibid., 273.

ety, and two years later *Holy Trinity, Perfect Community.* In this latter publication he wants to present in a more understandable manner what he wrote using technical terminology in his earlier publication. Since he believes "in God, Trinity of Persons, in eternal interrelationship and infinite perichoresis," he seeks for a society that will be more an image and likeness of the Trinity.[95] This means that the interrelatedness of the Trinity provides a model for liberation. Boff starts his reflections with the threefoldness of Father, Son, and Holy Spirit, stating that the unity of the three consists in their community. In the center of his considerations is the perichoresis, which serves as the structural principle of explaining faith in the Trinity.

> Because of its perichoresis and communion everything in the Trinity is triadic. Each Person acts in union with the others, even when we consider actions belonging to one or attributed to one: creation by the Father, the incarnation of the Son, the coming of the Spirit. The Father creates through the Son in the inspiration of the Spirit. The Son, sent by the Father, becomes flesh by virtue of the life-giving Spirit. The Spirit comes upon Mary and fills the life of the just, sent by the Father at the request of the Son.[96]

Unlike in traditional monotheism, in the Christian understanding of the Trinity there is not in the beginning the loneliness of the one God, but the story starts with the communion of the three divine persons.

Three questions concern Boff: How is God in God's self? How is the self-mediation of Son and Spirit, since the Son has his concrete reality in Jesus, and the Holy Spirit has it in Mary? And what kind of society does God want for his daughters and sons, because the social conditions today, in which most people do not find a place, cannot be pleasing to God? These questions are important for Boff because a strict monotheism can lead to a cold totalitarianism in a political or religious sense and the concentration of power in one single person. In a situation in which individualism is prevalent and there is little or no communion and solidarity among people, we must focus our view neither on the one God nor on the threefoldness but on the relationship between the divine persons and their communion as equals. The persons receive their personhood solely from the relationship they maintain with other persons. But the three divine persons are not like

---

95. Leonardo Boff, *Holy Trinity, Perfect Community,* trans. Phillip Berryman (Maryknoll, NY: Orbis, 2000), xiv.
96. Leonardo Boff, *Trinity and Society,* trans. Paul Burns (Maryknoll, NY: Orbis, 1988), 6.

three individuals who then relate to one another in communion and unite. Trinitarian persons constitute themselves as persons through the exchange of love and life. The eternal perichoresis of love and life between Father, Son, and Holy Spirit is the source and blueprint of any love, lifelines, and communion of creation patterned after the image of the Trinity. Boff sees in the triune communion a source of inspiration for societal praxis.

> The three "Differents" uphold their difference one from another; by upholding the other and giving themselves totally to the other, they become "Differents" in communion. In the Trinity there is no domination by one side, but convergence of the Three in mutual acceptance and giving. They are different but none is greater or lesser, before or after.... The sort of society that would emerge from inspiration by the trinitarian model would be one of fellowship, equality of opportunity, generosity in the space available for personal and group expression.[97]

Of course this Trinitarian vision of communion, nonoppression, and fundamental equality is important not only for changes in the world but also in the church. Boff points out that the ecclesial unity in the Western church is tied to a pre-Trinitarian or un-Trinitarian monotheistic concept. The heavenly monarchy is foundational for the earthly monarchy, which means the principle of concentration "of all power in one person, sole representative of the sole God."[98] There is a paternalistic trait, because everything is done for the faithful of the people of God but little or almost nothing with the faithful. One can either subject oneself or revolt. The latter leads to exclusion or severe canonic punishment. A perichoretic model of the church would subsume all ecclesial offices under the commandment of communion and the participation and codetermination of all the faithful in everything that relates to the well-being of all. Then, Boff maintains, the church would actually be the united people in the unity of the Father, the Son, and the Holy Spirit.

In the transition from the logical mystery of the Trinity to the mystery of salvation, we realize that the Trinity relates to the life of every person in everyday life in the struggle to live a righteous life of love and joy in undergoing suffering and tragedies of being. The Trinity is involved in the struggle, which accuses societal injustice and demands more human brotherly living together, with all the sacrifice and mar-

---

97. Ibid., 151.
98. Ibid., 153.

tyrdom that such striving not unusually carries with it. Similar to Moltmann, Boff discerns in the Trinity an urging to a more just society. God the Father generates the Son. "With the very same love which is responsible for begetting the Son, he gives origin to all the other beings in the Son, by the Son, with the Son, and for the Son."[99] Christ is the firstborn of all our brothers and sisters participating in Christ's sonship. Since Christ was born and not created by his Father, this fatherhood does not bear male features, since he could just as well have been born from God as his mother. Boff reminds us that in the Old Testament quite frequently God's love is expressed as a motherly love. But Israel also discovered Yahweh as its Father when he freed the nation from slavery. He is the God of liberation and protects the orphans, the widows, the foreigners, and those who are without protection of the law. The same is true for the Son. "The Son, the Word or Image also shows, in himself, traces of the eternal paternal Mother or the eternal maternal Father, traces received from his source of generation or revelation."[100]

While God is always triune, Boff realizes that we have no human symbols concerning the Holy Spirit. When we call him "Spirit," this refers to something that is common to all three. Yet the Holy Spirit is something special, since it unites Father and Son and is the bond of love between the two. According to Paul, flesh and spirit battle with each other, and the coming of the Spirit signals the liberation from oppression in our sinful situation. The presence of the Spirit also shows the differences of gifts and services that we enjoy in the congregational community. Similar to God the Father, the Holy Spirit also has some female dimension, taking over the function of mother. For instance, we are born again in the Spirit. In order to overcome the divisive issue of the *filioque*, Boff follows Moltmann's lead and refers to Russian church historian Vasilij V. Bolotov (1854–1900), who claimed that through the generation from the Father the Son is so intimately united with the Father that he is the logical presupposition and objective condition of the spiration of the Holy Spirit. Moreover, the Holy Spirit is the Trinitarian condition of the generation of the Son through the Father. In other words, the Trinity is so closely interconnected that one can have neither a single-handed procession of the Spirit from the Father nor a double-handed procession from the Father and the Son. There is total equality among of the three persons even with regard to their

---

99. Ibid., 168.
100. Ibid., 185.

emergence. Therefore they continuously cooperate from the beginning of creation to its fulfillment. "The Trinity is in creation because the Father creates all things from the inexhaustible source of his life and love, through the Son in whom all things are enclosed as in an eternal prototype, by the power of the Holy Spirit which unites all things from their heart of all things and leads them back to the Father."[101] That Trinitarian movement from beginning to end leads to final liberation and communion of all creation of the triune God. This optimistic vision bears close affinity to Moltmann's approach.

---

101. Ibid., 230.

8

A Systematic Discernment

For Karl Barth, "God, the Revealer, is identical with His act in revelation, identical also with its effect."[1] This means for Barth that the doctrine of Revelation must begin with the doctrine of the triune God. Yet, as Paul Althaus contends, the Trinity can only be established on a christological and pneumatological basis.[2] Otherwise the doctrine of the Trinity, which ought to establish the doctrine of revelation, is suspended in thin air. It is simply a contention on which all further deductions are based. This seems to be the case with most present-day conclusions that are derived from the Trinity. The doctrine of the Trinity is simply presupposed as a fact without much further consideration. Yet this is a very dangerous undertaking because it resembles building a house without first constructing its foundation. Moreover, much of what is going on today in Trinitarian reflections seems to go against the essentials of Protestant Reformation insights, especially of the Lutheran variety.

---

1. Karl Barth, *Church Dogmatics*, vol. 1, *The Doctrine of the Word of God*, part 1, trans. G. T. Thomson (Edinburgh: T&T Clark, 1960 [1936]), 340.
2. Paul Althaus, *Die christliche Wahrheit: Lehrbuch der Dogmatik*, 5th ed. (Gütersloh: Bertelsmann, 1959), 689.

A Lutheran Caveat

When we consult the Augsburg Confession, the authoritative confession of Lutherans, we see that its first article focuses on God. There the decree of the Council of Nicea is reaffirmed, and all anti-Trinitarian positions are rejected. There follows an article on original sin, and the next one is on the Son of God. Yet there is no article on the Trinity. Evidently the Trinity was not so high on the agenda for Lutherans. They must have remembered that Luther insisted that "In the Godhead there is highest unity."[3] He also cautioned:

> If reason holds [the doctrine of the holy Trinity] as folly, why do we ask for it? Since it is not difficult to reason in such matters. I could do it as well as others do it. But thanks be to God I have grace that I do not want to discuss much about it. If I know that it is God's word and God has talked in this way, then I do not ask any further how it could be true and am satisfied with God's word alone, whether it goes together with the reason as it may. This is how a Christian should do it in all the articles of our holy faith that one does not reason and discuss much about it, whether it is possible but only look at it and ask whether it is God's word.[4]

One might think that this approach is some kind of fideism, simply holding that whatever is God's word is true, regardless what reason might say. Yet this is far from Luther's own approach. For him the issue of the Trinity is an issue we cannot dissect with reason, and neither is it one we must simply accept as part of our Christian faith. This is also the approach the Augsburg Confession takes in article 1. It simply reiterates the decisions of Nicea without elaborating on the why or the how. Luther was always opposed to speculative theology and rather talked about the mystery of God, focusing his attention on Scripture. But exactly this reference to Scripture is what is often missing in today's Trinitarian reflections.

Neither the term *Trinity*, nor *triune*, nor any of their variety can be found in the New Testament. Without any emphasis on unity, we only encounter triadic formulas. Even the baptismal formula in Matthew 28:19 ("in the name of the Father and of the Son and of the Holy Spirit") seems to be preceded by an earlier formula that Peter used in his speech in Acts: Baptism "in the name of Jesus Christ" (Acts 2:38). The implication is that the Holy Spirit will be conferred to those who

---

3. Martin Luther, WA 46:436.7–8 (sermon of June 16, 1538).
4. Martin Luther, WA 41:273.40–274.11 (sermon of May 23, 1535).

are baptized in Christ's name. From these humble beginnings developed "an intellectually highly demanding speculation on the Trinity. It is almost something like higher Trinitarian mathematics which regardless of all the endeavors for conceptual clarity hardly attains lasting solutions."[5] Once Emperor Constantine realized that the decision of Nicea did not bring about the unity of the church, he became more conciliatory toward Arius and attempted to steer toward a middle course to bring together the warring factions. Yet even this move did not bring lasting peace. Under the reign of his sons we see a continuous going back and forth between favoring Nicea and opposing it. Athanasius too, who is the symbol of the ardent defense of Nicea only gradually came to the conclusion of the *homoousious* of Father and Son. Moreover, his battles were christological in nature and not Trinitarian, though the controversies in the fourth century are traditionally called the Trinitarian controversies. Until the Pneumatomachians entered the fray, the main concern was about Christ, whether he is equal to God the Father or not. The three Cappadocians then developed the doctrine of the Trinity, which as a result gave more attention to the Holy Spirit at the Council of Constantinople in 381. There the Nicene Creed was expanded to the Nicene-Constantinopolitan Creed, which is still used today under the name of the Nicene Creed. "While not stating explicitly that the Spirit was of the same substance as the Father and Son, it elaborated his role (which Nicaea did not), 'Lord and giver of life,' 'who spoke through the prophets.'"[6] There was still enough resistance at that time to accord the Spirit full equality with Father and Son.

When we consult Scripture, which ought to be normative for the Christian faith, we can perceive the unity of God, Jesus Christ, and the Spirit. Especially in the farewell discourses in the Gospel of John, the "Helper" and "Advocate" (John 14:16), whom Jesus promises that the Father will send and who is generally equated with the Holy Spirit, bears decidedly personal features. But neither in that Gospel nor in the Apostles' Creed do we find an actual Trinitarian doctrine of one God in three persons. We only encounter triadic assertions concerning Father, Son, and Holy Spirit. We could even venture to say that Christians by themselves did not arrive at a doctrine of the Trinity. It was only under the cloud of Emperor Theodosius the Great (347–395) that such a doc-

---

5. So rightly Hans Küng, "Die Trinitätslehre im Dialog mit dem Islam," in *Der lebendige Gott als Trinität: Jürgen Moltmann zum 80. Geburtstag*, ed. Michael Welker and Miroslav Volf (Gütersloh: Gütersloher Verlagshaus, 2006), 300, in his critical but perceptive contribution.
6. W. H. C. Frend, *The Rise of Christianity* (Philadelphia: Fortress Press, 1984), 638.

trine was affirmed, in 381. And such a decision, arrived at under political considerations, should make us doubly apprehensive about calling the Trinity the foundational dogma of the Christian faith.

Trinitarian Fascination

From the very beginning of the Christian faith the Trinity was not decisive—all-important was Jesus as the Christ. As Paul affirms: "If you confess with your lips that Jesus is Lord and believe in your heart that God raised him from the dead, you will be saved" (Rom 10:9). Jesus as Lord is set in parallel with his resurrection from the dead. As British New Testament scholar N. T. Wright (1948–) says: "Paul then explains this with a remarkable statement, one of the clearest in all his writings, of what precisely Christian faith consists of. It is not, for him, a vague religious awareness, a general sense of the presence of a benevolent deity. It is the confession of Jesus as Lord and the belief that God raised him from the dead."[7] The resurrection as God's decisive act was the turning point in history and the foundation of hope for each person. From then on it was also evident that Jesus was indeed the one who he said he was the Christ, God's human face, the actual Messiah.

But what about the Trinity?

In religion and mythology the number three is understood as a divine and holy number. It symbolizes completeness, since it contains in itself beginning, middle, and end. In many cultures the cycles of the year and of life are seen in three steps: growth, fertility, and decay; or childhood, adulthood, and senescence. There are the three elements that make up the world, earth, water, and air; and in ancient anthropology one often distinguishes between body, spirit, and soul (1 Thess 5:23). In many religions there exists also a trinity of gods. In Hinduism, for example, we have Brahma as the creator god, Shiva as the god of fertility but also of death and destruction, and Vishnu as the sustainer of life. In ancient Egypt we also encounter trinities. In a hymn to God Amon we read: "All gods are three: Amon, Re and Ptah, and there is no second to them. 'Hidden' (*imn*) is his name as Amon, he is Re in face, and his body is Ptah."[8] In Greek mythology the trinity of Zeus, Poseidon, and Hades shares rule over humans and gods. Kerberos, the awe-inspiring dog with three heads, guards the entrance to Hades, the

---

7. N. T. Wright, *Commentary on Romans*, in *NIB*, vol. 10, on this passage.
8. As quoted in Siegfried Morenz, *Egyptian Religion*, trans. Ann E. Kemp (Ithaca, NY: Cornell University Press, 1984), 144. See also the whole section "Unity in Plurality: Egyptian Trinities," in ibid., 142–46.

netherworld, from which no one can escape. At the oracle of Delphi in ancient Greece the priestess Pythia was sitting on a three-legged chair.

Even in Christianity the number three is of significance. Next to the Trinity of Father, Son, and Holy Spirit, we have the holy family of Mary, Joseph, and the Christ child. Then we encounter the three kings, Caspar, Melchior, and Balthazar, often also referred to as the three wise men. Before Jesus began his ministry he was tempted three times by the devil (Matt 4:1-11), and Peter denied his Lord Jesus three times (Matt 26:69-75). We could also adduce the resurrection on the third day, which actually was only two days in today's counting, to show the popularity of the number three even in Christianity. With the evolvement of the concept of the Trinity we may find an analogy to the evolvement of seven sacraments. The number seven consists of the number three, the divine completeness, and the number four, symbolizing the material world, which consists of the four elements of fire, water, earth, and air. Therefore seven sacraments can be interpreted to stand for the union of the divine and the material and also for completeness. Initially the number of the sacraments was much more fluid depending on what one understood a sacrament to be. Only in opposition to the Reformation movement did the Council of Trent stipulate the number as seven and also list these sacraments. A similar move seems to have occurred much earlier with the Trinity. In the post–New Testament disputes over whether Jesus Christ is indeed equal with God and even one with him, not only was the equality of Father and Son affirmed but also their relationship to the Holy Spirit. The Spirit, who undeniably is closely associated with Father and Son, was incorporated into a Trinity to emphasize the completeness of the divine. But at what price?

As the Roman Catholic church historian Norbert Brox (1935-2006) affirms, the faithful perceived the Hellenistic speculations on the Trinity largely as a threat to the faith in the one God, speculations that also jeopardized the unity of the church. They vehemently resisted the Trinity, claiming that with it a doctrine of two or even three gods was promulgated. "The beginnings of a theology of the Trinity by the church were understood as polytheism and rejected as heresy in the name of the biblical God."[9] Still today the three persons of the Trinity are often understood as the subjects who each have their own consciousness, an understanding that leads to some kind of tritheism. This

---

9. Norbert Brox, *Kirchengeschichte des Altertums*, 5th ed. (Patmos: Düsseldorf, 2008 [1983]), 172.

is reinforced in Eastern iconography if the Trinity is depicted in the form of three angels, as in the famous icon by fifteenth-century Russian painter Andrei Rublev. The icon, painted in the early fifteenth century, depicts the three angels who visited Abraham at Mamre (Gen 18:1–8). The painting is full of symbolism and is interpreted as an icon of the Trinity. In the fifteenth century the Trinity was considered the embodiment of spiritual unity, peace, harmony, mutual love, and humility. Yet today most people would hardly interpret it as symbolizing the unity of Father, Son, and Holy Spirit. It reinforces the idea of three gods. The notion of one God who successively appears in three modes as Father, Son, and Holy Spirit, as in modalism, is not satisfactory either. It is difficult to explain how, according to the biblical account, the Son can dialogue with his Father, if Father and Son are just different modes of the same God.

Following the Biblical Mandate

In the New Testament there is a unity of revelation and action between Father, Son, and Holy Spirit. We see this most graphically in Jesus's Baptism: after Jesus is baptized by John, "he saw the heavens torn apart and the Spirit descending like a dove on him. And a voice came from heaven, 'You are my son, the Beloved; with you I am well pleased'" (Mark 1:10–11). The Spirit of God descends on Jesus, and the voice, none other than God's voice, affirms the relationship to Jesus as God's Son. As New Testament scholar Pheme Perkins (1945–) explains this passage: "Elements of apocalyptic symbolism—the open heavens (Isa 63:19), the descent of the Spirit, and the divine voice—also call attention to the fact that Jesus is the agent of God's salvation."[10] The central focus is on Christology, who Jesus is, and not on the Trinity. Yet the passage leaves no doubt that the Spirit of God, Jesus, and God's own self belong together.

Another example of the relationship between Father, Son, and Holy Spirit is given in Stephen's speech to the council just prior to his being stoned to death. We read about Stephen that, "filled with the Holy Spirit, he gazed into heaven and saw the glory of God and Jesus standing at the right hand of God" (Acts 7:55). The phrase "filled with the Holy Spirit" designates Stephen as one who is enabled by the Spirit to give bold and powerful witness to the risen Messiah. The Spirit also elevates Stephen's prophetic consciousness to envision "the glory of God"

---

10. Pheme Perkins, *The Gospel of Mark*, in *NIB*, vol. 8, on this passage.

and "the Son of Man standing at the right hand of God" (Acts 7:56). The Spirit who filled Stephen is the connecting link between him, Jesus, and God. Since God is invisible, only "the glory of God," in Hebrew *kābôd*, can be discerned by Stephen. This is his power, symbolized by the radiance issuing from God's own self, which remains hidden. But Jesus becomes visible as the Son of God standing at God's right hand, which signifies that he is of equal power and glory with God. He has been raised from death and received into God's eternal glory as God's Son and his representative for us. At the same time, Jesus represents us before God. The Holy Spirit is in Stephen. Evidently it is the invisible power and might issuing from God who fills Stephen and allows him to perceive the glory of God. This means that the Spirit is the one who allows humans to perceive and understand God and Jesus the Christ. The three, God the Father, Jesus Christ the Son, and the Holy Spirit, are intimately connected but have very different functions.

Coming from the New Testament, the doctrine of the Trinity has the task of appropriately describing these functions and also of showing the proper relationship between Father, Son, and Holy Spirit. As the continuous battles during the first four centuries show, with excommunications being carried out by one side and then the other, it might be reasonable to question whether either the Hellenistic solution of the *homoousios* ("of the same being") or the Latin phrase *tres personae et una substantia* ("three persons and one substance") has really caught the meaning of the biblical correlation between God the Father, the Son, and the Holy Spirit. One should also remember that the decisive issue in the early church was not the Holy Spirit, but whether Jesus was indeed equal to God and therefore superior to all the Hellenistic divinities and demigods, who could not lastingly solve the human predicament.

British New Testament scholar James D. G. Dunn (1939-) says with regard to Christology that the issue is whether we encounter here an unfolding or an evolution.[11] An unfolding would mean the outworking of what was always there in principle or *in nuce*. The christological formulations of the later centuries could then be traced back to Jesus and the apostles. According to Dunn, this is in fact that classic view of christological development. "The alternative view is that early as Christology developed by accretion, that is, in crude terms, by adding

---

11. For the following see Dunn's perceptive essay "The Making of Christology—Evolution or Unfolding?," in *Jesus of Nazareth: Lord and Christ. Essays on the Historical Jesus and New Testament Christology*, ed. Joel B. Green and Max Turner (Grand Rapids: Eerdmans, 1994), 437-52.

on new ideas and claims which were not implicit in or native to the earliest response to Jesus. This can be characterized more carefully as the model of 'evolution.'"[12] Dunn concludes that the process of the development of Christology in the first centuries cannot simply be described as evolution. Yet he also contends that whether it can be described simply as unfolding is less clear. Nevertheless, he states that there was an inner dynamic involved "and that it was understood by the participants as an unfolding of the truth of Christ."[13] We certainly must agree with his conclusion. Jesus has always acted as if he stood in God's place. The development of Christology is therefore retroactive recognition of this fact.

Yet we wonder whether the same distinction that Dunn applied to Christology should not also be used for the development of Trinitarian reflections. As far as we can see, it would be nearly impossible simply to talk about an unfolding of that which is present in the biblical corpus. Yet should we call this development just an evolution, by which new ideas and claims were added in the development of the doctrine of the Trinity? To agree with this latter position would certainly be an exaggeration. In some way or other the postbiblical claims concerning the Trinity are not totally foreign to the biblical sources. Yet they are not the Bible's rectilinear conclusions either. But concerning the development of Christology, the scales tilt much more closely to the "unfolding," while with regard to the Trinity they are closer to the mark of "evolution." Is the doctrine of the Trinity then just a result of a postbiblical development that has some roots in the Bible but is steered by other interests?

The Doctrine of the Trinity in Peril?

The issue concerning the Trinity does not get easier then we consult the confessional documents of the sixteenth century. In the opening sentence of article 1, concerning God, we read in the Lutheran Augsburg Confession: "The churches among us teach with complete unanimity that the decree of the Council of Nicaea concerning the unity of the divine essence and concerning the three persons is true and is to be believed without any doubt."[14] In the Heidelberg Catechism we read in article 53 that the Holy Spirit "is, together with the Father and

---

12. Ibid., 438.
13. Ibid., 452.
14. Robert Kolb and Timothy J. Wengert, eds., *The Book of Concord: The Confessions of the Evangelical Lutheran Church* (Minneapolis: Fortress Press, 2000), 37.

the Son, true and eternal God." And in article 25 we read that "these three distinct persons are one, true, eternal God." Should we simply say that this is no longer true, since most people, whether Christians and non-Christians, will understand this doctrine as speaking of three gods instead of the one triune God? On the one hand, we realize that this affirmation of the Triune God is indeed the one doctrine that ties almost all of Christendom together regardless of any other differences. But we must also acknowledge in the same breath that the interpretation of the Trinity has often been shrouded in mystery and caused serious questions. We may only think here of Spanish medical doctor, lawyer, and Renaissance humanist Michael Servetus, who called the doctrine of one God in three persons a monster with three heads, a congregate of four phantoms that one neither could nor should accept.[15] He not only rejected the personal Godhead of the Holy Spirit but also that of Jesus Christ. The Father alone was essentially God, while Son and Spirit only participated in the Godhead and were different and subordinated appearances of the one God. Since the doctrine of the Trinity was affirmed by all the Reformers, it is no surprise that at that time Servetus could hardly challenge the traditional doctrine of the Trinity.

As we have noticed, however, in the sixteenth century anti-Trinitarian confessions and churches were formed in Transylvania (present-day Romania) and in Poland. They still exist today, and of course there are Unitarian denominations in the United States. More important is that most "orthodox" Christians do not understand the traditional doctrine of the Trinity and simply brush it aside as unintelligible. This means that more and more an ugly broad ditch has opened up between faithful Christians and professional theologians in their understanding of the Trinity.

We must also remember Schleiermacher's dictum concerning the Trinity: *"We have the less reason to regard this doctrine as finally settled since it did not receive any fresh treatment when the Evangelical (Protestant) Church was set up; and so there must still be in store for it a transformation which will go back to its very beginnings."*[16] Schleiermacher observes here that the Reformation has simply accepted the ancient doctrine without any further consideration. He also claims that this doctrine therefore is not finally settled, and any transformation of the doctrine has to go

---

15. So Nicolas de la Fontaine in his theses 8 and 9 against Servetus in CO 8:728 (Plainte portée par Nicolas de la Fontaine contre Servet).
16. Friedrich Schleiermacher, *The Christian Faith*, ed. H. R. Mackintosh and J. S. Stewart (New York: Harper & Row, 1963), 747 (§172).

back to its biblical roots. Implied here is the charge that in its development this doctrine has veered off from its biblical foundation. Schleiermacher also contends that many people refute the Trinitarian faith simply because it is unintelligible to them. Therefore he calls "for a thoroughgoing criticism of the doctrine in its older form." He also refutes the idea that the acceptance of the doctrine of the Trinity is the necessary precondition for faith in redemption. Such ideas only leave the door wide open "to the influx of speculative elements."[17]

Schleiermacher gives some indications of the task before us. The first and foremost difficulty he sees in the relation to the unity of the essence to the Trinity of the persons. He questions the original and eternal existence of distinctions within the divine essence. Is this idea really so clearly and definitely present in the New Testament? Schleiermacher seems to opt for an alternative between the Athanasian hypothesis, that indeed from the very beginning there is a distinction in the divine essence of Father, Son, and Holy Spirit, and the Sabellian idea of three different and perhaps successive modes within the one Godhead. The next issue Schleiermacher raises is the equality of the three persons if the first person is designated as Father and the second as the Son of God. Here he notes that by "Son of God" Scripture always and exclusively means the whole Christ and recognizes no difference between "God" as the Supreme Being and "the Father of our Lord Jesus Christ." He implies here that in Scripture the distinctions in the one God are not that clearly and definitely present, as the doctrine of the Trinity leads us believe. Yet in this perceptive critique, to which he asks for "new solutions," Schleiermacher does not provide any.

Jewish Monotheism and the Trinity

The issues that Schleiermacher raised are indeed noteworthy. Are there really distinctions in the Godhead from the very beginning, so that we can talk of the Triune God? As we have seen, there has always been the distinction between Yahweh and his spirit. Yet this *rûaḥ Yhwh*, this spirit of God, is always second to Yahweh, which most likely implies a subordination. Concerning the divine Sonship, we cannot go back further than to the expectation connected with the lineage of David. Yet to contrast Jewish monotheism with Christian Trinitarian thinking does not agree with historical reality. The best example for this is the so-called prologue in the Gospel of John. The prominence

---

17. Ibid., 749–50.

here of the *logos*, the Word, is thoroughly rooted in the Old Testament Jewish tradition. Especially wisdom theology comes to the fore. But the *logos* also figures prominently in early Stoicism as the term for the rational principle of the universe. Stoicism taught that the world is held together by an order that can be detected through reasonable insight and recognition. This means that all order has its transcendent origin in God, whose word is the power through which everything came into being and is kept alive. "God said" ... "and it was so" (Gen 1:3) is the key insight in understanding the relationship between God and the world. "It is likely, however, that the Fourth Evangelist's reading of logos was more influenced by Jewish and early Christian interpretations of Stoicism than by Stoic philosophy directly."[18]

The best place to look for the background of *logos* is within Judaism. Jewish philosopher Philo of Alexandria (ca. 25 BCE–ca. 50 CE) is an excellent example of a Jewish contemporary of the fourth evangelist who melded Greek philosophy, particularly Stoicism and Platonism, with Jewish exegesis of the Old Testament. In Philo, the *logos* figures prominently as a way of speaking about the creative plan of God that governs the world. Yet the fourth evangelist's use of *logos* does not seem to be directly a derivative from Philo but is a christocentric reading of the meaning of the *word* in Judaism by someone steeped in the same Hellenistic culture.

The role of the Word in creation and in human history in the opening verse of the Gospel of John thus draws on the word of God in the Old Testament. God's spoken word makes the difference between being and nothingness, not just in the creation accounts; God also spoke through the law at Mount Sinai and then again through the prophets. The Word encompasses both word and deed. The Word also brings with it associations from Jewish wisdom tradition. In wisdom theology the creative and almighty word of God and wisdom creating order come together. Wisdom can even become a preacher who beckons humanity: "Does not wisdom call, does not understanding raise her voice? . . . I, wisdom, live with prudence, and I attain knowledge and discretion" (Prov 8:1-12). Wisdom was God's companion "before the beginning of the earth" (Prov 8:23), working alongside God to accomplish God's plans. This might even infer wisdom's preexistence. In later Judaism Wisdom becomes a personal being, standing next to God, and "in the assembly of the Most High she opens her mouth" (Sir 24:2). While Wis-

---

18. So Gail R. O'Day, *The Gospel of John*, in *NIB*, vol. 9, in her comments on the prologue.

dom is decidedly feminine, John refers to the Logos as masculine in order to introduce the incarnation of Jesus as "the Word became flesh" (John 1:14).[19]

In the Testament of Dan we read of "the angel who intercedes for you, because he is the mediator between God and men" (6:2). In Exodus 23:21 we hear that Yahweh will send to the Israelites an angel with the admonition: "Be attentive to him and listen to his voice; do not rebel against him, for he will not pardon your transgression; for my name is in him." Yahweh's name, meaning Yahweh himself, is in that angel. Again the identification of God with that angel is very close, and moreover we are reminded here of the hymn in Philippians 2 where the crucified Christ is given by God "the name that is above every name" (Phil 2:9). Both in Israel and in Judaism God is not the solitary monolithic figure, but there are others around him who share in his divinity and execute his work. This becomes also evident from Psalm 110, where we read: "The Lord says to my lord, 'Sit at my right hand until I make your enemies your footstool'" (Ps 110:1). This verse was frequently used in the New Testament as a reference to Jesus's exaltation to the right hand of God (Mark 12:36; Acts 2:34-35; Heb 1:13). When the question is raised as to who is allowed to sit next to God on the throne, we read: "You are a priest forever according to the order of Melchizedek" (Ps 110:4). We gather from Genesis 14:18 that "he was a priest of God Most High." There was one who sits at the right hand of God executing a priestly function, something that the letter to the Hebrews prominently attributes to Jesus.

When we look at the New Testament, we realize that there is no interest there in a specific Word of God, or a specific Wisdom, or a specific Messiah, or in what way any of these shared in God's divinity. Decisive for the New Testament was that all these figures and metaphors became incarnate in Jesus of Nazareth, who died on the cross and was resurrected to new and eternal life against all expecta-

---

19. We notice that at least in the intertestamental period that there are figures who share in God's Godhead. Especially prominent is the divine Wisdom and also the personified Word of God. With regard to Wisdom and *logos* we could always say that their status is only metaphorical; they are no entities in their own right. But the story is different when Philo calls Moses mediator and reconciler (according to Christoph Markschies, "Jüdische Mittlergestalten und die christliche Trinitätstheologie," in Michael Welker and Miroslav Volf, eds., *Der lebendige Gott als Trinität: Jürgen Moltmann zum 80. Geburtstag*, 205). And in the Testament of Moses we hear Moses say: "But he did design and devise me, who (was) prepared from the beginning of the world, to be the mediator of his covenant" (Testament of Moses 1:14). Though in the next verse we read that Moses is going to sleep with his fathers, that is, he is going to die, this verse seems to imply his preexistence. This is not too unusual, since Philo can identify Moses and Aaron with the holy *logos* of God and can even call figures within the divine sphere "God" or "second God." So ibid., 205-6.

tions. Such a suffering, dying, and rising Messiah was unique in the Jewish concept of the divine mediator. Therefore it proved to be a stumbling block for most Jews. For example, Justin Martyr, in his dialogue with the Jew Trypho, quotes this Jew as saying: "Let him be recognized as Lord and Christ and God, as the Scriptures declare, by you of the Gentiles, who have from His name been all called Christians; but we who are servants of God that made this same [Christ], do not require to confess or worship Him."[20] This means that Trypho could agree to call Jesus Christ and God as long as he would not be required to confess him as his Lord. Jews could attribute to Jesus divine qualities, but not that he was their Lord.

Historian of early Christianity Larry Hurtado (1943–) emphasizes two characteristics of ancient Jewish religion:

1. A remarkable ability to combine a genuine concern for God's uniqueness with an interest in other figures with transcendent attributes which are described in the most exalted terms and which we may call 'principal agent' figures who are even likened to God in some cases; and

2. an exhibition of monotheistic scruples, particularly and most distinctively in public cultic/liturgical behavior.[21]

For the Jewish faithful there was only one principal deity, who was distinguished from all the divine and heavenly beings, but as some kind of high God or monarchical God quite often accompanied by them. There was the characteristic reservation of worship for this one God only, even at the expense of one's life.

Justin Martyr explains: "God begat before all creatures that Beginning [who was] a certain rational power [proceeding] from Himself, who is called by the Holy Spirit, now the Glory of the Lord, now the Son, again Wisdom, again an Angel, then God, and then Lord and Logos."[22] We note that there is a wide variety of divine mediators in Judaism on which Christian theology could draw to explain the significance of Jesus. Since the Jews, however, were reluctant to offer public, corporate worship to such a principal agent next to the one God, this made the early Christian pattern of worshiping God the Father and the Son genuinely innovative and striking. As Hurtado states: "God's uniqueness was characteristically manifested and protected in religious prac-

---

20. Justin Martyr, *Dialogue with Trypho* 74 (ANF 1:229).
21. Larry H. Hurtado, *How on Earth Did Jesus Become a God? Historical Questions about Earliest Devotion to Jesus* (Grand Rapids: Eerdmans, 2005), 111.
22. Justin Martyr, *Dialogue with Trypho* 61 (ANF 1:227).

tice, by directing prayer (especially in the cultic/liturgical setting) and worship to God alone, withholding such devotion from any other heavenly being, including God's closest ministers and agents."[23] Therefore the Christian reverence for Jesus was considered heretical by pious Jews. It must have taken powerful experiences, such as the appearance of the resurrected one to the disciples or to Paul on his way to Damascus, for the cultic veneration of the glorified Jesus to emerge among his first Jewish followers in such relatively close proximity to his life on earth. Jesus was not just recognized as the Christ but also as the one to whom prayers could be offered. We might refer here again to Stephen, who in his vision saw in heaven the glory of God and Jesus standing at God's right hand. Having recognized Jesus's privilege and divinely approved status as God's plenipotentiary, Stephen prays, "Lord Jesus, receive my spirit" (Acts 7:59). Praying to the heavenly Jesus is the sort of specific early cultic devotion otherwise reserved for God in Jewish tradition. It comes a no surprise that the Jews, including Saul before his conversion, approved of killing Stephen because of this obvious blasphemy, which contradicted Jewish monotheism. Here we encounter the roots of considering Jesus Christ equal with God. But this is still a far cry from any Trinitarian affirmations.

Reconsidering the Trinity

Karl Rahner muses "that already before Christ there was in one way or other faith in the Trinity."[24] He discerns this faith in the Word, which God establishes, and in the Spirit, who takes hold of the prophets and the charismatics. Word and Spirit take the place of God in Israel, though they are distinguished from him and nevertheless belong to him. In this Rahner perceives "a true secret prehistory of the revelation of the Trinity in the Old Testament."[25] If it is indeed a secret prehistory, then it is open to all kinds of speculation. But exactly this kind of speculation we must avoid in order to be credible to our own intellect and to other people. There has been so much talk about "the mystery of the Trinity" that most people, whether faithful or nonbelievers, have renounced any interest in the Trinity. Yet most still care about Jesus, the central figure of the Christian faith.

Jesus and his relation to God came to the fore in the Israelite and

---

23. Hurtado, *How on Earth Did Jesus Become a God?*, 131.
24. Karl Rahner, "Der dreifaltige Gott als transzendenter Urgrund der Heilsgeschichte," in Karl Rahner, *Sämtliche Werke* (Freiburg: Herder, 2013), 22/1b:561.
25. Ibid., 22/1b:563.

Jewish context and therefore should be best understood in that context. For instance, when Jesus enters Jerusalem and the crowds are shouting, "Hosanna to the Son of David! Blessed is the one who comes in the name of the Lord! Hosanna in the highest heaven!" (Matt 21:9; Ps 118:26), the crowd does not just legitimize Jesus as messenger of God. According to Matthew, this greeting implies that Jesus brings with him the name of Yahweh; that is, God is entering the holy city. This mode of presence is prefigured in the Old Testament. There is a differentiation between God whom "even heaven and the highest heaven cannot contain" (1 Kgs 8:27) and his name and the form of his presence in the temple and in Jerusalem. Since God is hidden, there are worldly figures to represent him such as the Word, Wisdom, or the messengers of Yahweh, who talk to humans in the name of God.

According to systematic theologian Christian Link (1938–), "we encounter here the Old Testament root of the doctrine of the Trinity: the self-representation of God in Jesus of Nazareth and his effective presence in the Spirit of sanctification are revelational images of the *name* of Yahweh."[26] Link then concludes that a corresponding Trinitarian theology need no longer contradict the monotheistic confession of Israel. Such a doctrine could do without the metaphysical frame of the early church expressed by "substance, nature, and person." As we have seen, Judaism does not deny the different historical figures in which the divine name becomes present. But by refusing cultic devotion to these figures, Judaism wants to make sure that they are just manifestations of the one God and of his coming. They are not considered as a second or third mode of the divine being. There is only one divine being, namely the one God. But exactly here we see the limit of drawing a connection between the Old Testament and later Judaism and the Christian faith. Though the Christian faith vehemently affirmed the unity of the one God by insisting on the *homoousios*, it also insisted on the cultic devotion to Jesus by offering prayers to him.

A faith in the Trinity prior to Christ, as Karl Rahner suggested, or to perceive Old Testament roots for the doctrine of the Trinity, as Christian Link proposes, is difficult to detect. We can discern the Old Testament roots of the implied divinity of Jesus and also of the divinity of the Spirit. But from these manifestations of the one God it is difficult to arrive at a doctrine of the Trinity. While the metaphysical terminology of the early church leads to such a doctrine, the biblical witness

---

26. Christian Link, "Trinität im israeltheologischen Horizont," in *Der lebendige Gott als Trinität*, 227.

could only arrive at a doctrine of the Trinity in a mediated way. Should we then abandon this doctrine, as Unitarians and Jehovah's Witnesses have done? Even if we wanted to do this, we would not abandon the Christian tradition altogether. We would simply follow a minority position that existed throughout the history of the Christian faith. But by doing this we would endanger our faith in Jesus as the Savior. As Jesus himself affirmed and as theologians of the early church tenaciously held onto, there is a oneness of Father and Son.

The Presence of God in Jesus Christ

From the very beginning of Jesus's ministry the decisive question was whether Jesus was the Christ, the promised Messiah. When John the Baptist is imprisoned, he sends some of his disciples to Jesus to ask him, "Are you the one who is to come, or are we to wait for another?" (Matt 11:3). Jesus refers them to his words and actions. "Go and tell John what you hear and see: the blind receive their sight, the lame walk, lepers are cleansed, the deaf hear, the dead are raised, and the poor have the good news brought to them" (Matt 11:3–4). With this response Jesus claims implicitly that in him the Old Testament promises connected with the time of salvation (Isa 35:5–6) are being fulfilled. The claim that he is the bringer of salvation at the end time is frequently attested. For instance, Jesus tells his disciples: "Blessed are your eyes, for they see, and your ears for they hear. Truly I tell you, many prophets and righteous people longed to see what you see, but did not see it and to hear what you hear, but did not hear it" (Matt 13:16–17). His disciples are experiencing what was promised for the end time: the Messiah has arrived.

While Jesus acts as if he stands in the place of God, as we previously noted, and while he also allows for *proskynēsis*, he is still the representative of God and not God's self. Otherwise his intimate interaction with God, whom he calls his Father, would not be possible. The confession of Jesus as Lord, as the *kyrios*, emerges from the Christian faith in Jesus as the Christ. The divine Lordship of Christ as expressed in the gospel cannot be recognized prior to or apart from Christ. To think that the Lordship of Christ can be discerned in the Old Testament or in the writings of later Judaism is to be mistaken. We should also be careful applying here the notion of preexistence. It expresses the conviction that the Son participates fully in the deity of the Father. As Udo Schnelle perceptively notes: "The preexistence statements underscore the claim of the human being Jesus, showing that his words are at the same time the words of God, his works are at the same time the works of God, that as a human being he is at the same time 'from above.'"[27] There is no equal to Jesus as the human face of God, either in ancient Israel or in Judaism. Yet both provide the contextual background for that Lordship, since after all Jesus was a Jew. In a unique way, Jesus connects the one God with humanity, being one with God as his representative and at the same time fully human from birth to death. In an unexpected way, however, his humanity becomes supplemented or rather re-created to new life in the resurrection and exaltation to God's own being (see Phil 2:9–11). This then allowed for and even necessitated cultic devotion to Jesus as the Lord. When we apply to Jesus as the Lord the criterion of being *homoousios* with God, then we encounter a both/and. Jesus is of the same being as God, and yet he is different. In him transcendence and immanence meet; the invisible God becomes visible. Jesus therefore is the human face of God, of the God who is invisible and unapproachable.

The Presence of God in the Spirit

In order to arrive at the Trinity, we must also consider the Spirit. As we noted, in the Old Testament, the Spirit is so to speak that tool through which God works in humans and in the world in general. The *rûaḥ Yhwh*, the Spirit of God, is always closely associated with Yahweh but can also be imparted to humans. It enables humans to live, to be skillful, intelligent, and discerning, and to follow God's ways. As the divine power, it also makes the difference between life and death, not just for humans but for all living beings.

There is a strong continuity between the Old Testament understanding of God's spirit and the Holy Spirit in the New Testament. Right at the beginning of Jesus's ministry, we read that Jesus "saw the heavens torn apart and the Spirit descending like a dove on him" (Mark 1:10). Having been endowed with God's spirit, Jesus could drive out the unclean spirits. The people noticed the power and authority by which Jesus performed his deeds (see Luke 4:36). As the mediator between God and humans, Jesus promises his followers a *paraclete* or comforter who will continue his activities once Jesus is no longer physically among them. Indeed, at the day of Pentecost, when they are all

---

27. Udo Schnelle, *Theology of the New Testament*, trans. M. Eugene Boring (Grand Rapids: Baker Academic, 2009), 670.

together in one place the Spirit of God descends on them, and "all of them are filled with the Holy Spirit" (Acts 2:4).

It was a matter of fact for the first Christians that their ministry in word and deed was conducted in the name of Jesus and through the power of the Holy Spirit. Addressing the crowd at Pentecost, Peter emphasizes that the fulfillment of the prophecy given by Yahweh to Joel has come true: "in those days I will pour out my spirit" (Acts 2:18; Joel 2:28). Peter explains that God promised to Jesus the Holy Spirit, which he has poured out on his followers. This means the Spirit is given by God through Jesus Christ. Of course, this Spirit, as God's life-giving power, was also involved in Christ's resurrection, as Paul shows: "If the Spirit of him who raised Jesus from the dead dwells in you, he who raised Christ from the dead will give life to your mortal bodies also through his Spirit that dwells in you" (Rom 8:11).[28] As a result, Paul states to the Christians in Rome that if they are led by the Spirit of God they are children of God, and if children of God and led by the Spirit, they should live as such (see Rom 8:13-14). It is characteristic of the Christian understanding of the one God that he is not considered distant but through Christ and the Spirit God is active in those who follow him. This leads again back to the Old Testament understanding that God's Spirit can be imparted to humans. The Holy Spirit therefore can be considered as the connecting link between the unapproachable God and those who try to follow God's commandments. Yet, different from Jesus the Christ, there is no enfleshment of the Spirit. He is only active as God's divine agent in that the Word became flesh (see Luke 1:35). So where does this leave the Trinity?

The Trinitarian Conclusion

We have seen that in the New Testament we encounter no doctrine of the Trinity or Trinitarian formulations. At the most, we have triadic formulations, as in the famous commission to the disciples when the resurrected Christ says to them: "All authority in heaven and on earth has been given to me. Go therefore and make disciples of all nations, baptizing them in the name of the Father and of the Son and of the Holy Spirit, and teaching them to obey everything that I have commanded you. And remember, I am with you always, to the end of the age" (Matt 28:18-20). The impetus for transforming such a triadic for-

---

28. See N. T. Wright, *Paul's Letter to the Romans*, in NIB, vol. 10, on Romans 1:3-4, where he mentions the resurrection of Jesus by the Spirit.

mulation into a Trinitarian formula arose once Christianity had left Palestine and entered a new religious and philosophical context.

As mentioned above, there were triads of gods in many different religions. Often there was one supreme god with whom two other gods were associated, such as in Egypt and Babylonia, and in Rome with Jupiter, Juno, and Minerva. In these other religions there is often the genealogical triad of father, mother, and son. Generally triads were patterned after the nuclear family, a union of the male and female principles, and a son as the result of that union. The head of that family was often a creator god. We should not forget that in early Christianity some also talked about God the Father, the divine Sophia, and Jesus Christ as the Son of God. The preference for triads is also found in the number three, since this means a totality with beginning, middle, and end. It also denotes the human being, consisting of body, soul, and spirit, as well as the world, with heaven, earth, and the surrounding waters. Yet Christianity went a decisive step further beyond genealogy and numerical considerations. It developed a Trinitarian doctrine, attempting to show the intrinsic and extrinsic relations between the three members of the triad, Father, Son, and Holy Spirit.

The development of this doctrine was at great cost. As with most new doctrinal affirmations, there are always some who oppose them, and therefore dissensions and divisions in unity become almost unavoidable. This has also been the case with Christianity. Some segments of Christianity left the mainstream church and established their own churches, such as the Arians, Nestorians, and Monophysites, just to mention a few. And finally there came the split over the Trinity between the Western church under Rome and the Orthodox Church in the East. But most lamentable today is that most average Christians lack even the basic understanding of that doctrine. Moreover, the frequent argument of Muslims, Jews, and even of Christians that the doctrine of the Trinity amounts to worshiping three gods shows how easy it is to misunderstand this doctrine. Should we then simply give up this doctrine, admitting that we have overextended ourselves in the attempt to fathom intellectually the unapproachable and supreme God, on whom we depend in this life and in the hereafter?

The answer must be a flat *no*. At the same time, however, we must refrain from undue speculation and practice intellectual modesty. If God is in heaven and we are on earth, as Karl Barth so forcefully claimed, we can only know about God that which he has disclosed to us in his human face, Jesus Christ. Only through the human being Jesus can we approach God, because "the humanity is that holy ladder of ours, mentioned in Genesis 28:12, by which we ascend to the knowledge of God."[29] Only through the impression and impact made by the life and destiny of Jesus do we realize that God loves us. Only through Jesus do we obtain the appropriate understanding of God and God's activities. This means that Jesus is not important because he was such an effective preacher or because of the miracles he performed or the saintly life he lived. Jesus is decisive for us because he is the mediator of God's salvific activity, shown most importantly in the resurrection. With this emphasis on the salvific activity of God in Christ, all the other ways by which medieval Christians proposed to approach God and to understand God's will or to dispose him favorably to them collapse. Christ alone was Luther's decisive insight.

The reason for "Christ alone" was founded in God's decision to disclose God's self only in Jesus. Yet Luther realized that this divine self-disclosure hinged on the unique relationship between God and Christ. In order to mediate God completely, Christ could not be just a saint or an avatar. He had to be completely and totally God. Otherwise he could not have mediated God. At the same time, Christ also had to be completely and totally a human being. Otherwise he could not have reached us and identified himself with us. In being one being with the Father, a point that Luther affirmed, with the Council of Nicea, Christ could mediate God. How Jesus can be one being with the Father and yet still be different from him belongs to the mysteries of God, as Luther might say, which must be adored and not explored. Ontological categories do not suffice in matters of existential significance. This was the shortcoming of the *homoousios.*

What Jesus Christ mediated to us was God's love. Yet how God is in himself, which intrinsic Trinitarian theology wants to unearth, is no business of ours. It is simply undue speculation. To talk about the one God who from the very beginning was triune overextends the biblical warrant. An extrinsic economic Trinitarian theology suffices showing how the one God, the Father of us all, has acted and is still acting for our benefit by the power of the Holy Spirit and through his Son, Jesus Christ. At this point we differ from Paul Althaus, who claims: "Yet the step to the immanent, i.e., the eternal and essential Trinity of God is indispensable. It is founded in Christology and pneumatology. The recognition of Christ and the recognition of the Holy Spirit lead in prin-

---

29. Martin Luther, *Lectures on Hebrews* (1517/18), in LW 29:111, in his comments on Hebrews 1:2.

ciple to the Trinitarian dogma."³⁰ Faith in Jesus, according to Althaus, includes the certainty that the communion with the Father is eternal. Yet such eternal communion between Father and Son cannot be established in the Old Testament tradition. It is based solely on a few assertions from the New Testament. Whether it has to be taken literally or can be taken metaphorically seems debatable. Swiss New Testament scholar Eduard Schweizer (1913–2006) rightly claims: "Pre-existence is not in the strict sense content of the faith but describes the dimension of salvation brought by Christ.... Its theological import lies in the fact to characterize the one who has died for us, was exalted and is present in baptism, Lord's Supper, and the proclamation of the Word as the one in whom all the wisdom of God which has been effective since the creation for salvation has found its final realization."³¹

Preexistence, not in a strictly temporal sense but much more in a metaphorical and nevertheless existential sense, shows the significance of Jesus. It does not necessitate a doctrine of the Trinity in terms of an intrinsic Trinity. An economic Trinity still suffices. But how is it with the Holy Spirit? Does it necessitate an intrinsic Trinity?

The presence and the working of the Holy Spirit is the presence and the working of the one God through Christ or the presence and the working of the living Christ. This is what the New Testament accounts imply. One and the same event can be attributed to God, Jesus Christ, or the Holy Spirit. Yet then we encounter the Paraclete in Scripture as distinguished from Jesus. When Paul talks about the varieties of gifts that Christians enjoy, he mentions first the Holy Spirit as the giver of these the different gifts (1 Cor 12:11). Yet this does not contradict the conviction that God is the ultimate originator and giver of all gifts, who works in our world through Jesus Christ and the Holy Spirit. God is present and active in the world through Jesus Christ and the Holy Spirit. On account of his incarnation, a personification of Jesus of Nazareth is clearly given. But this seems to be different with the Holy Spirit. He is more the extended arm of God and/or of Christ than a personified figure of the Trinity. This again would lead in the direction of an economic Trinity. Through the Holy Spirit God is active in the world in general and in Christians in particular. As Paul emphasizes, Christians enjoy the gifts of the Spirit and are expected to walk in the Spirit, meaning according to God's precepts. Contrary to the assertion of Althaus, it is not "the confession of the eternal intrinsic

---

30. Paul Althaus, *Die christliche Wahrheit*, 5th ed. (Gütersloh: Bertelsmann, 1959), 692.
31. Eduard Schweizer, "Jesus Christus. I: Neues Testament," in *TRE* 16:681.

Trinity" that secures the borders to any kind of pantheism but the confession of Jesus the Christ, God's human face.[32] As Luther adamantly asserted, though God is everywhere, he is not to be sought there but only where he has shown himself, in Jesus Christ. The attempt to trace God prior to his salvation-historical self-disclosure to arrive at some kind of primordial Trinity has no existential relevance and must be termed pure speculation. We should also remember Christian Link's insight that the doctrine of the Trinity could do without the metaphysical frame of the early church, which was expressed with the words "substance, nature, and person." This would also apply to the distinction between an intrinsic and an economic Trinity. The emphasis on the economic Trinity renders the charge of tritheism untenable. We can only know God concretely in an existential and not just a philosophical way because Jesus Christ, the Son, has disclosed God as our Father. And we can ascertain the ongoing activity of God in the world, the church, and in the faithful, since Jesus has promised the Holy Spirit as God's enlivening, discerning, and redemptive Spirit.

In interreligious dialogue the debate with Islam and Buddhism will not be one over the triune identity but whether Jesus, Mohammed, or Buddha can show us the way to the Father. But by starting with the Trinity we set out on the wrong foot, because it obscures more than it explains. It puts the cart before the horse since it begins with that which may serve as a tenable conclusion. The Christian faith, however, started the other way around. It entered the scene proclaiming that salvation is in Christ alone. This proclamation is as valid today as it was at the beginning of the Christian story.

We dare not forget that the doctrine of the Trinity evolved only as an offspring of christological reflection. From the beginning almost to the very end, the discussion during the first centuries was dominated by the quest for Christology: Who is the one whom we call Christ? Once it was clarified that he is indeed God, then the question had to be addressed of how the divine and the human "aspects" are related in him. Again we could assume that this was basically a speculative question. Yet salvation was at stake here too, because the conviction soon emerged that if God had not really come down to us in Jesus Christ we could never ascend to him. Others, however, were more afraid that the divine might be too much dragged down into our sphere and thereby

---

32. Althaus, *Die christliche Wahrheit*, 694.

lose its salvific power, so they objected to the *homoousios* of Christ with God.

The unresolved christological problems, similar to those regarding the Trinity, go right back to the New Testament, since the New Testament had neither a conceptually and intellectually developed Christology nor an actual doctrine of the Trinity. It was clear for the New Testament sources that Jesus Christ had been an actual human figure in whom God had been truly present. For reasons of adhering to a strict monotheism, Jesus is seldom referred to as God. Yet the early church had always considered Jesus to be God. Paul set the tone for the dominant strain of subsequent christological reflection when he asserted that Jesus Christ "was descended from David according to the flesh and was declared to be Son of God in power according to the spirit of holiness" (Rom 1:3-4). Contained therein is an understanding of Christ's twofold status, both human and divine.

Christ being truly human and truly divine was then finally accepted as doctrine at the Council of Chalcedon (451), at which then also the Niceno-Constantinopolitan Creed resurfaced. It was concluded at Chalcedon that Christ is not a composite being but is of two natures, the human and the divine. After stating that Jesus is truly God and truly a human being, the council did not actually state what this new being was like but decided to establish parameters or boundaries outside which the unity could no longer be affirmed. Four negatives were set forth: "unconfused" (*asynchytos*) and "unaltered" (*atreptos*), which were safeguards against Apollinarian thought that Christ is a human/divine mixture; and "undivided" (*adihairetos*) and "unseparated" (*achoristos*), which were safeguards against Antiochian tendencies that the divine just dwelt in the human person of Christ. These four negatives plus the Western affirmation of truly God and truly a human being may have looked like a compromise.[33] They were indeed a compromise. The church finally admitted that while it must affirm *that* Jesus Christ was truly divine and truly human, it cannot positively assert *how* he could be such. It could only state, and so it did, how one should not talk about that unity.

With regard to the Trinity, that theological restraint did not take place. In speculative fashion, people wanted to fathom the mystery of

---

33. See the reservations by Wolfhart Pannenberg, *Jesus—God and Man*, trans. Lewis L. Wilkins and Duane A. Priebe, 2nd ed. (Philadelphia: Westminster, 1988), 285, where he calls the formulation "problematic," since it does not take the concrete unity of the historical human being Jesus as its point of departure but rather the difference between the human and divine creaturely being.

the Trinity. The result was that the biblical warrant was far exceeded and conclusions were reached that were never really satisfying to inquisitive minds. Perhaps in our present situation, in which the Christian faith is challenged by a secular mind-set and by the reawakening of the major world religions as hardly ever before, it would be good to show more restraint in Trinitarian reflections. Would it not be sufficient to state that we believe in one God, the Creator and sustainer of everything that is, who showed his heart to us in Jesus the Christ, his human embodiment? Through Jesus's life and destiny, God indicated that there is eternal life beyond this present one. This God is present in us and the world around us through his enlivening and sustaining Spirit, which he mediates to us though his Son Jesus Christ.

It suffices that there is a unity of action of Father, Son, and Holy Spirit, without the need to fathom the mysteries of the Trinity with regard to their exact mutual relations and their status over against each other. As the New Testament affirms, decisive is that God was and is in Christ for our salvation and that God is present through his Holy Spirit so that there is life.

In Conclusion

We have come to the end our investigation on the long history of Trinitarian reflection. We could have cited many more authors and considered many more implications of Trinitarian reflection, whether for creation, the human personhood, or the salvific process. Yet the most salient points in the history of the doctrine and its unfolding have become clear.

1. In the Old Testament there developed a strict monotheism over against the polytheism of Israel's neighbors. Many Israelites, however, worshiped other gods, as the prophets Amos and Micah tell and as present-day archaeologists show us with their findings of figurines of various deities. Yet the covenant at Mount Sinai between Yahweh and Israel attests that Yahweh was their only God. The important link between Yahweh and the created world was the Spirit of God. This Spirit could be imparted to humans and nonhumans alike and made the difference between life and death. This Spirit or *rûaḥ Yhwh* endowed humans with special gifts, such as wisdom and craftsmanship. But it is not an independent entity. It is always imparted by Yahweh, who can give it and taken away. Though there are other spirits, they are also under God's control. The Spirit of God signifies God's presence and guiding function throughout creation.

When we come to the Son, the second member of the Trinity, the Old Testament leaves no doubt that Yahweh would not father a son. This was different from the religions of Israel's neighbors, in which the gods could have actual children of their own. But Yahweh told King David that he would be like a father to him and that David would be to God like his own son. This had nothing to do with a divine kingship. Though David's kingship enjoyed divine protection, he was a mortal like everybody else. Since God had promised him that his throne should endure forever, this promise gave rise to messianic expectations, which culminated in Jesus of Nazareth. Among all the turmoil Israel endured through the centuries, messianic expectations never ceased.

Since *Christos* is the Greek equivalent for the Hebrew *māšîaḥ*, and since in the New Testament this title was most frequently applied to Jesus, he was understood as the Messiah and as the fulfiller of the Old Testament promise given to David. Though the title "Messiah" is not used in the Old Testament in an eschatological context, the hope is already present for a God-provided figure who will usher in the eschaton. This figure seems to have originated from a retrospective glorification of David and from the promise given to him through Nathan (2 Sam 7:12–15). In the period of apocalyptic, the Messiah enjoyed a more independent position. He will destroy the enemies of God and of Israel and bring about the salvation of Israel. There is also an increasing emphasis on his preexistence, and as the Son of Man he ushers in the final triumph of God's people in God's kingdom at God's appointed time. While all of Israel and also individuals can be called son(s) of God, the Davidic kingship seemed to have an enduring effect and entailed a messianic promise of an end-time fulfillment. Though the term *sonship* was more metaphoric and never conceived of as biological, it showed the close connection between God and this special figure of God's son or of his Messiah.

While the Old Testament documents lead up to Jesus of Nazareth as the Messiah of God and as the Savior of the whole world, there is nothing in these documents about a plurality of persons in the one Godhead. Such plurality would have mitigated against the strict monotheism of the official Israelite faith. This monotheism did not exclude, however, that God used his Spirit and the Messiah to bring about God's purposes.

2. In the New Testament it is no longer Yahweh or the Lord God who occupies center stage but Jesus of Nazareth, or rather Jesus Christ. In the Gospels the divine Sonship of Jesus plays a leading role. There is an interesting phenomenon connected with this new situation: in the Septuagint, the Greek translation of the Old Testament, the term *kyrios*, that is, "Lord," is generally used to render the Hebrew term *Yhwh* ("God") into Greek. In the New Testament the term *kyrios* is still used for God in quotations and allusions to the Old Testament (see Mark 1:3), and in pronounced references to God. But generally Jesus Christ is called the *kyrios*, and God is referred to with the generic term *theos*, meaning "God." This would indicate that Jesus is now considered on a

par with Yahweh, while Yahweh himself remains in the background as the only God. Jesus is understood as the *bringer of salvation*. But little attention is given to the way he is related to the Lord God as the *sender of salvation*.

That Jesus is not just a human being but God(like) can be seen in many instances in the Gospels. He acts as if he stands in God's place, he allows *proskynēsis*, which was reserved for the godlike king in other religions, and he affirms his oneness with God. The divine fullness dwells in Jesus, as we hear at his Baptism, and the whole world is reconciled to God through him. At the end of his life Jesus even uncovered the messianic secret and declared himself to be the Messiah, an act that finally led to his death. Through the power of God's Spirit, Jesus was resurrected to new life as a signal that those who will follow him will not be contained by death.

While this unique relationship with God showed Jesus's equality with God, where does this leave the Holy Spirit?

In Judaism one encounters a more independent Spirit who interacts with humanity. Yet the Spirit is still God's, as we can see in Jesus's relationship with the Spirit, who comes to him from God, allows him to work miracles, and guides him in his various activities. Similar to Moses, Jesus can impart the Spirit to his followers. While the Spirit descended on Jesus in his Baptism, for believers the Spirit becomes a reality only after Jesus's death and resurrection. Then there is the outpouring of the Holy Spirit at Pentecost. The Spirit is intimately related to God the Father and to the Son as God's gift. But there is no personal unity of the three. For Paul, and with him for the whole New Testament, it was decisive that God was acting in the risen Christ through the power of his Spirit for the benefit of the faithful. God as the sender of salvation had acted through Jesus as the bringer of salvation and continued to be present in his Spirit, dispensed by the risen Christ. Any question about the exact relationship between Father, Son, and Spirit was considered unnecessary. All-decisive was that salvation was provided by God through Jesus the Christ.

3. In the early Christian community, outside the New Testament we initially encounter no reflection about the Trinity, but rather reflection about the relationship between God the Father and Jesus the Son. Entering the Hellenistic environment, Christians were confronted with demigods and sons and daughters of gods. Many of them had salvific significance, albeit of limited range. It no longer sufficed to assert that God the Father was the provider of salvation and Jesus as the Son was

the bringer of salvation. Decisive was now the exact stature of Jesus in relation to God the Father. Was he one of these demigods or of one of the sons of the Godhead? If so, salvation in an all-encompassing way was in danger. Jesus had to be really and actually God to provide salvation as announced in the New Testament. But how was this compatible with the Father also being God? Would the Christian faith not become polytheistic? Such an idea was untenable for Christians influenced by Jewish monotheism. For those coming from a Hellenistic background, such polytheism would also mean that Christianity was just another religion that claimed to provide salvation.

To steer away from sliding into polytheism and yet affirming that Jesus was truly God, there was a lot of dogmatic experimenting. There was no precedence from which to glean a satisfactory vocabulary. One talked about monarchianism and modalism, and subordination, adoptionism, generation, and offspring, but none of these terms sufficed to indicate the proper relationship between Father and Son. The Holy Spirit received only minor consideration over this issue.

These theological issues tormented the minds of laypersons and theologians alike and often erupted into violent dissensions, since salvation was at stake. Once the Christian faith was given privileged status by the Emperor Constantine, this evident disunity concerned the emperor. He felt responsible for the unity of religion and convened a council at Nicea to arrive at a dogmatic solution. The result was the Nicene Creed, which affirmed that Jesus Christ was of the same being (*homoousios*) as the Father. Here the equality of Father and Son in terms of their divinity was sanctioned by imperial decree. The Holy Spirit, however, was only briefly mentioned. Those who dissented from the decision were exiled. Yet soon the emperor wanted to bring everybody together and became more lenient against those who had disagreed. He had considered the issues simply "petty" and "unintelligible." After Constantine's death, the battle went back and forth between those who affirmed the full divinity of Christ and those who were afraid that this might endanger Christian monotheism and therefore diminished somewhat Christ's full divinity. This struggle between Arius and Athanasius finally ended in favor of the latter, who unwaveringly fought with all means available for the *homoousios*, the full divinity of Christ.

While at Nicea the Holy Spirit had received little attention, the situation changed once the Pneumatomachians claimed that the Holy Spirit should not be given equal rank with the Father and the Son. This move united those who felt that Father, Son, and Holy Spirit belong together and are of equal rank. One could still distinguish among them in the one Godhead by attributing to the Father the unbegottenness, to the Son the generation from the Father, and to the Holy Spirit the procession from the Son. This solution advanced by the three Cappadocians—Basil the Great, Gregory of Nyssa, and Gregory of Nazianzus—decisively shaped the doctrine of the Trinity. There is not simply a numerical distinction or one by name among the persons of the Trinity but one that highlights the respective peculiarities of the persons. In the Nicene-Constantinopolitan Creed of 381, we read that with the Father and the Son the Holy Spirit is together worshiped and together glorified. Though this creed essentially claims the *homoousia* of the Spirit, it scrupulously avoids the term so as not to alienate those who did not want to elevate the Spirit to the status of God. There was still enough resistance among the faithful to fear that such elevation would lead to polytheism.

The decisive steps with regard to the Trinity were made in the East under the influence of Greek terminology and Greek thought patterns. Even the Western representation at Nicea and Constantinople was rather sparse. When Greek finally gave way to Latin as the common language of the empire in the fifth century, the main dogmatic decisions concerning the Trinity were already settled. But then came the rift between East and West through the *filioque*, meaning that the Holy Spirit proceeds from both the Father and the Son. While the Eastern church maintained the original decision of Constantinople that the Spirit proceeds from the Father through the Son, the Western church wanted to tie the Spirit closer to Father and Son by emphasizing that the Spirit proceeds from the Father and the Son. This way one could more easily reject any Arian leanings that would see in the original wording three levels in Trinity (of significance), Father, Son, and Holy Spirit. The East, however, objected that tying the Spirit to both Father and Son splits the unity of the Godhead in favor of a twofoldness and therefore leads to polytheism. Instead of abandoning the unity of the church, those involved should have heeded Augustine's insight that the Trinity and its activity through the individual persons in the Trinity is beyond human comprehension.

4. In the early church and in the subsequent formative centuries of the Trinitarian dogma, existential issues prevailed. But eventually they gave way to intellectual concerns, as we can see most prominently in scholasticism. Theologians wanted to demonstrate the truth of the

Trinitarian dogma. For instance, Anselm of Canterbury elevated the doctrine of the Trinity to an axiomatic truth, but in so doing it lacked salvific relevance. An exception was Joachim of Fiore, who mined the doctrine of the Trinity for his apocalyptic interpretation of history, which had far-reaching effects.

The Reformers led back to the salvific significance of the Trinity. They emphasized, in accordance with tradition, the three persons of the Trinity. Yet, as Luther declared, in the Trinity there is utmost unity, and our vocabulary is inadequate to explain its mystery. Similar to Luther, for Calvin Scripture is the starting point for his perception of the Trinity, while tradition informs him of the vocabulary to be used. Yet for Calvin the Trinity was of such existential import that someone who denied it, such as Michael Servetus, was treated as a heretic with dire consequences for his life.

The Reformation movement was by no means uniform. It also gave rise to unitarian thinking, in which religion had to correspond to reason and be explainable by reason. Therefore the concept of the Trinity was rejected. Underlying this judgment was a literal interpretation of Scripture and the use of reason unguided by tradition. As a countermovement there emerged in the post-Reformation period an orthodoxy both in Protestant and in Roman Catholic circles in which reason was liberally used to affirm the traditional dogma. On the other hand, the use of reason also led to the Enlightenment period, with its disregard for the Trinity.

5. Only in the nineteenth century did Trinitarian thinking reemerge with vigor, especially through the influence of Hegel, whose dialectic thinking was easily adaptable to the doctrine of the Trinity. His influence was felt far into the twentieth century. Especially for Karl Barth, the Trinity was the starting point for dogmatic reflections. Since then the Trinity has been mined for various concerns, from liberation theology to process thought and to feminist issues. Often, however, the caution of Karl Rahner remains unheeded in such reflections: "How do we know?" Friedrich Schleiermacher already cautioned that we should express this doctrine without doing harm to the biblical witness. Theological reflections cannot start with the doctrine of the Trinity but in biblical fashion must begin with God the Father. This starting point we hold in common with Judaism. What separates us from Judaism is not Jesus as a divine figure, because such figures are also known in Judaism, such as the Wisdom or the Word. But they were never the focus of prayer and adoration.

IN CONCLUSION

It is interesting that the Augsburg Confession does not contain an article on the Trinity. It simply reiterates in article 1 the decisions of Nicea without elaborating on the why and the how. Martin Luther too was opposed to speculative theology and talked about the mystery of God. His main focus was Scripture. But this reference to Scripture is often missing in today's Trinitarian reflections. When we consult Scripture, which ought to be normative for the Christian faith, we perceive a unity of God, Jesus Christ, and the Spirit. But neither in the Gospels nor in the Apostles' Creed do we find an actual Trinitarian doctrine of one God in three persons. We only encounter triadic assertions concerning Father, Son, and Holy Spirit. We could even venture to say that Christians by themselves did not arrive at a doctrine of the Trinity. It was only under the cloud of Emperor Theodosius the Great that such a doctrine was affirmed, in 381.

From the very beginning of the Christian faith, the Trinity was not decisive; all-important was Jesus as the Christ. Father, Son, and Holy Spirit have different functions but are intimately connected with one another. The doctrine of the Trinity has the task of appropriately describing these functions and also of showing the proper relationship between Father, Son, and Holy Spirit. As the continuous battles during the first four centuries show, with excommunications going back and forth, none of the dogmatic terms seems to have satisfactorily captured the proper relationship between Father, Son, and Holy Spirit. One wonders whether these time-honored terms still have binding value today. Moreover, one should remember that the decisive issue in the early church was whether Jesus was indeed equal to God and therefore superior to all the Hellenistic divinities and demigods who could not lastingly solve the human predicament. Should we then simply discard the doctrine of the Trinity, since its proponents are often prone to speculation, and the doctrine itself causes often more confusion than it provides insights?

Our answer should be as strict *no*. But we must refrain from undue speculation and practice intellectual modesty. We also must get straight that decisive for the Christian faith is that God showed God's self in Jesus of Nazareth in such wise that he was understood to be the Christ, the awaited-for Messiah, for the salvation of the whole world. As "proof" of Jesus's Messiahship, God resurrected him to new life through the power of his Holy Spirit. Jesus Christ mediates to us God's love. Yet how God is in himself, which immanent Trinitarian theology wants to unearth, is no business of ours. It is simply undue speculation.

An extrinsic economic Trinitarian theology suffices, showing how the one God, the Father of us all, has acted and is still acting for our benefit through his Son, Jesus Christ, by the power of the Holy Spirit.

Recommended Reading List

Ayres, Lewis. *Augustine and the Trinity*. Cambridge: Cambridge University Press, 2010.
Boff, Leonardo. *Holy Trinity, Perfect Community*. Translated by Phillip Berryman. Maryknoll, NY: Orbis Books, 2000.
_____. *Trinity and Society*. Translated by Paul Burns. Maryknoll, NY: Orbis Books, 1988.
Boyd, Gregory A. *Trinity and Process: A Critical Evaluation and Reconstruction of Hartshorne's Di-polar Theism towards A Trinitarian Metaphysics*. New York: P. Lang, 1992.
Bracken, Joseph A. *God: Three Who Are One*. Collegeville, MN: Liturgical Press, 2008.
Bray, Gerald. *The Doctrine of God*. Downers Grove, IL: InterVarsity, 1993.
Dünzl, Franz. *A Brief History of the Doctrine of the Trinity in the Early Church*. Translated by John Bowden. London: T&T Clark, 2007.
Grant, Robert M. *Gods and the One God*. Philadelphia: Westminster, 1986.
Grenz, Stanley J. *Rediscovering the Triune God: The Trinity in Contemporary Theology*. Minneapolis: Fortress Press, 2004.
Gulley, Norman R. *Systematic Theology: God as Trinity*. Berrien Springs, MI: Andrews University Press, 2011.
Gunton, Colin E. *The Promise of Trinitarian Theology*. Edinburgh: T&T Clark, 1991.
Heim, S. Mark. *The Depth of the Riches: A Trinitarian Theology of Religious Ends*. Grand Rapids: Eerdmans, 2001.
Helmer, Christine. *The Trinity and Martin Luther: A Study on the Relationship between Genre, Language and the Trinity in Luther's Works (1523-1546)*. Mainz: P. von Zabern, 1999.
Johnson, Elizabeth A. *Consider Jesus: Waves of Renewal in Christology*. New York: Crossroad, 1990.

Kärkkäinen, Veli-Matti. *Trinity and Religious Pluralism: The Doctrine of the Trinity in Christian Theology of Religions*. Aldershot, UK: Ashgate, 2004.

———. *The Trinity: Global Perspectives*. Louisville, KY: Westminster John Knox, 2007.

Kasper, Walter. *The God of Jesus Christ*. London: Continuum, 2012.

LaCugna, Catherine Mowray. *God for Us: The Trinity and Christian Life*. San Francisco: HarperSanFrancisco, 1991.

Letham, Robert. *The Holy Trinity: in Scripture, History, Theology, and Worship*. Phillipsburg, NJ: P&R, 2004.

Moltmann, Jürgen. *The Trinity and the Kingdom of God: The Doctrine of God*. Translated by Margaret Kohl. London: SCM, 1981.

Papanikolaou, Aristotle. *Being with God: Trinity, Apophaticism, and Divine-Human Communion*. Notre Dame, IN: University of Notre Dame Press, 2006.

Peters, Ted. *God as Trinity: Relationality and Temporality in the Divine Life*. Louisville, KY: Westminster John Knox, 1993.

Phan, Peter C., ed. *The Cambridge Companion to the Trinity*. Cambridge: Cambridge University Press, 2011.

Rahner, Karl. *The Trinity*. Translated by Joseph Donceel. New York: Crossroad, 1997.

Ricks, Thomas W. *Early Arabic Christian Contributions to Trinitarian Theology: The Development of the Doctrine of the Trinity in an Islamic Milieu*. Minneapolis: Fortress Press, 2013.

Stăniloae, Dumitru. *The Holy Trinity: In the Beginning There Was Love*. Translated by Roland Clark. Brookline, MA: Holy Cross Orthodox Press, 2012.

Studebaker, Steven M. *From Pentecost to the Triune God: A Pentecostal Trinitarian Theology*. Grand Rapids: Eerdmans, 2012.

Taylor, Iain. *Pannenberg on the Triune God*. London: T&T Clark, 2007.

Torrance, Thomas F. *The Christian Doctrine of God, One Being Three Persons*. London: Bloomsbury, 2016.

Vander Pol, Allen. *God in Three Persons: Biblical Testimony to the Trinity*. Phillipsburg, NJ: P&R, 2001.

Volf, Miroslav, and Michael Welker, eds. *God's Life in Trinity*. Minneapolis: Fortress Press, 2006.

Ward, Keith. *Christ and the Cosmos: A Reformulation of Trinitarian Doctrine*. Cambridge: Cambridge University Press, 2015.

Index of Subjects

Abba, 25n20, 26, 26n23, 27, 27n24, 33
Adoptionism, 40, 100, 202
Alexandri, 17, 37, 39, 41–43, 48, 49n45, 50, 53, 55, 57–60, 66, 146, 185
Antioch, 26n23, 36–37, 41–43, 47–48, 52, 53n55, 62, 62n13, 68
anti-Trinitarian, 91, 97, 101–2, 121, 176, 183
apocalyptic, 11–13, 12nn13–15, 12n18, 86, 86n26, 103, 157, 180, 200, 204
Arianism, 50, 59–60, 68–69, 76, 100
Augsburg Confession, 91, 91n45, 103, 103n81, 176, 182, 205

Baptism, 15, 18, 27–29, 31, 33, 40, 67–68, 95, 98, 102, 107, 114, 123, 139, 176, 180, 195, 201
Biterrae, Synod of, 70

Caesarea, 19, 38, 42–43, 53, 63, 107
Cappadocian Fathers, 64, 68
Chalcedon, Council of, 67, 133, 197
Christology, 15n1, 35, 50, 66, 139–40, 157, 166, 166n86, 168, 180–82, 181n11, 194, 196–97, 207

Coinherence, 146
Communion, xii, 32, 52, 57–58, 74, 129, 148–49, 154–55, 157–58, 160, 162–64, 163n77, 170–71, 173, 195, 208
Constantinople, Council of, xii, 65, 68n31, 77, 133, 146, 177
Creed, Apostles', xi, xii, 35, 177, 205
Creed, Athanasian, xii, xiii, 76
Creed, Nicene, xii, 60, 66–67, 71, 76, 129, 142, 145, 177, 202
Creed, Nicene-Constantinopolitan, xii, 177, 197
Cyrus Edict, 9

Dogmatics, xi, xin2, 43, 109n11, 123, 123n49, 124–25, 124n53, 163, 175n1
Dominus Iesus, 77

emanation, 45, 49, 51, 129
eschatological, 5, 8–9, 8n8, 10n12, 11, 22–24, 88, 103, 139, 144–45, 154, 156–57, 163–64, 168, 200
eschaton, viii, 9, 156, 200
Eucharist, xii, 163–64
evolution, 181–82

209

feminist theology, 144n23, 167
filiation, 84
filioque, 69, 74, 76–77, 77n61, 129, 142, 146, 149–50, 152, 159, 172, 203
Franciscan Spirituals, 88

generation, xi, 3, 11, 39, 64, 70, 83, 84–85, 87, 109, 120, 165, 172, 202–3
gnostic, 39, 49, 100, 131

Heidelberg Catechism, 182
homoios, 58–60, 62
homoousios, 41–42, 45, 47, 54, 58–61, 123, 146, 155, 181, 189, 191, 194, 197, 202
homoousion, 41–42, 64, 71n41, 147, 155
hypostasis, 44, 47, 54, 63–64, 66, 74, 93, 96, 99, 111, 160, 165

inter-Trinitarian, 129, 159

Johannine Comma, 33

kābôd, 181
kingship, 6–7, 13–14, 199, 200
kyrios, 15–16, 17n3, 19, 31, 157, 190, 200

liberation, vii, 91, 107, 135, 165, 167, 170, 172–73, 204
liberation theology, vii, 135, 204
logos, 185
Lyons, Second Council of, 77

Messiah, 8–9, 8n8, 9n9, 10–11, 12n14, 13–14, 17, 23, 25, 107, 168, 178, 180, 186–87, 190, 200–201, 205
messianic, 7–9, 9n10, 10, 10n11, 11–14, 24–25, 27, 88, 90, 200–201
Milan, Edict of, 48
millennialism, 90
modalism, 41, 119n36, 158, 180, 202
modalistic, 38–39, 98–99, 119, 143
monarchianism, 37, 40–41, 202
monarchy, 40, 46, 146, 149, 171
monotheism, 36, 38–40, 50, 98, 140, 170, 184, 188, 197, 199, 200, 202
Mühlhausen, 103
mystery, 71, 92, 95–96, 106, 132, 142, 156, 160–62, 162n73, 165–69, 171, 176, 183, 188, 197, 204–5
mythology, Greek, 49–50, 61, 178

Nicea, Council of, 182

orthodoxy, Lutheran, 106–7
Ousia, 47, 54, 59, 63–64, 69, 74, 106, 134, 160

paraclete, 30–31, 33, 33n36, 107
patriarchy, 143, 144n23, 167
patripassianism, 46
perichoresis, 127, 141, 143, 144n23, 155, 165, 170–71
person(a), xii, 4–5, 9, 14, 32, 80, 106, 131, 141, 149, 156, 185, 195
pietism, 92, 108–9
Platonic, 48
Platonism, 185
Pneuma, 2, 157
Pneumatology, 194
Pneumatomachians, 62, 65, 177, 202
Poland, 91, 101–2, 183

polytheism, 36–37, 46, 77, 99, 111, 120, 179, 199, 202–3
preexistence, 12, 38, 157, 185, 186n19, 190, 195, 200
procession, eternal, 42, 49, 94
proskynēsis, 22, 190, 201

Qumran, 20, 23

rabbinic, 5, 20, 26
revelation, xi, 6, 24, 26, 39, 71, 75, 83, 86–87, 89, 94, 110–11, 112–13, 118, 122–29, 131–32, 134, 139, 141, 145, 154–55, 159, 161, 172, 175, 180, 188
Rome, 31, 40–43, 46, 53, 58–59, 63, 68, 76–77, 192–93
rûaḥ, 1–5, 184, 191, 199

Sabellianism, 98, 100
Serdica, Council of, 59
Shekinah, 137, 168
Son of God, 6, 6n5, 8, 13, 13n19, 14, 22, 29, 40, 42, 48, 51, 54, 69, 98, 102, 112, 114, 122, 158, 176, 181, 184, 193, 197
Son of Man, 12, 12n14, 23, 27n26, 181, 200
sonship, 13–15, 24, 64, 70, 157, 172, 184, 200
Sophia, 165, 167–68, 193
Sozzinianism, 101
speculation(s), vii, 39, 75, 86, 91–92, 100, 110, 121, 123–24, 131, 135, 140, 145, 152–55, 160, 177, 179, 188, 193–94, 196, 205
spiration, 83–84, 172
subordination(ism), 39, 45, 47, 70–71, 110, 149, 158, 167, 184, 202

subsistence, 49, 62, 69–70, 94–95, 132, 140
substance, xiii, 31, 42, 45, 47, 51, 54, 58, 65, 67–68, 71–74, 80–83, 88, 93, 95, 99–100, 111, 115, 137, 142, 163, 165, 177, 181, 189, 196

Thalia, 49n46, 49n50, 50n48
theophany, 23
Thessalonica, Edict of, 66
third age, 88–89
Third Reich, 88n31, 90, 90n42, 103
Toledo, 69
tradition, vii, xi, xiii, 20, 66, 73–74, 86, 86n26, 91, 93, 95–96, 105, 108, 111, 120–21, 124, 137, 150, 152, 160, 168–69, 185, 188, 190, 195, 204
Transylvania, 91, 101–2, 183
Treveri, 58
triad(s), 75, 193
triadic, xii, 32, 34, 170, 176–77, 192, 205
Trinitarian theology, 82, 116, 131, 135, 144, 144n23, 152, 153n47, 162, 189, 194, 205–6
trinitas, 93, 106
Trinity: economic, 94, 119, 123, 132, 141, 145, 147–48, 150, 153, 159–62, 162n73, 195–96; immanent, 94, 131–32, 141–42, 145, 153, 156, 159–60, 162; intrinsic, 195; ontological, 147, 153–54
tritheism, 65, 99, 101, 127, 134, 146, 152, 179, 196
tritheistic periodization of history, 89
triune, 92, 96, 103, 115, 117, 125,

136, 141, 145, 147–48, 151, 156, 169, 171–73, 175–76, 183, 194, 196
Triunity, 146, 150

unitarian(ism), 100–102, 134, 183, 190, 204

utopia(n), 89, 90n42, 103

wisdom, 36, 38–40, 62, 81–82, 91, 96, 139, 165, 168–69, 185–86, 186n19, 187, 189, 195, 199, 204

Index of Names

Aaron, 3, 186n19
Abraham, 87, 92n49, 180
Aetios of Antioch, 62
Ahab, 4
Alexander (bishop), 48–49, 50, 57
Althaus, Paul, 175, 175n2, 194, 195n30
Ambrose of Milan, 76
Amon (god), 178
Angelici, Ruben, 80, 80n1
Anselm of Canterbury, 81, 81n6, 204
Aquinas, Thomas, 83, 83n13, 86, 106, 147, 161
Arius, 48–49, 49n45, 49n50, 50n48, 51–53, 55, 57–58, 96, 140, 177, 202
Arndt, Johann, 108
Athanasius, xiii, 41n19, 49n46, 49n50, 50n48, 50nn57–58, 58n1, 59–60, 60n5, 61, 61n9, 62, 62n11, 63, 63n15, 67, 67n28, 70–71, 121, 177, 202
Augustine, 72, 72n42, 73–76, 80–81, 85–86, 92, 94, 123, 131, 134, 158, 160–61, 203
Azazel, 12

Baal, 8

Barth, Karl, xi, xin2, 109, 109n11, 116, 124, 124n53, 133, 135, 140, 145, 162, 175, 175n1, 193, 204
Basil the Great, 42, 42n22, 63–65, 65n26, 67n29, 160, 203
Baumgärtel, Friedrich, 5n1
Baylor, Michael J., 103
Benedict (St.), 87
Bengel, Joahnn Albrecht, 110, 110n14
Benz, Ernst, 89n37
Berdyaev, Nikolai, 137
Billerbeck, Paul, 20n12
Bloch, Ernst, 89, 89n33
Boff, Leonardo, 169, 170nn95
Bolotov, Vasilij V., 172
Boring, M. Eugene, viin1, 20n11, 29n28, 34n37, 191n27
Brox, Norbert, 179, 179n9
Bucer, Martin, 97

Callixtus I, 40
Calvin, John, 91, 94, 95n58, 95n97, 97n62, 98n64
Capito, Wolfgang Fabricius, 97
Charlemagne, 76
Chemnitz, Martin, 106
Chrysostom, John, 26

Cohn, Norman, 90, 90n41
Comte, August, 90
Constans, 58–59
Constantine, 48, 51–53, 53n56, 57–58, 177, 202
Constantine II, 58
Constantius II, 58–60, 63
Cudworth, Ralph, 111, 111n16
Cyrus the Great, 9

Damasus, 66, 68
Dannhauer, Johann Conrad, 92, 92n49
David, 6–10, 17, 184, 189, 197, 199–200
Decius, 43
Denzinger, Heinrich, 77n62, 83n12
Deutero-Isaiah, 11, 23
Diocletian, 48
Dionysius, 41, 41n19
Dunn, James D. G., 181

Elisha, 4
Elliger, Walter, 103n79
Engels, Friedrich, 89, 90n40
Epiphanius, 67
Esau, 3
Eunomius, 62, 62n12, 64
Eusebius of Caesarea, 19, 38, 53, 107
Eusebius of Nicomedia, 51, 53, 58–59
Evans, Craig A., 27n26

Farel, William, 97
Foerster, Werner, 16, 16n2
Fohrer, Georg, 7n7, 10n11
Fontaine, Nicolas de la, 183n15
Fortman, Edmund J., 14, 14n20, 33n35
Fossum, Jarl, 6n5, 13

Frederick II, 88
Frend, W. H. C., 177n6
Friedman, Jerome, 100n72
Fuchs, Ernst, 19, 19n10, 21, 24

Gerhard, Johann, 106, 106n1, 109
Goppelt, Leonhard, 20n11
Green, Joel B., 181n11
Gregory of Nazianzus, 64, 160, 203
Gregory of Nyssa, 62, 62n12, 63–64, 69, 69n33, 160, 203
Grenz, Stanley J., 132n78, 157, 157n58
Gritsch, Erich, 103n78
Gunton, Colin, 152

Hahn, Ferdinand, 15, 15n1
Harner, Philip B., 24
Hegel, Georg Wilhelm Friedrich, 116, 116n30, 117n32
Hilary of Poitiers, 70, 71n38
Hildebrand, Stephen M., 37n3, 43n25
Hippolytus of Rome, 40
Hitler, Adolf, 90
Homer, 22, 22n15
Hosius of Cordoba, 52–53, 58
Hurtado, Larry H., 187n21

Ignatius of Antioch, 37
Irenaeus of Lyon, 38

Jacob, 9, 17n4, 92n49
Jefferson, Thomas, 115
Jenson, Robert W., 150, 150n40, 151n43
Jeremias, Joachim, 25, 25n20
Jervell, Jacob, 17n4
Joachim of Fiore, 86, 87n27, 88n31, 103, 143, 145, 204

INDEX OF NAMES

John of Damascus, 69, 69n32, 143, 143n19
John Paul II, 77
Johnson, Elizabeth A., 166, 166n86, 167n88
Julian Apostata, 60
Julius I, 59
Juno, 193
Jupiter, 193
Justin Martyr, 37, 37n7, 107, 187, 187n20

Kant, Immanuel, 115, 115n28
Kehl, Medard, 87n28
Kelly, J. N. D., 35n1, 67n30
Kinkel, Gary Steven, 110, 110n15
Kolb, Robert, xiiin4, 91n45, 182n14
Küng, Hans, 177n5

LaCugna, Catherine Mowray, 160n68
Lessing, Gotthold Ephraim, 89, 89n39, 112, 112n20, 113n22
Liberius, 60
Licinius, 48, 51
Link, Christian, 189, 189n26, 196
Locke, John, 112, 112n19
Lohse, Eduard, 13, 17, 17n3, 31n33
Lombard, Peter, 88, 124
Louth, Andrew, 69n33
Löwith, Karl, 88n30
Luther, Martin, xi, 88, 91, 91n44, 92, 92n46, 93n53, 94n57, 103, 105, 116, 117n31, 176n3, 194n29, 205
Luz, Ulrich, 17n5

Magnentius, 60
Maier, Paul L., 38n8
Mamaea, 43
Marcell of Ancyra, 59

Marcion of Sinope, 46
Markschies, Christoph, 186n19
Mary, 37, 40, 67, 99, 102, 117, 170, 179
Matthews, Victor H., 5n2
McGinn, Bernhard, 86n26, 87n27
Melanchthon, Phillip, xi, xin1
Melchizedek, 186
Minerva, 193
Moltmann, Jürgen, 116, 135, 136n1, 144n23, 165, 177n5, 186n19
Morenz, Siegfried, 6n4, 178n8
Moses, 2–4, 7, 12, 23, 28, 30, 107, 186n19, 201
Müller, Hans-Peter, 8n8
Müntzer, Thomas, 102, 103nn78

Nathan, 6–7, 9, 200
Nebuchadnezzar, 3
Noetus of Smyrna, 41

O'Day, Gail R., 29n29, 185n18
Odysseus, 22
Oecolampadius, Johannes, 97
O'Regan, Cyril, 119n36
Origen of Alexandria, 37, 39

Pannenberg, Wolfhart, 116, 135, 157, 157n59, 197n33
Papanikolaou, Aristotle, 165n85
Paul, 16–17, 26, 28–29, 31–32, 40–42, 89, 95, 98–99, 157, 172, 178, 188, 192, 192n28, 195, 197, 201
Paul of Samosata, 41
Perkins, Pheme, 180, 180n10
Perrin, Norman, 24n18
Peters, Ted, 156, 156n54
Philo of Alexandria, 17, 185
Photios I of Constantinople, 77
Poseidon, 178

Powell, Samuel, 110, 119
Praxeas, 37, 37n4, 46, 46n41, 76n58
Preus, Robert D., 107, 107n7
Ptah, 178

Rahner, Karl, 130, 130n72, 131n73, 140, 160–62, 188, 188n24, 189, 204
Ratramnus, 76, 76n60
Reimarus, Hermann Samuel, 113, 114n23
Richard of St. Victor, 80, 80n2
Ritschl, Albrecht, 122, 122n45
Ritter, Adolf Martin, 45n38, 53n54, 58n2
Rowley, H. H., 12n14
Rublev, Andrei, 180
Rusch, William, 53n55
Russell, D. S., 12n13

Sabellius, 63
Sampley, J. Paul, 32n34
Samson, 4
Saul, 4, 188
Sauter, Gerhard, 89n37
Schäfer, Rolf, 123n49
Schleiermacher, Friedrich, xi, xin3, 120, 120n40, 183n16, 204
Schlusser, Michael, 42n21
Schmeisser, Martin, 102n75
Schnelle, Udo, viin1, 20n11, 34, 34n37, 190, 191n27
Schrenk, Gottlob, 27n25
Schweizer, Eduard, 195, 195n31
Seeberg, Reinhold, 45n39, 50, 75, 76n57
Septimus Severus, 43
Servetus, Michael, 96, 98n65, 99n69, 100n71, 183, 204
Silvanus, 60

Sjöberg, Erik, 27n27
Socrates, 50n51, 51, 52n53, 53n57, 60n8, 63, 63n14
Sozzini, Fausto Paolo, 101
Sozzini, Lelio, 101
Spangenberg, August Gottlieb, 109n12
Spener, Philip, 92
Stauffer, Ethelbert, 23, 23n16
Stephen, 114, 180–81, 188
Stinglhammer, Hermann, 86n25
Strack, Hermann L., 20n12

Tertullian, 37, 37n4, 42–43, 46, 46n40, 47, 76, 76n58
Theodoret of Cyrus, 51
Theodosius the Great, 66, 177, 205
Theodotus of Byzantium, 40
Theophilus of Antioch, 36
Tillich, Paul, 133, 133n79
Toland, John, 113
Torrance, Thomas F., 145, 145n26, 147n29, 148n34
Trypho, 37n7, 187, 187n20
Turner, Max, 181n11

Unamuno, Miguel de, 137
Urban, Waclaw, 101n74

Valens, 60, 66
Victor of Rome, 40
Vishnu, 178
von Rad, Gerhard, 9n9, 10n11, 13

Wall, Robert W., 29, 29n30
Wengert, Timothy J., xiiin4, 182n14
Wilbur, Morse, 98n65, 100, 100n73
Williams, Rowan, 43n24
Witherington, Ben, III, 33n36
Woude, A. S. van der, 9n9

Wright, N. T., 178, 178n7, 192n28

Zerubbabel, 11
Zeus, 178

Zinzendorf, Nicolaus Ludwig von, 109, 109n12, 110
Zizioulas, John D., 163, 163n77

www.ingramcontent.com/pod-product-compliance
Lightning Source LLC
Chambersburg PA
CBHW071157070526
44584CB00019B/2827